THE MEN OF 64

CW00545371

THE MEN OF 64

WEST HAM UNITED & PRESTON NORTH END IN THE FA CUP

BRIAN BELTON

TEMPUS

Dedicated to the men of '64 – the West Ham United and Preston North End managers and players.

First published 2005

Tempus Publishing Limited
The Mill, Brimscombe Port,
Stroud, Gloucestershire, GL5 2QG
www.tempus-publishing.com

© Brian Belton, 2005

The right of Brian Belton to be identified as the Author of this work has been asserted in accordance with the Copyrights, Designs and Patents Act 1988.

All rights reserved. No part of this book may be reprinted or reproduced or utilised in any form or by any electronic, mechanical or other means, now known or hereafter invented, including photocopying and recording, or in any information storage or retrieval system, without the permission in writing from the Publishers.

British Library Cataloguing in Publication Data.
A catalogue record for this book is available from the British Library.

ISBN 0 7524 3549 3

Typesetting and origination by Tempus Publishing Limited
Printed in Great Britain

CONTENTS

Acknowledgements

I would like to say thank you to all the players and fans who took the time and the patience to contribute to this book by face-to-face interview, letter, fax, email and telephone. Many of these people, all over the world, invited me into their homes and allowed me access to their memories. This has been an education and an honour.

A special thank you to Bob Bond for allowing the reproduction of his Sporting Caricatures of Preston players (please see www.elbobbo.org.uk for further examples and details of how to purchase the same).

Brian Belton
July 2005

Introduction

For me, the sixties was a time when I got to know football. Although my first visits to Upton Park were in the 1950s, my consciousness of 'being West Ham' grew as the sixties dawned.

I was born less than a John Bond free kick away from the Boleyn ground and on the odd match days when I couldn't get to the ground, I could clearly hear the Upton Park roar as goals were scored or narrowly missed. In these days of the gravitational pulls to Chelsea, Manchester United or Arsenal, those from another football generation can't change their background or betray their first soccer love. In the third of a century I have been writing this book, talking to players who trod the path of West Ham United and Preston North End to Wembley in 1964, this has only been reiterated.

I have had the great fortune to have watched football practically all over the world. But there will and can never be for me another club quite like West Ham.

You're only born once, I was born a Hammer.

Any number of people watching football in the early 1960s would agree that at that time there was no team in Britain that would do better in Europe than West Ham. But equally, most folk understood that the Hammers lacked something. It wasn't skill, flair, or the feeling for football at its highest tactical level. The East Enders possessed all this. Some said West Ham were not brave enough or did not have the determination to succeed, others called this 'character'. But from Boxing Day 1963, following a humiliating home defeat by Blackburn Rovers, West Ham's youngsters somehow added the steel of determination to the velvet of their style.

Not five months later, they stood just ninety minutes from the gateway to European Soccer; victory at Wembley.

West Ham had always shown a curiosity in terms of international football. In 1921 the club organised a four-match tour of Spain. They won every game, scoring eleven goals and conceding none. Up to 1964, apart from the war-time break, only three years out of forty-three were bereft of international experience. Since 1960 they had played twenty matches against teams from fourteen countries, losing two, drawing five and winning the rest. Admittedly, some victories were against the emerging teams of Southern Africa, but in New York in the summer of 1963 they had won a prestigious international tournament, and only lost the two-leg New York Cup by a single goal. During these ten tense matches they pitted their skills and know-how against teams like Dukla Prague, Gornik, Ore and Mantova.

West Ham had become a side prepared to learn. Skipper Bobby Moore, showing the Malcolm Allison influence, once said:

> I have never played in a match against a strange team, no matter how weak they were, when I haven't seen some phase of the game that was worth thinking about, worth talking about, worth trying in practice.

It was from this willingness to watch and keep an open mind that much of West Ham's insight and inspiration came. The side did little by accident. They charted the strengths and weaknesses of opponents. Climate, atmosphere, diet and strategy were all considered.

It was in the frying pan heat of New York that Ron Greenwood, who was not prone to prediction, summed up his feelings on West Ham's triumph in mastering teams from seven other lands to become International Soccer League champions. He said of his side:

> This could be a great team in two or three years' time. It would have taken us three years at home to accomplish this experience

He saw the cup final as just another stepping stone towards the realisation of a soccer ideal of thinking and coaching; the precursor of his vision. West Ham had grown up as a team in the USA. In a few weeks, boys had developed character playing against club sides with their varying styles and patterns and become men, the men of '64.

But on their return to England, the Hammers knew that there was a much bigger fight waiting. The English game was still one of the most powerful in the World, and if West Ham were truly to succeed, they had to better it. As such it was fitting that the Irons met one of the great representatives of the football traditions of these islands, Manchester United, in the last four of the FA Cup. Matt Busby had developed a United side that called on the skills of men from all corners of Britain to produce one of the greatest club sides to take the European and world stage. The Manchester Reds of the mid-1960s were the zenith of four proud nations, the oldest footballing nations, plus some of the best of what the 'garrison game' had produced in Eire. It was an awesome creation, but in the rain of Sheffield the men from London's Docklands destroyed this mighty phenomenon; they overcame it by skill and will.

The semi-final was a high point for West Ham United, they would never again 'fly so high'. But there was one more obstacle waiting. A Wembley encounter with a football institution that represented Albion's bedrock of football history; the Invincibles of former days, the North End Lilywhites, profound in the pride of northern purity, Proud Preston. With them, they brought to Wembley everything that meant anything in the British game. As such, as the tulips bloomed in the early days of May 1964, the world saw a mighty clash of football tradition and the future of 'working man's ballet'. Nothing like it had been seen before and will never be seen again; this was the best of the past against that which might be; it was the known against the possible and it would shape what is the single and only 'world sport' for the next forty years.

It has been said that if you can remember the 1960s you were not there, but I remember it and I was there. I saw and felt it happen. Its music, its television, its sport all merged into one to make it literally 'swing'. This book attempts to capture something of the ethos of the period. This cannot really be done just by reporting football facts, so I have provided some memory jerks of the period and words from those who experienced it as young people and literally lived the dream that the era was to so many of us. I have also tried to provide a historical context to demonstrate the enormity of that Wembley encounter between the soccer heritage of the East End and the North End; whatever came of it was the fruit of that which was before it.

I have talked to many of those who played at Wembley in 1964 and some who were left in the wake of their onslaught to, what seems now, their inevitable meeting. This book looks to bring something of that time and that encounter to you. It was a fantastic phase, when freedom seemed possible, when hope lay in the stars and in us who looked excitedly to the future. It is the hope of the pages that follow that you will remember it, or if you were too young to have its breezes blow on you, that you will at least feel its red hotness and how the men of '64 were part of it all.

West Ham Emerge from Winter

We didn't start too prosperously in the league, but then the cup games came and we seemed to blossom.

Peter Brabrook – West Ham United and England

The first part of West Ham's 1963/64 season had not been impressive. The Hammers, sitting in the bottom third of the First Division, had only managed six wins in twenty-three League matches and had gone seven games without a single victory. But things got worse on Boxing Day when Blackburn came to Upton Park for the 11 a.m. kick-off. The Rovers from Lancashire were undefeated in ten games and looking down on everyone else in Division One. The Hammers were beaten 8-2 and although they got some revenge a few days later by defeating their punishers at Ewood Park, it was really not much in the way of consolation after crashing to a record home defeat. For all this, the trouncing by Blackburn was the ironic turning point in West Ham's season.

Jack Burkett, a West Ham defender at the time, recalled that the Hammers were leading 2-0 at one point

> ... but everything they hit went in, including one from near the halfway line.

After the game the West Ham side went straight to a hotel in Manchester before the return game the following day.

Jack remembered some frank words and a few 'home truths' at a team meeting that went on until 2 a.m.:

> Next day we went out and beat Blackburn 3-1 and, from that moment on, success came. No one likes to get beat 8-2 but it was a turning point.

The Irons were drawn at home to Charlton Athletic in the third round of the FA Cup. The Addicks would finish in fourth place in the old Second Division at the end of the season, one place below, but eight points (four wins then) adrift of Preston North End.

However, well before the seeds of fate were conjured from the ball-bag of destiny at Lancaster Gate, West Ham had also fought their way to the last four of the League Cup and this trophy, given that the second leg of the semi-final tie with Leicester City would be played in East London, seemed a much more likely target, alongside First Division survival, for the Upton Park club than a protracted run in the Football Association Cup.

Facing Charlton

Those who lined up in the cold streets that snuggled around Upton Park to purchase the 6d programme for the third-round contest at Upton Park on the fourth day of 1964 were informed that the meeting with Charlton was West Ham's forty-third FA Cup tie since the Second World War. The imparting of such knowledge is in the tradition of most West Ham publications in that, from this, fans could conclude that the next tie would be the forty-fourth since the Second World War and that the last one, the defeat at Anfield in March the previous year, was the forty-second. Readers were also made aware that the British Rail return fare to Sheffield for the coming League game against the Blades at Bramall Lane would cost them 33s 6d, around £1.67. It doesn't sound much but the average wage in Britain at the time was £18 2s 2d. I sold sixty-seven half-hundred-weight bags of firewood to get the money; it was a part-time job I had in the days before central heating was widespread and the ritual lighting of the living room fire was a daily practice in many homes. I had worked most of Sunday and every evening after school to get the money to go up north. Sadly, I was rewarded by watching my side defeated 2-1.

The atmosphere in which the match against Charlton Athletic took place was typical of England's winter game. The windless chill stiffened the very air so as one cheered or shouted it seemed to crack the ether almost without resonance. As you expelled breath from your lungs it froze into a cloud and the icy starch of coldness gripped every inch of exposed skin. The game kicked off as a feeling that evening was well on its way enveloped you; the day struggled with the forces of twilight and the Upton Park floodlights gradually went from dip to full-beam. The daylight hours of Saturdays in the early sixties felt like a cross between the Sundays of that era but with shopping and Fridays without work; the day had a spirit of no-man's land about it, especially around 3 p.m. This was even more profound less than a week after the Christmas holidays; a sense of 'What are we doing here?' dominated the background of the collective mind. It certainly made little practical sense to be standing crushed together on the freezing cold, ice-hardened terraces with 34,154 other shivering souls. But in 1964 I, like everyone else to a greater or lesser extent, was there on the North Bank because I was there. I 'was' (and still am) along with every other supporter of the claret and blue enigma... West Ham.

The last time the Hammers and Charlton had met in the Cup had been in the 1931/32 season, when the travelling Irons visited The Valley, again in the third round. Vic Watson, West Ham's all-time top goal getter, netted twice for his side in the 2-1 Irons victory. It had been a hard-fought game, the visitors finding it a challenge to deal with centre-forward Ted Watkins, and it had seemed almost impossible to get anything past Addicks 'keeper Peter Robertson. But West Ham appeared to be taking no prisoners that day. The home side were truly the 'Valliants' (although the club's fans didn't vote for the adoption of that particular nickname until 1963, at the same time the now familiar club emblem of the sword was introduced) for even though they were reduced in numbers during the second half, the nine Charlton men that finished the game managed to avoid a massacre.

In 1964 Charlton may not have been a First Division outfit, but the club posed a challenging prospect for a struggling West Ham side so early in the competition. The manager of the Robins (what Charlton lack in glory they make up for in nicknames), Frank Hill, a former Scottish international wing-half and three times League Championship-winning Gunner, who had started his coaching career with Preston North End in 1944, was able to select the blooming, Wisbech-born Michael Alfred Bailey, who would honour his Cambridgeshire roots a few months later by gaining the first of his two England caps for his robust, all-action wing-half part in the 10-0 destruction of the USA in New York. Mike, an experienced Under-23 international in January 1964, had started his football career on the ground staff at The Valley before turning pro in March 1959. He made his League debut in December

1960 against Plymouth at Home Park. He would move from South East London and adopt the old gold of Wolverhampton early in 1966, becoming a stalwart of Molineux for a dozen years before finishing his playing career with Hereford and Minnesota.

The Charlton strike force included inside forward Dennis Edwards, an England amateur international before he moved to Charlton from Wycombe Wanderers in February 1959 and Eddie Firmani, who was, at the time, the 'golden boy' of The Valley. Firmani was intelligent striker, who signed pro for Charlton in 1950 along with fellow South African Stuart Leary. He went to Italy and Sampdoria in 1954, a quite novel move for a British-based player in those dour days of English football, but Eddie had returned to The Valley just three months before facing the Hammers in the Cup. Firmani would be the pioneering manager of a number of clubs after he hung up his boots, including his beloved Charlton. John Hewie was yet another South African import, born in Bornat, Pretoria; he played for Arcadia Shepherds before he joined Charlton in 1949. He had appeared in nine different positions for the club (including goalkeeper). Hewie had made his 450th appearance for Charlton over the Christmas period of 1963. Apart from representing his country at Under-19 and Under-23 level he was also an able baseball player.

The Charlton boss, Frank Hill, was the man who would make William Arthur Bonds a Charlton professional just eight months after the FA Cup third-round game with West Ham in 1964. Billy was the boy who would become the man who would lift the cup in 1975 and 1981 in a Hammers shirt. Hill was an astute and cunning manager of the old school, and alongside Michael Gliksten, who at the age of twenty-three became the youngest ever League chairman when he took command of The Valley in February 1962, was building a team that during the spring of 1964 would make a real effort to return to the First Division.

Charlton took the field in their white shirts with red shoulder flashes and white shorts, a strip that was pioneered by the club at the start of that season (these were the times when a change of kit colours marked a real departure from tradition rather than the annual commercial ploy it has become). The furtive fenland official Mr J.R. Osborne from Ipswich blew the game to its start in the strangely still atmosphere of New Year at Upton Park. It marked the start of an afternoon of magic from the feet of West Ham's Johnny Byrne. This, together with the faultless stream of supply to wingers Peter Brabrook and Sissons (this was the first FA Cup tie that teenager Johnny had played) took its toll on Charlton after just ten minutes. The immaculate Bobby Moore glided a graceful pass to Sissons, Johnny moved elegantly before delivering the ball to Hurst, who wasted not a fraction of a second in putting the Hammers into the lead.

Just a quarter of an hour later Byrne flowered into what was an amazing run through centre field, only to be confronted by one time Manchester United centre half, Frank Haydock. He had joined Charlton the previous August for a fee of

£10,000 having made his debut for United three years previously. A product of the Old Trafford nursery, Frank had spent three years undertaking an engineering apprenticeship before turning professional in the grim days after Munich. Although not being able to break into the first team on more than the odd occasion, Haydock only made half a dozen appearances for the Manchester Reds, Matt Busby thought a lot of Frank, admiring his bravery (he had a number of bad injuries as a direct result of his courage) and whole-hearted approach. As such, West Ham's artistic Byrne was facing a dangerous opponent. With split-second decision-making Byrne sent the ball on a quick amble to Brabrook. The iron flank man hit a hammer shot. Mike Rose, the South Londoner's custodian, might have got in the way of the Brabrook bomb, but he was beaten by the sheer pace and power of the strike.

Sissons concluded matters in the final sixty seconds of the game, effortlessly driving home from twenty-five yards. The buoyant, brash Byrne was bequeathed the bounteous bonus of Man of the Match.

Two days after West Ham cleared the first hurdle in their 1964 FA Cup campaign, the Rolling Stones started their first tour as a headline act, supported by the Ronettes, whose *Be My Baby* had been amongst the top selling records throughout the winter. Their second big British hit *Baby I Love You* entered the British charts at number 40 five days after West Ham progressed into the fourth round of the 1964 FA Cup.

1

The Third Round

We all liked a bit of music... all the latest stuff... like Top of the Pops and that...
Johnny Byrne – West Ham United and England

It's Number One...

A few days before the first kick of the 1964 FA Cup was taken, at 6.36 p.m. on 1 January 1964, a Wednesday evening, the first *Top of the Pops* was broadcast on BBC1 from a disused church in Manchester. The original opening music to the show was a percussion piece written by Johnnie Stewart and Harry Rabinowitz and this became a theme for kids like me who grew up in the 1960s.

This first show was presented by Jimmy Saville and his cigar. The acts that appeared were (in order) the Rolling Stones, who had just made number 13 in the chart with *I Wanna Be Your Man*, Dusty Springfield smashed out *I Only Want to be With You*, the Dave Clark Five banged and boomed the fact that they were feeling *Glad All Over* (I always wondered what Glad thought of that), the Hollies did *Stay* and the Swinging Blue Jeans shook *The Hippy Hippy Shake* (for goodness sake!). The show was completed by filmed pieces with Cliff Richard and the Shadows followed by Freddie and the Dreamers. The finale was the Beatles, who played the week's number one, *I Want To Hold Your Hand*.

Originally there were six *Top of the Pops* (TOTP) commissioned but in one format or another it would last for more than forty years, celebrating its 2,000th show in 2002, making it the longest-running pop show in the history of television. It moved to a Thursday night, but was later scheduled for Friday evenings, a change which was not altogether well received. After all, if you were into rock music you were out (or getting ready to go out) on Friday evening, and TOTP had been a mid-week life-saver for most young people as the television of the 1960s threatened to pulp the brain with the likes of Hughie Green and Michael Miles to the fore.

TOTP was originally a response to ITV's hugely successful *Ready, Steady, Go* (opening credits depicted Mods on scooters, waiting at traffic lights to roar of when the green light signalled 'go man go') and from the start, record executives and agents fought for their artistes to appear when they realised that being seen on

TOTP could mean the difference between reaching number ten in the 'hit parade' or being a 'chart topper'. Those were the days when the vinyl 45rpm ruled the scene. Most weeks from the mid-1960s on I would make my way to Selman's on the Barking Road, Canning Town and buy anywhere from half-a-dozen to twenty singles. Selman (coincidently the name of the bloke who owned Selman's) always made sure he was the first in the East End to stock the new releases. My dad (who was a great record collector) and I would look at the new releases and choose titles that appealed to us, or artistes that we liked. This was the way of music consumption at the time, the immediate musical past had been informed by 'Light Programme' and the crackling 'Radio Luxembourg'; when Joe Brown and his 'Bruvvers' were seen as the cockney answer to Elvis (not that I ever liked Elvis much).

For a band or singer to stay current they had to get as many as six new singles in the shops every year (although few got past one or two). Bill Cotton, Assistant Head of Light Entertainment for the BBC from 1962 to 1967 recalled the immediate impact of TOTP:

> After the second show I got a call from Brian Epstein asking if the Beatles latest record could be played. I said 'Sure, if they turn up at Dickinson Road.' He said to me 'Do you know what will happen if the Beatles turn up at Dickinson Road?' I said 'I certainly do!'

Soon it wasn't just British artistes that saw the value of appearing on TOTP. Indeed the show gave many British viewers their first sight of American stars like Diana Ross and the Supremes, 'Little' Stevie Wonder, Marvin Gaye and the Ronettes.

The original format for TOTP was created by Johnnie Stewart, the show's first producer (1964–1973). Alongside the production team he set guidelines for how things should be done. The most rigorous regulation was that performers would only be featured if their singles were in the top 20 and going up the charts. Artistes appearing would mime to their records, which were visibly placed on a turntable in front of the DJ (in those early days Jimmy Saville shared the presenting on alternate weeks with David Jacobs, Alan Freeman and Pete Murray). The records were 'spun' by an assistant and these included Denise Sampey (on the first programme), Diane Hefforan and Samantha Juste, who eventually married Micky Dolenz of the Monkees after they met on the show. Robin Gibb of the Bee Gees remembered:

> Top of the Pops was a catalyst for the swinging sixties... It represented a great period of music.

However, as British pop music grew into an international industry it became increasingly difficult for bands and singers to commit themselves to appearing on TOTP, and so more filmed inserts were added.

As Keith Richards of the Rolling Stones said:

> If we were touring Australia or somewhere far away we'd phone them up and say 'how about we record a film of us singing the record or larking about' and they'd say 'fine'. It was the caveman version of the later pop video that I guess we and the Beatles invented.

As an alternative to the filmed inserts TOTP also introduced a trio of girl dancers called the *Go-Jos*. The name was a corruption of 'Go-Go', the title given to professional discothèque (yes, that's where the word 'disco' comes from) dancers. The TOTP troop were led by dancer and choreographer Jo (hence *Go-**Jo***) Cook. Pop star Lulu remembered seeing them for the first time:

> They mostly wore white boots to the knee and short skirts and the camera would go up the skirt and it was all very risqué.

Like many a boy who grew up in the mid-1960s, sexual preference becoming set in adolescence, I spent my early teenage and young adulthood looking for a *Go-Jo*, but no one really danced like that (did they?). In the late 1960s, and through most of the 1970s, the dancing girl idea was taken a step further with *Pan's People*, a group of six dancers led by Flick Colby. *Ruby Flipper* took the tradition on, bringing at times a child-like surrealism to their routines, which can't really be described in words and had to be seen to be believed. The last incarnation was *Legs & Co.* who whilst having skimpier costumes (or rather a lack of costume) and being much more provocative, never really tapped into the deep traumatic urges of male pre-pubescence in the same way as the *Go-Jos*.

Ticker

Ronnie was a player's player. He had a very high work rate and would find space and get the ball to you when you had made space.
Johnny Byrne – West Ham United and England

West Ham's Ronnie Boyce was a hard-working midfielder, a very good passer, who kept the game simple and supplied the bullets for the likes of Geoff Hurst and Johnny Byrne to fire. A local lad who grew up just a throw-in away from the Boleyn Ground in East Ham, Boyce followed the Hammers as a young fan in the '50s. He joined the Upton Park cause as a hopeful schoolboy in 1954.

From his earliest days Ron fought with his own self-doubts and nervousness. He was about thirteen years of age when he was invited to Upton Park for the traditional Tuesday and Thursday evening training nights by Wally St Pier, the legendary 'star maker' of West Ham United. Ron remembered:

> … those nights, under the tunnel, Noel Cantwell and Malcolm Allison coached the younger players. We didn't have much in the way of facilities but the training was fun and helped to get us fit and improve our skills.

This was a time before the arrival of Ron Greenwood, when Ted Fenton was the manager of West Ham. According to Boyce,

> He was a nice man but not really a coach in the same way Allison was. Ernie Gregory thought he'd be a good chief scout and he did bring some great players to the club.
>
> Then you could leave school in the fourth year and most boys who got taken on at a football club, on the ground staff, finished school at that point. But my Mum thought I should stay on and take O-Levels, so I did the fifth year. I was on holiday when my Mum sent me the results. I did eight exams and didn't pass one.
>
> I suppose that year was a bit of a waste as I was going to join West Ham, but at the same time I never saw myself as being good enough to make a professional footballer. [Ron laughed]. I never saw myself as being successful at much at all. I always thought I would fail at the things I did.

Ron, who was also a good tennis player, represented East Ham, London, Essex and England at schoolboy level. He joined the Hammers' youth section and played for the England Youth side. He was always nervous before games, regardless of standard. He recollected:

> Before home matches I'd have boiled fish at about twelve o'clock round at Dawn's mum's house [Ron and Dawn, formerly Ames, were married in July 1964] in East Ham. Then I'd walk to the ground, getting there for around quarter-to-one. I can't see many players doing that these days. Some players relaxed before the match but not me. I would worry about not doing well. Like my mum, I'm a worrier.

For all this, as Ron said himself, if he had not been so nervous he would not have played as well as he did.

At the age of seventeen, having signed professional forms in the summer of 1960, Ron was introduced to first-team football at Upton Park against Preston North End that first year of the 1960s. On 22 October, only he and Eddie Bovington were one-club men. It was Ted Fenton's last term at Upton Park. Ron recalled:

> The year before, I was sixteen, I played against Millwall in the Southern Floodlit Cup [as an amateur at Upton Park on 13 October 1959] so I had a bit of experience at senior level. We beat Preston 5-1; Malcolm Musgrove got a hat-trick. I had to wait a few months for my next match at Leicester. We were beaten 5-1 [Ron laughed].

At the time Boyce was still very young and Fenton did not feel he was ready for regular first-team football. Ron played just a few games over the next couple of years, but when one of West Ham's most experienced international players was sold to Aston Villa he got a chance. The 5ft 9in, twelve-stone Boyce gained a regular first-team place on the departure of Phil Woosnam in November 1962. The Welshman had been a popular player at the Boleyn Ground and Boyce was not well received at first. Woosnam was able to imprint his personality on a game; in contrast Ronnie was a relatively quiet player who got on with his midfield job of grafting, unnoticed and mostly unheralded. He reflected:

> I just thought 'wait a little while, it will come'.

Maybe Ron learnt some of his patience and meticulousness from the thrillers he used to like to read but gradually his fortitude paid off, getting the recognition he deserved from the Upton Park congregation. When Ron Greenwood came to Upton Park and worked with Boyce to develop his relatively uncomplicated 'up and down' inside forward style to produce a more cultivated midfield role, the England team manager Alf Ramsey began to take note.

For Ron, when Greenwood became manager, everything at the club seemed to change. Along with the other young players, the former Arsenal and England Under-23 coach taught Boyce things about the game he would probably have never learnt from any other manager in the country. According to Boyce Greenwood was

> … definitely a training ground manager. Ron opened your eyes because he could put his ideas over and explain the reasons for the things he wanted you to do.

Some have said that Greenwood could, at times, be hard on people, but Boyce always got on well with his manager, who he saw as giving him confidence by letting him and other players know what he wanted from them and why. For Boyce:

> If you took notice of what he said, you couldn't disagree with his ideas about the game. He had a tremendous knowledge of football. I think he lost some people but I had no problems understanding him.

In 1964 Boyce described his role in the West Ham team in an unspectacular way: '... working behind the front line... I play the way the manager wants me to play. If he is satisfied, I am satisfied.' Greenwood once said of Boyce that he was 'the quiet man' of the West Ham side and it is true that before the 1964 FA Cup he was not one of the Hammers' players who made the headlines. In this respect he was like his dad, who I knew fairly well as my family used to supply his business with 'carrier-bags' of firewood that he retailed from his greengrocers shop, which was situated equidistant from my home and the Boleyn Ground. I often saw Ronnie there helping out, even after he broke into the West Ham first team. Despite being a man of few words, Boyce senior was Mayor of West Ham and was referred to as 'Alderman'. But he was also true to the innate kindness of his old Labour principals. Between the ages of around six and ten I used to deliver the wood to him in a small barrow made for me by my grandfather, I was paid 3d for filling each brown paper bag, each about the size of a contemporary plastic shopping bag. I think my youthful industriousness appealed to the other side of Alderman Boyce, his entrepreneurial persona. He'd point to where he wanted the bags lined up outside the shop and I'd unload the barrow. On completion he would look at my work and wordlessly slip me two bob. That florin nearly always paid me into West Ham's North Bank, with enough left for a bag of Percy Dalton's (was that peanut with legs in a top-hat, spats and monocle scary or what?) and a drink.

When in the ground I'd watch Ronnie Boyce and, to me, the management of his game reflected many of his father's principals. It was based more on pragmatics and seemingly tireless work-rate than pointless flourish. It seemed to mirror what the great Celtic manager Jock Stein once said of football, that it was 'a type of Socialism'. Boyce was indeed the pumping heart of the West Ham team, linking the side together as a unit. However, Ron was also a clever player and, like his colleague Bobby Moore, able to read games almost to perfection. The boy who stood on the terraces to support the Hammers had modelled himself on the artistry of Johnny Haynes and, much like Fulham's England skipper, Boyce's first-time passing was of exceptional quality. Indeed, it was this ability that proved to be a vital factor in West Ham's successful mid-sixties era. He certainly was one of the most important players in the Irons' tactical formation, despite perhaps being the least conspicuous.

Forest Fired

Both of the Forest games were very hard work. They gave nothing away...it was do or die... a real battle for survival.
Alec Ashworth – Preston North End

In the first months of the 1960s, 'Proud' Preston North End, the one-time rulers of Lancastrian soccer, fell out of the top flight of English football. The town, steeped in soccer history, home of 'The Invincibles' of the first days of the game was made mute at the shock of such a debacle. There seemed little to do but wait for the resurrection that few thought less than certain. The initial signs were not good, however:

FAMOUS
FOOTBALL
CLUBS
1/-
OFFICIAL HISTORY OF
PRESTON NORTH-END
THE EXCITING STORY OF PRESTON NORTH END. SIXTY-SIX YEARS OF FOOTBALL THRILLS . . . GREAT GAMES AND GREAT PLAYERS OF THE PAST AND PRESENT
by
ALEX JAMES
& LAINSON
WOOD

The cover of *The Official History of Preston North End.*

the first hint at a possible Deepdale renaissance came in the form of a fine FA Cup run in 1962, which included the defeat of Liverpool over three games and taking Manchester United to a replay in the sixth round. But by 1963 many of North End's brightest prospects were attracting the attention of football's giants, particularly Liverpool and their manager, former Preston stalwart Bill Shankly. It was clear that North End had to get back into Division One swiftly, before the means to achieve such a feat was denied them by the dictates of soccer economics.

Although the Lilywhites showed little sign of cup form in the first part of the 1963/64 season, suffering an early exit from the League Cup after a sluggish start in Division Two, the Deepdale legion produced a brilliant 5-4 win at Southampton to begin an impressive run of results that caused them to look like promotion prospects. This was in no small part due to their manager, Jimmy Milne, being able to keep a fairly settled side together. The improved standard of play was especially noticeable from the points picked up away from their home ground. Reaping harvests of points on 'foreign' turf was not a trait that Preston had been known for during the first part of the 1960s, but through the autumn, winter and on into the spring, North End would battle it out with Sunderland and Leeds United for the championship title. However, 1964 was still young when an already exciting campaign gained added spice from a determined assault on the FA Cup by Milne's marauders, although there was little indication of the coming cup crusade as the Preston potentate brought his troops home for the third-round FA Cup replay, following an inauspicious goal-less away draw against Nottingham Forest.

The team that Milne built

In the great Tom Finney's final playing year, Preston North End, the club that his name had been synonymous with, and still is, achieved a negative balance of over £10,000. This figure, in its time, was relatively comparable to some of the crisis-provoking football debts of the current era. By 1963, the Deepdale board effectively staked everything on an attempt to return to the elite sphere of the English game. The gamble brought a number of fine players into the ranks of the Lilywhites.

After the arrival of Alex Dawson, Jimmy Milne began to build his side in earnest. Before the Christmas of 1962, Doug

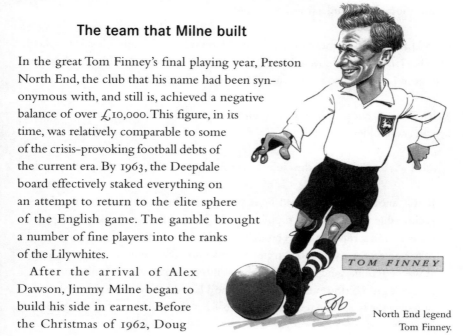

North End legend Tom Finney.

Holden and Ian Davidson had joined the former Manchester United progeny. Norbert Lawton, another former Old Trafford graduate, signed up with Milne's brigade. Nobby was a huge influence on the side's good form in the early part of 1963. At the same time that Milne was building via the chequebook, young players like Peter Thompson, who many thought to be 'the new Finney', were coming up through the youth ranks. It was becoming clear that Milne had an eye for talent and many were of the opinion that in particular his acquisition of Dawson and Lawton had been two masterful moves on the transfer market. Other players showed excellent form too, and both Dave Wilson and George Ross attracted the attention of the international selectors from England and Scotland, respectively.

A dour struggle

As Preston approached the replay of the third round of the 1964/65 FA Cup they were beginning to gel as a unit, as Alec Ashworth recalled:

> When Alex Dawson or myself were out, Brian Godfrey could come in. That made the chances of scoring pretty good. Nobby, Ian Davidson and Alan Spavin were playing brilliantly in the midfield, and at the back George Ross and Jim Smith were always reliable. Alan Kelly was a great 'keeper, at the time he had played for the Republic of Ireland for a couple of seasons and Doug Holden was always making his presence felt. Of course, at centre half Tony Singleton was a local bloke and a tower of strength.

On 13 January 1964, Jimmy Milne brought Howard Kendall into his side to take the role that Ian Davidson covered in the first game with Forest. Davidson in turn took over from Jim Smith, so the Preston side was:

Kelly, Ross, Davidson, Lawton, Singleton, Kendall, Wilson, Ashworth, Dawson, Spavin and Holden.

Kendall was a youngster at the club at the time and recalled something of those days:

> It was another era, sure, and light years from the millionaire's row of the Premiership, but you weren't spoiled then. Cleaning the tide mark off the players' bath and scrubbing boots brought you down to earth and gave you a sense of perspective as a young boy trying to make it in the professional game. I look at Wayne Rooney and he's got Robbie Williams and Atomic Kitten coming to his eighteenth birthday. A few years ago he'd have been painting the tea-hut or sweeping the Goodison terraces, but football has changed beyond all recognition. These boys are the new pop stars and it takes a lot of handling.

First Division Nottingham Forest made Milne's men work hard. Ashworth recalled:

> Forest fought us for every ball and were determined not to be shown up by a side from a lower division. I don't think that fact helped us a lot. Maybe it put us off a bit as they played a bit like a Division Two side. It was a battle really. I don't know if anyone had even expected a replay. There wasn't even time to print programmes. There was just a single sheet for people.
>
> Forest had a decent side: Peter Grummitt in goal, he'd played for the Football League and was an England Under-23 man, as was Henry Newton and Jeff Whitefoot. Frank Wignall would play for England up front a bit later on as would Ian Storey-Moore of course. They gave us a tough game – we were underdogs of course. But Howard Kendall got the only goal in extra time and we went through. I think we earned it.

Kendall recalled the game:

> I'd played a few games that season, but the one tie that really sticks out is scoring that extra-time winner against Nottingham Forest in a fourth-round replay. There were twenty-nine thousand there and the game finished with Deepdale under a couple of inches of snow.

The fates were pulling West Ham United and Preston North End together; two football institutions from different ends of the country and opposite poles of the soccer continuum. The matches that would follow in the quest for the cup would dictate the destiny of these clubs, their players, their managers and their supporters. This was not, however, just the start of the road to Wembley, it was also a path that would change the history of the 'world contest'; the sport most hallowed by humanity – the planetary pursuit – the greatest game.

The Managers

Jimmy Milne

Jimmy Milne was a good manager. He knew what football was about and he knew how to handle players.
Alec Ashworth – Preston North End

The phrase that describes an individual as being the club 'through and through' is, in the contemporary era, to be subjected to the most severe questioning, but in the mid-1960s Jimmy Milne was second only to Tom Finney in terms of being inextricably associated with North End. Milne joined Preston from Dundee United as a promising left-half in 1932 for a fee of £900 and made his debut for the club on 29 October 1932 in a Division Two game at Lincoln. A goal from Bert Hales didn't prevent Preston from going away from Sincil Bank as losers.

Milne soon became noted for his consistency and ability to give of his all in match after match. He had great composure on the ball but was a strong tackler and almost instantly became a regular in North End's first team. Although he was often overshadowed by his more illustrious teammates, Jimmy's contribution in his second season with the club helped Preston win promotion to Division One, pushing deadly rivals Bolton Wanderers into third place (keeping them in the lower flight for another season) by a single point. Milne was a rock as North End pushed through to the sixth round of the FA Cup in the 1934/35 term. They were only to be stopped by an excellent West Bromwich Albion side. But Jimmy went to the final in 1937 playing left-half for the Whites. Preston were the underdogs against Sunderland, who, skippered by Raich Carter, had finished as League Champions the previous season. The Black Cats dominated the match, winning 3-1. However, 1937 had its compensations for Jimmy. His son Gordon had been born on 29 March of that year. He would follow his father into the Preston side as a stylish wing-half and win fourteen England caps.

The following season Preston found themselves level on points with Arsenal at the top of the First Division when the Gunners came to Deepdale. Great things were expected of North End as Milne and his comrades had knocked Arsenal out of the cup at Highbury. It was a vital match but the North Londoners won 3-1 and were crowned champions. It might have been different if Milne had not broken a collarbone after a collision with Alf Kitchen, leaving Preston with ten men. With Milne out of the side Preston faltered and finished the season in third place. However, a week after being beaten by the Gunners, the Deepdale men, contesting the FA Cup final for the second successive year, met Huddersfield at the Twin Towers. Jimmy watched his side win 1-0 with a last-minute penalty.

Preston had gone from strength to strength after Milne had joined the club's cause. He had become a permanent fixture in the North End side, and as the shadows of war overtook the happenings of the football pitches of Britain, Jimmy was becoming recognised as one of the finest uncapped half-backs of his era. He played for Preston during a period when the club were amongst the football elite of England and as such, at that time, were one of the best sides in the world. His defensive partnership with Bill Shankly, who would become immortalised as perhaps the finest manager in the history of Liverpool Football Club, became renowned. Other stars of that Preston side included Tom Smith, Bob and Andy Beattie and George Mutch.

Whilst with Preston, Jimmy worked under two managers (a club committee had run Preston from 1932 to 1936 and again from 1937 until the outbreak of the Second World

War). The first, Lincoln Hyde, he barely got to know, but the second, Tommy Muirhead, had a lasting effect on the young Milne. Muirhead joined North End in April 1936 having managed in the USA, and taken St Johnstone into the top echelon of Scottish football in 1931/32. He had also guided the Saints to the last four of the Scottish Cup. In his playing days Muirhead worked well in a number of positions. He turned out 352 times for Glasgow Rangers, scoring forty-nine goals in his thirteen years at Ibrox, gaining eight Scottish caps, eight Scottish League Championship medals and a Scottish Cup winners medal in 1928 (although he did not play in the final) in the process.

At Preston, Muirhead quickly saw that the English game was not to his liking, for him it lacked the aesthetic qualities of Scottish football and the Caledonian purist became frustrated by what he saw as a lack of flair and artistry. After the 1937 cup final he walked away from Deepdale, seeing the team as being in little need of his direction. This was instructive for Milne in that it gave appropriate responsibility to honest and able players. The side he built in the early/mid-1960s had similar qualities.

During the Second World War Milne became a police officer. From time to time he played for Preston but in common with most players of the time his football career suffered. But in all he turned out in 272 League and cup games for Preston. With the coming of peace, Jimmy became player/manager of Wigan and later, in 1947, the first ever manager of Morecambe FC (he was again player/manager), before taking up the role of trainer with Doncaster Rovers. He returned to Deepdale and served the club for eleven years as a trainer, again going to Wembley in 1954; this time he watched his side defeated by West Bromwich Albion. Jimmy became the twelfth manager of Preston in 1961, taking over after the resignation of Cliff Britton; it was the year that North End fell out of English football's upper strata.

As a manager, pipe-smoking Milne was a fair but hard taskmaster. He would tell players that if they played below form he would drop them, despite any excuses. But if an individual lost his place through injury Jimmy would restore him to the side as soon as he was fit. Milne was to achieve much given that the basis of Preston's former successes had been limitations imposed on players by the maximum wage. With the abolition of the restrictions on player salaries in 1961, North End found it hard to hold on to their younger players and compete with the big clubs of the time. One such loss was Jimmy's only son Gordon.

Gordon Milne came into the Preston side as a wing-half. He made ten first-team appearances in two seasons deputising for Tommy Docherty and Frank O'Farrell. He turned out for Morecambe before he came into his dad's side. In August 1958, now in the Army and with Docherty transferred to Arsenal, Milne junior turned out on twenty-nine consecutive occasions for Preston at right-half, playing in three FA Cup ties. Gordon was picked to play for the British Army against the French Army in Paris and the following season he made thirty-eight first-team appearances, ten of them as a makeshift inside right.

After the first three games of North End's relegation season of 1960/61 failed to yield a single point, Gordon Milne became one of the scapegoats, probably to soften the fans for the blow of his imminent transfer. In August 1960, three days after being dropped, Milne the younger moved to Liverpool for £17,000, joining his father's former defensive partner Bill Shankly. He had played eighty-one games for North End and scored three goals.

In 1962 Gordon won a Second Division Championship medal with the Anfield Reds having made a huge contribution to his side's campaign, playing in all forty-two matches. To Preston fans this could only illustrate the nature of the times and what they had lost in the departure of 'one of their own'.

Jimmy Milne was a soccer guru. As a manager he had habituated going for long walks in search of peace and the perspective gained from taking in the glories of nature. It was his safety valve and a form of meditation. His tactical awareness and football intelligence were second to none, as exemplified when he effectively extended Tom Finney's career by suggesting that the England legend and Preston god switch from right-wing to a Di Stefano game, playing as a deep-lying centre-forward. Had Preston done that in 1954, they might have won the FA Cup.

After North End plummeted out of the First Division and deep, deep down into Division Two, it had been Jimmy who salvaged their pride. In the 1960s he came near to doing for Preston what he had done for the club in the 1930s. There was a touch of the Midas about Jimmy Milne.

Ron Greenwood

Ron Greenwood was a tremendous coach. Ron was far in advance of anyone else as a manager and when I came from Chelsea it was an entirely different ball game.

Peter Brabrook – West Ham United and England

Ron Greenwood's dad had been on the ground staff at Wembley and as a boy working in the great arena he had painted many of its signs, but he had always had an inner desire to go back to the stadium with a less humble status.

In 1946, Greenwood, a solid half-back, played for Bradford Park Avenue in an FA Cup tie against Manchester City at Maine Road, which resulted in an 8-2 victory for Bradford. In 1952, Ron captained an England 'B' team to a 1-0 victory against Holland's full national side in Amsterdam. He made twenty-one League appearances for Chelsea in the 1954/55 season – the last time Chelsea won the League Championship in the twentieth century, before moving to Fulham to play alongside the impiously precocious, prodigiously perceptive, brusque, 'Brucey-chinned' Jimmy Hill.

Ron started coaching with Oxford University and Walthamstow Avenue, before moving to Eastbourne United. He subsequently managed England's Youth team before Arsenal signed him as assistant manager and coach, and for nearly three years he was coach to England Under-23 teams.

Although many have cited Ron's coaching sessions and clinics as bringing them out of the darkness with his ideas and insight, he once said:

> Coaching is nothing mystical. It is a question of common sense, of encouraging players to think for themselves, getting them to react in the right way to situations as they arise in the game. There is a tendency to forget that errors are never intentional, that even the greatest players make mistakes. As long as I can put my tracksuit on and get down amongst my players I can appreciate that I can make a bad pass or mis-trap a ball. I can pick out the wrong player to pass to when others are in a better position.

Greenwood respected ability but insisted that it was backed with effort. He allowed individual expression within the framework of his side, but demanded that the each person sink himself into the team effort when it was required. To that extent he was a purist. According to West Ham winger of the 1960s, Peter Brabrook,

> … he baffled me a little bit because he was so far advanced. It was unbelievable really and things he used to do back then are even being done at West Ham now. That's how far-sighted he was.

Greenwood emphasised passing and holding the ball. He encouraged players to use space and move off the ball. Most of the West Ham professionals of the mid-1960s had been playing this way since their earliest days at the Boleyn ground, under the influence of Malcolm Allison, but Greenwood had organised and developed the West Ham game and made it work in the 4-2-4 system. This was cultivated football. Greenwood has often faced criticism of his 'man-management' but for Johnny Byrne, the man for whom Ron broke the British transfer record to bring to Upton Park:

> Ron had enough faith in me to pay a lot of money for my contract. He never stopped believing in me as a player and I always believed in him as a manager.

2

The Fourth Round

Playing in the snow! That was always fun... everyone liked doing that...
Johnny Byrne – West Ham United and England

The Tyrolean city of Innsbruck was host to the Winter Olympics that commenced on 29 January 1964. Despite being a traditional winter sports resort, there was a lack of snow and ice during the Games, and the Austrian army was called in to bring 'the cold stuff' to the sport venues.

Just a few days after the fourth round of the 1964 FA Cup the bobsleigh returned to the Olympics, having not been included in the Games of 1960. For aficionados of the bobsleigh the Olympics had double importance in 1964 as this was one of the years when the Bobsleigh World Championships would be combined with the Olympian event, so in effect each gold medal carried two titles.

The clear favourites in the four-man contest were the hometown Austrians and the mighty Italians. Experts gave the good-looking Canadians an outside chance. However, in the first heat Canada 1 broke the Olympic record and had a half-second lead on the rest of the field. But on that record-setting first run the Canadians went into the last turn too fast, hitting the ice wall of the Igls run and were propelled up on two runners. The accident damaged the sled axle, causing it to seize. If the Canadians failed to fix it they would be disqualified.

The Italian team included Eugenio Monti. Alongside the rest of his teammates Monti had no desire to win unless victory was attained against the best, on equal terms. He was the most successful bobsled pilot the world had known. In the 1956 St Moritz Games, Monti had picked up silver medals in both the two- and four-man races. He had been World Champion in the two-man event every year from 1957 to 1961 and led the Italian four-man team to victory in 1960 and 1961. The year before Innsbruck he had regained the World two-man title. Monti was the brains behind many Italian successes in bobsledding. He attached more importance than most people to practising push-off starts, being acutely aware of the valuable fractions of a second to be saved at this crucial stage. For Monti the correct position and speed of the bob as it entered a major bend was a matter of scientific precision.

Fifteen minutes before Canada's second run, their pilot, Victor Emery, reached the top of the track to find his sled upside down. The Italians had torn it apart and

Monti's mechanics where doing their best to fix the damage. With Monti's help, Canada 1 was able to race and hold on to its lead. By the fourth and final run, they were so far ahead only a disaster would keep them from the gold medal. When the Canadians came to a stop the gold medal was theirs. In the end, Eugenio and his team received the bronze medal.

After the four-man event, Monti and brakeman Sergio Siorpaes began their defence of their two-man World title and bid for Olympic glory. The British pair, Anthony James Nash of the RAF and his brakeman Grenadier Guards Captain, Robin Thomas Dixon, were seen as contenders. Although Britain did not have a strong tradition in bobsleighing – the British had not won a World Championship since 1937 and a British bob had never won an Olympic title – in 1963 Nash and Dixon, despite always being obliged to compete on foreign ice, had finished third in the World Championship in the two-man boblet event and fourth in the four-man contest, joined by crewmen David Lewis and Guy Renwick. That World Championship had been staged on the same Igls course as would be used in Olympics.

Nash saw the ninth corner, Hexenkessel, which was situated about halfway down the course, as the vital point of the run. He had discovered that if the sled took the turn correctly at this stage, it could more easily dive and gather extra momentum for the rest of the run. By trial and error Nash and Dixon found the precise manner in which to take that bend. This was to give the British a crucial advantage.

In their first run Nash and Dixon recorded the fastest time of the competition, but their axle had been cracked in the process and withdrawal seemed inevitable. Eugenio Monti, who was about to steer the Italian number one sled down the track said, 'Get an Englishman and a spanner to the finish and they can have my axle'. True to his word and ignoring inquiries from mystified Italian journalists, the British bob was repaired just in time and Nash and Dixon took home Britain's only gold of the games.

Eugenio Monti, yet again, made do with the consolation of a bronze medal having been beaten into third place by the Italy 2 pair.

However, perhaps a greater solace was the decision of the Comité Internationale des Trophées du Fair Play Pierre de Coubertin in Paris to award Monti the Fair Play Trophy for his unselfish and sportsmanlike behaviour. For all this, Monti was viciously criticised in the Italian press for his acts of sporting charity, but he was steadfast:

> Nash didn't win because I gave him the axle… He won because he had the fastest run.

But Eugenio proved himself to be a rarity in modern sport, understanding the Olympic ideal. He wanted to achieve victory over his opponents on their best day.

For him there would have been no glory, only disappointment, when top competitors were injured or disqualified.

Nash and Dixon went on to successfully defend their World title in St Moritz, Switzerland the following year. Nash was a powerful influence behind a British bobsleigh resurgence, not only inspiring others with his steering skill but also as a keen brain behind his country's technical developments in the sport he loved. He achieved a remarkably close racing understanding with Dixon and even after their retirement in 1968 they remained of great value to British bobsleighing, passing on the benefit of their experience to younger team colleagues. Robin Dixon returned to his home in Northern Ireland, set up a successful business and eventually became Lord Glentoran. At the time of writing he was actively involved in promoting London's bid to host the Olympic Games.

Monti took his two bronze medals from Innsbruck and went on to win yet another two-man World title in 1966, and in 1968 he won the Olympic titles that had eluded him throughout his career when he raced his way to both the four-man and two-man gold medals in Grenoble. Monti's skill, experience and sportsmanship led to his being appointed Italian team manager after his retirement in 1968. Apart from his achievements as an Olympian, between 1956 and 1968 he had won eleven World titles together with three silver and two bronze World Championship medals. But it was his willingness to lose that earned him a prominent place in Olympic history. His acts of sportsmanship represent the best of human endeavour in competition: the pursuit of victory with zeal and passion, recognising that there is no true victory without honour. The real glory of sport is in the striving, not the winning. But maybe a West Ham supporter finds that easier to say than the 'remote' Arsenal fan or the so-called 'London Red' for whom the motivation to 'wear the shirt' has more to do with gaining some insipid 'reflected glory' rather than the giving of support – there are indeed many brands of poverty in this world.

In these days, when so many sportsmen and women are willing to cheat by using drugs, when footballers are willing to dive or urge that fellow professionals be sent off in order to improve their chances of winning at any cost, even their integrity, we need reminders of the noble potential of sport as embodied in Eugenio Monti, he and his Italian teammates of 1964 represent everything that is important in life. They gave the best of themselves, but also gave their best to everyone around them.

In Milan, Italy on 30 November 2003, Eugenio Monti died at the age of 75. He had been suffering from Parkinson's disease. In the 2004 World Championships in Koenigssee, Germany the International Bobsleigh and Skeleton Federation, FIBT, commemorated and honoured Eugenio Monti. The little Italian (but a giant of a man) was, in his time, the most successful bobsleigh pilot of the World Championships and one of the most successful sportsmen ever to take to the ice.

Ousting Orient

The next round was at Orient, a lovely old club where I ended up going a few years later. There were 34,000 at Brisbane Road that day. Imagine that now? But we had a star-studded side with the quality of Martin Peters, Geoff, Bobby and Budgie – world-class players of the day – and those were the kind of crowds we drew. We were a big attraction wherever we went.

Peter Brabrook – West Ham United and England

West Ham had about a fifteen-minute journey to bring them face to face with their fourth-round adversaries, the same opponents they had vanquished in the second round of the League Cup earlier in the season. At Brisbane Road the Hammers were greeted by a record crowd for the stadium (34,345 – a record that stands to the present day). Many more than half of them were Irons supporters.

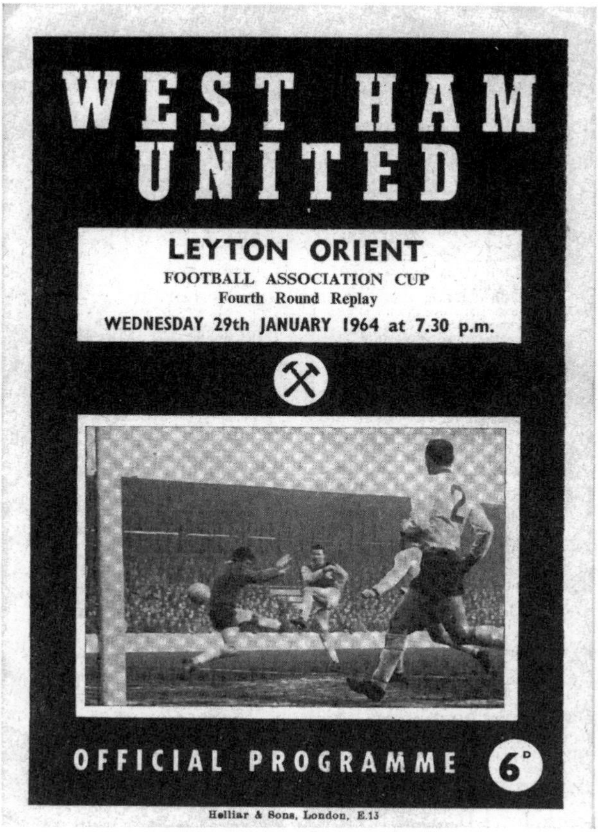

West Ham United *v.* Leyton Orient, 29 January 1964 programme cover.

In 1962, Orient had accompanied Liverpool into Division One. However, their time with the 'big boys' had been limited to that single season. They were relegated in 1963 as bottom club. Maybe in part because Orient have historically (post the First World War) been something of the poor relation to West Ham in East London, Hammers fans have seen the Leyton club just down the road from Upton Park as being 'mostly harmless' (to coin a phrase). The Irons and the Os have traditionally been the most convivial of rivals. Brisbane Road had also long been a place that many former West Ham players had retreated to following their peak years. But although Orient *v.* West Ham is nearly always a 'friendly derby' – the complete antithesis to, for example, a Millwall *v.* West Ham encounter – there is always pride at stake, and Orient had to be respected having seen off First Division Leicester City, just getting the majority of goals of a thrilling handful at Filbert Street.

The danger Orient posed was quickly made manifest when Norman Deely, who, in 1959 had turned out for England as a Wolves player against Brazil in Rio de Janeiro and played in the side that defeated Peru 4-1 in Lima on the same tour, nodded home the former England youth midfielder Gordon Gregory's corner after just two minutes. This kept West Ham on the back foot for much of the first half. However, shortly before the break John Sissons glided away from the one-time England Amateur international centre half Stan Charlton to facilitate Brabrook's equaliser.

So, it was back to Upton Park to do it all over again.

Instant Replay

The replay took place three weeks later on 25 January. The Orient side (like the referee – Mr D.W. Dawes of Norwich) were unchanged. Ken Lenton, the manager of the Os, who had at one time been on the playing staff at Upton Park, had put a capable team together. Mike Pinner was the Orient 'keeper. In his seventeen-year career Mike gained forty-nine English amateur caps. He was born in Boston, Lincolnshire on 16 February 1934. Pinner played for Great Britain in two Olympic tournaments, Melbourne (1956) and Rome (1960) and visited more than thirty countries representing his nation and touring with the famous Middlesex Wanderers amateur side. He also appeared in four Cambridge *v.* Oxford Varsity matches at Wembley. Mike's goalkeeping days began in 1948 with the Boston side Wyberton Rangers. He joined Notts County in the summer of 1949, but moved to Aston Villa in 1951 before breaking into the Magpies' League side. Next, in 1957, he made his way to Sheffield Wednesday, to move on to QPR two years later. A year at Loftus Road led to a move to Old Trafford in 1960. Pinner became the first amateur to play League football for United since Les Olive in 1953. He had four First Division outings for the Reds before joining Chelsea in 1961. In the same year he appeared for both Arsenal and Swansea reserves, and signed for Orient in 1962. At long last, in October 1963, he turned professional at the age of twenty-nine.

Like Pinner, full-back Stan Charlton was also an England amateur international. His defensive partner was Eddie Lewis, who had spent a year at Upton Park before moving to Brisbane Road. Eddie was as talented as an inside forward as he was at full-back. Born in Manchester on 3 January 1935, Lewis was a confident footballer who joined the Old Trafford ground staff as a fifteen year old in 1950, signing professional in January 1952. Eddie spent almost five years at Matt Busby's academy as one of the original 'Babes' before transferring to Preston North End at Christmas 1955. He made twenty League appearances for United, contributing nine goals to the Old Trafford cause. He made a dozen appearances and netted twice for North End. West Ham secured his services in 1956, and he played thirty-one games for the Hammers League side, finding the back of the net on twelve occasions prior to moving to Leyton.

I spoke to Eddie a few years ago, whilst he was the coach of Batha in South Africa where he had lived since 1971. His view of one of his West Ham opponents in the fourth round tie of 1964 was forthright:

> John Bond was a big mouth. He was always moaning, he wanted the ball but lost his temper when he didn't get it.

But Eddie was honest enough to give Bond his due in terms of his influence at Upton Park before the arrival of Greenwood:

> ABC, Allison, Bond and Cantwell, ran the club.

Lewis' frankness didn't stop with the Hammers:

> Going to Preston was the biggest mistake of my life. Tom Finney was a brilliant player, but was a miserable sod and Tommy Docherty was uncouth. It's part of my life I'd like to delete. It was a disaster. Even down to the digs. I used to have a landlady who would blow smoke down the spout of the teapot before she'd pour it. You got no help at Preston. I didn't really want to move south, but I hated Preston. But if I had stayed at Old Trafford, if I'd have been that bit faster, I'd have been dead. The air-crash see. I lost my best man in that.

For all this, Eddie seemed to have a definite affection for West Ham:

> I was sorry to leave West Ham, I was sad to leave United (but not Preston) but I stayed in the area and saw the same people, the lads I knew from West Ham, so it wasn't so bad and Orient were really a friendly, family club. When I was at Orient we were going to come in for a fat overweight boy, who sweated so much that

> you could see his shirt through his shorts. If Ron Greenwood had arrived at West Ham two weeks later, we'd have got him. But Ron wanted to look at the whole squad before he did anything and he chose to hang on to Geoff Hurst.
>
> The crowd were great, especially in the Chicken Run. It was quite something when they sang 'Bubbles'... all swaying together.

Two more former Hammers, David Dunmore (who had been a Tottenham man before coming to Upton Park) and Malcolm Musgrove, would play forward with Deely. Musgrove had made his debut for West Ham in the 1953/54 season in a visit to Brentford that resulted in a 3-1 beating. He was to become part of the bedrock of modern football and his career would span almost the entire second half of the twentieth century. Malcolm signed for West Ham following his demob from the RAF. He recalled:

> I went down and was met by Wally St Pier at the station. Players were all together in those days, most of the club houses were together in the same area. The fans weren't very good to me at times, when I was going through a bad period. We had a feller, in the Chicken Run he used to get at me something terrible. I wasn't afraid of going out, but I preferred to play on the stand side for a time. He used to shout, 'I'm here again Muzzy', and he'd just keep going. The only way you could beat him was to score or win the game. Eventually I won him over. I never met him. The crowd were so near!
>
> It was never my intention to leave West Ham. Orient came in, I could have gone to Fulham, Johnny Haynes was inside left there. Trevor Chamberlain was outside left, I thought, 'why are they looking for another left winger?' I thought I'd be stuck in the reserves. I could walk into the Orient side, Eddie was there and I didn't have to move house. I thought, 'I'm not going over West'.

Malcolm played 301 games for West Ham, scoring eighty-nine goals including a hat-trick against Preston in 1960 in front of the Upton Park fans. His first goal, one of two in a 3-3 draw, helped West Ham to salvage a point in a confrontation with Bury at the Boleyn Ground, late in 1954.

David Dunmore was with West Ham between 1959 and 1961. He was born in Whitehaven, Cumbria in 1934. I met with him at his home in York. He looked back on his days with the Hammers and the Os:

> Ernie Gregory, John Dick and Phil Woosnam were very helpful when I came to West Ham. Came from Spurs in part-exchange for John Smith. It was the night before the deadline day, 16 March, and Bill Nic had asked me if I fancied going to West Ham – this meant that he was ready to get rid of me. Newcastle had shown some interest but I said it'll do me. We used to get a percentage of your

provident fund, and £150 benefit a year after five years' service, I left Tottenham in 1960, they won the cup in '61, then when I left West Ham they won it!

We played at Manchester United. Moore, Hurst and Peters were playing and the average age was about eighteen or nineteen. I was about twenty-seven; Noel Cantwell and John Bond were the only other experienced players.

I played thirty-nine first-team games for West Ham; the first was a win at Bolton. I got eighteen goals, including a hat-trick against Arsenal in the 6-0 win at Upton Park on firework night 1960. That must have been my best game for West Ham. Jack Kelsey was in goal for Arsenal, it was nice to put three past him. I hit one with my left foot from just outside the box, it was a bit of a Ginola effort – not quite, nobody can be that good. I'd gone from the right side then along the box and then smacked it in the left – that was maybe my best goal for West Ham. One in that game was a thirty yarder – bang! – from a long way out, instead of running, why waste energy running when you can hit it? Could have gone anywhere, but it went high into the net. I got one at Liverpool the same.

I got my first goal with West Ham's 5-3 win at Old Trafford in April 1960. I think we were winning at half-time, but they got on top in the second half. I went to Orient in 1961 as part of an exchange with Alan Sealey. That was the last day again. It was a carbon copy of the move from Spurs. I got a goal every third game. I didn't get enough games. It does just stick a bit, why they got rid of me. I did pretty good by most standards. I was just getting to know people; a year isn't a long time in football. I was just getting into the rhythm. I have to ask would I have been there for the Cup? When I left it was for York, not for £10,700 but £35,000, it was the record at the time, they got to the semi-final of the Cup and beat Spurs on the way. West Ham were a good footballing side, if you like playing football that's what it's about. They had players like Bobby Moore who could play balls into your feet rather than over your head. You don't want that every two minutes and chasing. Andy Malcolm was a very good winger.

I remember the crowd singing 'I'm Forever Blowing Bubbles' The Chicken Run was always very fair, but if you were having a bad game they'd let you know it. There was some good banter. You only do your best whatever it is. If it's not your day then it doesn't happen.

West Ham was a friendly club. They started me on £20. I don't think it went up until I'd been at Orient a couple of years, then it went up to about £25. He was only young, but Bobby Moore stood out at Upton Park when I was there, head and shoulders.

Ted Fenton was in charge when I went to West Ham and Benny Fenton was at Orient when I went there. I don't know if Ted was a player's man, he was all right. There were five of us, we'd been down to Plumpton Races, we were

> playing Flumenese or someone, we beat them 6-2 or something. They were all little blokes, not one over 5ft 6in. We were a bit late, but we still went into the café around the corner, Cassartari's. We were supposed to be in about an hour before kick-off and we overshot the mark by about twenty minutes. So he fined us £1 each. John Bond said 'I am not paying'.
>
> I was happy at the Orient. I still scored goals. I was a bigger fish at Brisbane Road. The training gear was rubbish. Bill Nic would come out on the training areas. You never saw Ted. Johnny Kelly was all right at the Orient. He was a quiet sort of bloke but he made you think you were a better player than what you were. Pull the others down and lift you up.

The Orient had its own 'Tafia' in Mal Lucas and Cyril Lea who were both Welsh internationals. The irascible Sid Bishop was a solid presence in the side, as was former England Youth player Harry Gregory and the energetic Gordon Bolland.

The fourth-round tie took place at a sad moment with West Ham announcing the end of the playing career of John Lyall. John had been with the club from his school days, signing professional forms in May 1957 when he was seventeen years old. After playing for England Youth he made his League debut against Chelsea in February 1960. John made a total of thirty League appearances during the next three seasons, but in the opening Combination match of 1963/64 he was obliged to leave the field with a leg injury; he returned at the end of September with the 'A' team, but after three matches was again incapacitated and underwent an operation. Lyall was always a tough player. Eddie Lewis recalled:

> John Lyall ended my first-team career at Upton Park. He was in goal during a practice match. We were mucking about a bit and John was saying that I'd never score against him. I was going past him and he kneed me in the thigh. I was out for six weeks, that's when Ted signed Vic Keeble. I can still feel the lump in my thigh. But I always got on well with John. I once saw him dragging Ron Greenwood around by the scruff of the neck – I thought he was going to give him a smack. Ron wasn't worth two bob as a person.

After lots of hard training it was thought that John had beaten his problems. But on 4 January, his first outing of 1964 proved to be his last, and his soccer-playing career came to an end at the age of twenty-three. However, Lyall was a qualified coach both of football and cricket and he did not allow injury to divert him from the pursuit of his passion.

The Hammers came to the replay with things looking a tad dodgy in the League. They were tottering in fifteenth place. The replay with Orient was the thirty-seventh game of the season for the Irons and they really could not afford another draw. At the same time, with the prospect of finishing the season with nothing to show but a relegation fight, Bobby Moore and his men could not allow the Second Division side to progress. Three goals in the first fifteen minutes, two from Hurst and the third from Byrne ended fears of a second replay that had been scheduled to take place at White Hart Lane on 3 February.

In the end, the West Ham victory had been decisive, but it could have been worse for Orient; Pinner, who despite the scoreline had a fantastic game, became one of the few men to have saved a Hurst penalty (in the fifty-first minute) and effectively denied the big Hammer and his fellow striker Johnny Byrne hat-trick glory. The spot-kick was, as was usual, well taken by Hurst, but Pinner knew that Geoff would send the ball to his right, it would be between waist and chest height and would go in between two and three feet from the right-hand stanchion; all he had to do was dive for that area. For all that, the save looked marvellous.

The Hammers seemed, at least temporarily, to have emptied their luck account when they visited Filbert Street for the first leg of the League Cup semi-final at the start of February. With little more than twenty minutes to play, the Hammers were trailing 4-1. But the Irons fought back whilst Leicester didn't score again and the Foxes finished the match with just a one goal cushion to take with them to Upton Park.

Injury-free Hammers?

The West Ham team that had played in the games against Charlton and Orient would remain unchanged right the way through the club's FA Cup run of 1964. This had much to do with Welsh-born, fifty-four-year-old Bill Jenkins, the West Ham physiotherapist. Jenkins, a rugby devotee from the Rhondda Valley, was seen as one of the new school in soccer, a development of the man with the sponge who treated ailments on the field with a douse of cold water. He had been at Upton Park only four years in 1964, having been involved with amateur clubs Clapton and Walthamstow Avenue. His son, Robert William, succeeded him as physiotherapist with Walthamstow Avenue, and reached Wembley in 1965 with that side. Bob would one day take his dad's place at the Boleyn Ground following Bill's passing.

Later on, when I was coaching athletics with Newham and Essex Beagles, I knew many local athletes who would look to Jenkins' clinic in Green Street, nearly opposite the main gates of the Boleyn Ground, for treatment. Jenkins was amongst the first to experiment with cortisone and whilst this was quite effective in the short term, I worried about this therapy, as through my coaching training I knew something of the possible long-term consequences of such treatment. West Ham played fifty-six games in 1963/64 in League, League Cup and FA Cup. Before the start of the season they had fulfilled near a whole summer of highly competitive fixtures in the United States and would repeat that experience in the summer of 1964. Most of the Hammers were involved in games with England at some level before, during and after the season. This meant that a good proportion of West Ham players were involved in near to a hundred games between the early summer of 1963 and the autumn of 1964, this was a time when training for injury prevention was nowhere near the standard it is today. Football was also a much more physically hazardous occupation than the contemporary professional game, a true contact sport, full of hard men and dangerous tackles. Yet the Upton Park injury list was, certainly compared with current standards, light.

It is folklore to say that 'players were tougher then' or contest that West Ham were blessed with the presence of genius in their backroom staff. Alternatively one can argue that top-flight football is much more demanding in terms of performance now, but if one looks down the list of players involved with West Ham in the 1960s it is striking that near to a whole team have passed away well before their sixtieth year:

Bobby Moore, Johnny Byrne, John Charles, Derek Woodley, Harry Cripps, Ron Brett, Alan Sealy, Brian Rhodes, Dave Bickles and Bobby Keetch.

Brabrook on the Wing

I felt that Peter would give us a new pace and drive… once we persuaded him to think more about his game he became a mature, much more effective player. He was strong. He scored in a League Cup tie at Walsall. He turned round to celebrate and saw his five team-mates who had been involved in the build-up had been laid flat on their backs. At times things weren't pretty.

Ron Greenwood – West Ham United and England

Peter Brabrook, the son of a London docker, played his schoolboy football for East Ham, Essex and London, and might have come to Upton Park for a nominal signing-on fee in 1952. Even though he was a West Ham supporter as a boy, his early career was not to have the Boleyn Ground as a backdrop due to a rare mistake on the part of West Ham's chief scout, Wally St Pier, who had recommended that manager Ted Fenton offer the fifteen-year-old Peter two nights training per week rather than a ground-staff post.

Brabrook took up the offer but a short while later, after scoring two goals for London Boys against the touring West German Boys at Highbury the Chelsea scout Jimmy Thompson offered him a place at Stamford Bridge. Visiting the Brabrook family home St Pier tried his best to retrieve the situation but Peter had made his mind up to go to Chelsea. Over half a century later, having recently retired as coach of the West Ham Under-17s Academy, Brabrook still had a letter from St Pier lamenting the fact that West Ham had made a mistake in not signing the talented young striker, but wishing him all the best at Chelsea.

Brabook arrived at Stamford Bridge as an inside forward and only eight days after signing professional forms in March 1955, he found himself in this role for the Chelsea League team. However, the then Chelsea manager Ted Drake experimented with his swarthy progeny, assigning him to the right flank. Peter's speed and skilful ball play together with his ability to switch wings at will, caused Drake to move Brabrook to outside right. The transition was a complete success and the tall, swift, talented lad added to his honours as an England Youth player by representing his nation eight times at Under-23 level (the first three coming in the 1957/58 term).

In the 1958 World Cup Finals in Sweden, the nineteen-year-old Brabrook made his England debut, lining up on the opposite wing to Preston North End legend Tom Finney for the game against the USSR. At thirty-six years old, Finney was nearly twice Brabrook's age. Peter was called up again for his country to face Northern Ireland on 3 October 1958 and Spain on 15 May 1960.

Peter played 270 times for Chelsea, scoring forty-seven goals. However Tommy Docherty took over as manager at the West London Club in January 1962 and, from the start, Peter was unable to get on with 'The Doc' to the extent that a transfer seemed to be the only recourse. West Ham made their interest known but Chelsea were not keen to sell Brabrook, especially to a rival London club. Everton were also interested in the international winger and the Goodison manager Harry Catterick persuaded Brabrook to visit Liverpool. When Peter got to Lime Street hundreds of fans greeted him with banners welcoming him to Everton Football Club. When he got to Goodison Park there was another huge crowd ready to claim him as a 'Blue'.

But on the way home to Greenwich, Brabrook decided that he wanted to stay in London and after nine months, following the payment of a £35,000 fee, a record for a winger, Peter came to Upton Park; this demonstrated how much Greenwood wanted Brabrook at the Boleyn Ground. Peter was also keen on the move. He had always played well for Chelsea at Upton Park and he knew Bobby Moore and the majority of the other players through schoolboy and youth soccer. He made his first appearance in a home draw against Burnley on 22 October 1962.

There had been allegations that West Ham had approached Brabrook illegally. Although he was hanging around the club before actually signing, the transfer negotiations did take months to complete. Chelsea insisted that Peter had refused to sign a contract at Chelsea following statements made by West Ham's Ken Brown and Ron Greenwood, and accused the Hammers of not making a decent offer because they thought they could get Brabrook on the cheap. The charge was a serious one as it threatened the whole contract system. Things were made worse as all this happened at a time when the Professional Footballers' Association was threatening to go on strike. The Stamford Bridge tirade was answered by the West Ham Board who issued a statement to the effect that it could answer any charge Chelsea might bring. But the West London club were fond of picking up promising East End players, and they knew one or two tricks of their own about enticing talent to Stamford Bridge. A League tribunal cleared West Ham of all charges.

Peter Brabrook's arrival at West Ham had coincided with the start of the Hurst/Byrne partnership and his contribution to the success of West Ham's twin strikers was critical. Brabrook's incisive right-wing raids provided an element of service that cannot be underestimated. Peter rated Byrne as an outstanding player, but thought that 'Budgie' was underrated in terms of his contribution and technical ability that allowed him to bring other people into games and so enhance the effectiveness of the whole team, but was to also to claim:

> … Ron's coaching got the best out of all of us.

Like Byrne, Brabrook could be brilliantly unpredictable and had the ability to win a game with one dazzling run. He could be relied on to score around a dozen goals a season, which was good for a winger, but his contribution to the Hurst/Byrne combination made West Ham an incredibly exciting side to watch.

Bolton Battered

Derbies against Preston were always memorable, but Cup matches were even more so.
Eddie Hopkinson – Bolton Wanderers and England

As was the tradition before the 'Hammerettes', 'Pooperscooper', 'Bubbles the Bear' and 'Herbie the Hammer', in the days prior to executive boxes, agents and football selling its soul to Russian oil barons and Thai politicians, times when a 'Beckham Burger' was just the nightmare of a crazed tattooist in Leyton, seemingly on the final whistle of the FA Cup third-round games, providence was called upon to decide the next set of confrontations and the outcome decreed over the radio waves by a monotone and anonymous Football Association official. Those who had just vanquished worthy opponents were immediately faced with yet another obstacle. There is something humbling about such an experience; you think you've done it, but you ain't.

Preston North End were again pitted against a First Division side, and once more were obliged to brazenly confront their superiors on their own turf. But as with chicken-ripple ice cream, there was something extra to chew on; the gateway to the fifth round was guarded by Lancashire rivals Bolton Wanderers.

Bolton Wanderers *v.* Preston North End, 25 January 1964 programme cover.

There were some scores to be settled. In April 1961 the Wanderers had held North End to a 1-1 draw in a Division One match. This had effectively sent Preston into the Second Division, relegation rivals Blackpool and Newcastle United having picked up points on the same day.

The Bolton manager was Bill Ridding. He had been in charge of the Wanderers for over thirteen years but his association with the club had begun in 1946 after Walter Rowley appointed him trainer. Ridding was one of the last of the old school of secretary managers. Born at Heswall, Cheshire, on the Wirral on 4 April 1911, he played centre-forward for Heswall PSA before, at the age of seventeen, turning professional with Tranmere Rovers. As a young man it was thought that Bill had similar potential to other Prenton Park notables Dixie Dean and Pongo Waring, and this was true enough to cause Manchester City to pay £3,000 for his services in March 1930. He moved to the other Manchester club on Christmas Eve 1931 in exchange for Billy Dale and Harry Rowley plus £2,000. Bill made the first of his forty-four appearances for United against Wolves at Old Trafford on Christmas Day 1931. He was to score fourteen goals for the Manchester Reds. He moved back to Tranmere in August 1935 but signed for Oldham the following October. However, a double cartilage injury forced his retirement from the game at the early age of twenty-four. Once more he returned to Tranmere as 'A' team trainer whilst working full-time as a tram conductor. Bill later qualified as a physiotherapist and chiropodist. He was the trainer and manager of Rovers throughout the years of the Second World War, following the death of Jimmy Morton.

In August 1946 Bill moved to Bolton. On Rowley's resignation in October 1950, Ridding was put in temporary charge. In the same year the Football Association appointed him as trainer to the England team for the World Cup in Brazil, where his experience in tram conducting was invaluable. Ridding was officially appointed secretary-manager of Bolton in February 1951 and also continued to act as trainer until the appointment of Bert Sproston (the Sandbach Super Sponge). The Wanderers reached two FA Cup finals during Ridding's reign, losing in 1953 and winning in 1958. That side had cost Bolton (by way of Ridding) just the signing-on costs (£110) and a pint of milk a week for each player.

Bolton continued to produce plenty of home-grown players but Ridding found it difficult to hold on to them, especially after the abolition of the maximum wage in 1961.

The 1964 encounter between Wanderers and North End saw Bolton in the throes of a season that would end in them being relegated and begin a long period of decline. This was the first of three consecutive FA Cup meetings between the clubs and was also the third post-war engagement of these antagonists of tradition. None of the cup combats had gone the way of the Lilywhites. Bolton had defeated Preston at Deepdale 3-0 in the third round on the way to winning the 1958 FA Cup and Wanderers had again won the laurels the following season, although North End took the Cup holders to three games. Jimmy Smith, who had played for Scotland as a schoolboy, was the only survivor of the of the Preston side of that year when he played left-half, and even he did not make the game in 1964, Jimmy Milne choosing to stick with the same side that had beaten Forest in the previous round, apart from Godfrey who came in for Ashworth. The first game resulted in a thrilling 2-2 result. The replay at Ewood Park had gone to extra time but the sides could not be separated in a 1-1 draw. The third game, again staged at the home of Blackburn Rovers, saw Wanderers go through to the quarter-finals on the strength of the only goal of the game.

That was the tenth FA Cup meeting between the two Lancastrian adversaries. The first had taken place in the 1885/86 season, predating the formation of the Football League in 1888. It was played out on Bolton's Pike Lane ground and although Preston won the game 3-2, both clubs were disqualified for an infringement of rules regarding qualification of professional players, many 'mercenary' Scots having found their way to Deepdale. In the first instance, Bolton lodged a protest concerning the eligibility of two Preston men, but this was answered by a protest from North End, and much to the surprise of the Bolton management, one of the Wanderers players, Jack Powell, who had taken a job in Ruabon without telling the club, had also infringed the same rule. Other cup battles were to follow:

1887/88	Second round (first series)	Preston 9	Bolton 1
1889/90	Quarter-final	Preston 2	Bolton 3
1920/21	First round	Preston 2	Bolton 0
1931/32	Third round	Preston 0	Bolton 0
	Replay	Preston 5	Bolton 2

So, in seven ties Preston had prevailed five times, winning four of the ten games. Bolton had overcome North End on just three occasions. Wanderers had scored fifteen times in reply to Preston's twenty-four goals.

The first League meeting between Bolton and Preston took place in 1888 at Deepdale. North End won 3-1 but the second-half of the game lasted just forty minutes because of 'lack of light'. Preston became the first Champions of the newly formed Football League, not losing a single match. Bolton finished in fifth place, a full eighteen points behind their Lancashire foe. This was when North End picked up the tags 'Proud Preston' and 'The Invincibles', and lived up to the same by retaining the League Championship the following season. They became the first double winners by lifting the FA Cup in that initial term of League contest, keeping a clean sheet throughout their Cup run.

Although not winning another Championship after 1890, Preston came close in 1953, only to be denied by Arsenal's superior goal average. Perhaps the next century would have been kinder to North End had they gained just one more point that season.

North End visited Burnden Park in September 1895 playing in a benefit match for Di Jones. The away team took the day, winning the friendly match by a goal from David Smith.

'Go on you Lilywhites'

It was Smith who first coined the Preston nickname the 'Lilywhites'. In the early 1880s the team wore blue and white hooped or striped shirts. However, by 1888 the club had adopted the now familiar white shirts and navy shorts. For all this, until 1895 Preston were still known colloquially simply as 'North End'. It was late in 1895 that Smith, having been diagnosed with 'trench foot' a few weeks earlier (a testament to the state of playing surfaces at the time perhaps) took responsibility for the care of the club kit, but subcontracted the job of washing the same to a local washer woman, Nora Brindley, who 'saw to' the laundry of several local football clubs (apparently she refused to have any truck with rugby as the apparel of that game became 'too caked'). Prior to an away game with Small Heath, the diligent Smith retrieved the newly laundered strips from Nora's steaming abode; shorts and socks in one bag, shirts in another. However, on arrival at the opponents ground, to the collective horror of the side, Smith had collected the wrong shirts. But there was no time for prevarication or recrimination. The referee was summoned to the dressing room and after protracted explanation/consultation, of which the match official made 'thorough and copious' notes, Preston took to the park, to the astonishment of all and sundry, in white shirts! As they ran out onto the field of play it was the redemptive Smith who was the first to cry, to the consternation and amusement of fans and players alike: 'Go on you Lilywhites!' Thus the affectionate epithet of Proud Preston was born. From then on Smith, a man dark in complexion and hair colouring, was known to North End supporters as 'Whitey Smith', which apparently left uninitiated opponents in a state of dangerous bemusement. It seems that during one encounter a teammate of Smith's (the laundry man on recovery having returned him to the fray) was urged by a supportive onlooker to, 'Give it to Whitey Smith' as the Preston forwards bore down on the opposition 'keeper. The said goalie looked about him for a person fitting the description and was distracted to the extent that he neglected to consider Smith, who duly received the ball and drove it past the confused custodian.

Hence the cry in support of 'The Whites' (that was far more 'snappy' than 'Proud Preston' or 'The Invincibles') became something of a Deepdale secret weapon for a while (and a bit of a 'rum caution'). But the Preston management did not share their supporters liking for the spreading of confusion in the ranks of the opposition, seeing it as a type of unsporting duplicity. For all this, it was acknowledged that censoring the expression of the fans would have been a near impossible and certainly an alienating task. So, by 1888 supporter power won through with the adoption of white shirts.

A Battle at Burnden

Throughout their history, the FA Cup had been central to the success of Bolton Wanderers. They had won the cup in 1923, 1926, 1929 and 1958 (they also took the Charity Shield that year) and made the final in 1894, 1904 and 1953. Their only other major glory had been the winning of the Second Division Championship in 1909. At Burnden Park 'The Cup' was a sacred thing, very much the Holy Grail of the club and what the Wanderers wandered for.

In the third-round encounter of 1964, Bolton met Southern League minnows Bath City. The Wanderers were 1-0 down in the West Country as the game neared its final ten minutes, but Francis Lee converted a blush-saving penalty to retrieve the tie for Bolton. Although the Trotters won the replay 3-0, Taylor and Wyn Davies grabbing goals either side of another Lee penalty. The fact that it took them two games to be rid of such lowly opposition allowed Preston fans to approach their encounter with Bolton doped with the opiate of optimism. The confrontation fired cultural memories of the monumental cup confrontations the two teams had fought out in previous, more glorious eras.

The only locally born player on either side was Preston's Tony Singleton. However, the good news for Preston was the absence of Roy Hartle from the Bolton line-up, the full-back having sustained an eye injury while playing with his four-year-old son.

Preston had experienced only four defeats all season (all away from Deepdale) and came to Burnden Park holding third place in Division Two. With the Manchester-born Doug Holden returning to their ranks, there were few that would not give North End a good chance of taking the day. At the age of thirty-two Holden had moved from Bolton to Preston the previous season to provide experience during an awful run of results. It was his first appearance at Burnden Park as a Preston player.

The 1964 FA Cup fourth-round battle of Lancashire was expected to be close, and it was. Preston had scored thirty goals away from home in their League forays, a figure bettered only by Spurs and Blackburn in the whole League. Probably the most distinguished player involved in the tie was Bolton goalkeeper Eddie Hopkinson. Edward Hopkinson was born at Wheatley Hill, County Durham, on 29 October 1935. As a boy, growing up in Lancashire, he was a good cricketer. He started football as a midfield player but given his natural agility it was not long before he found himself between the posts. He was selected for Lancashire Schools and, aged sixteen; he played three games for Oldham Athletic in the Third Division North as an amateur in the 1951/52 season. He moved to Bolton to sign professional forms.

Looking back on his early career he remembered:

> I was twenty-one before I got into the first team, after doing National Service in the RAF. Lancashire Cricket Club wouldn't release Ken Grieves at the start of the season. He was their wicketkeeper but also Bolton's goalkeeper. So I made my debut against Blackpool.

Hopkinson's talent was soon noticed, and he won six Under-23 caps before making his full international debut for England against Wales in a 4-0 victory in Cardiff during October 1957. He was England's first-choice goalkeeper in the late 1950s. In 1958 he was a central figure in Wanderers FA Cup final victory. He recalled:

> United came to Wembley with Bobby Charlton and everyone wanted them to win after Munich. Their team was made up with players on loan, kids and whoever they could get. But we wanted to win. The club had not forgotten losing to Blackpool in the 'Matthews match' a few years earlier.

> In the third minute Nat Lofthouse put us ahead. I was a bit lucky early in the second half, a shot by Charlton came off the post and I caught it. But in the second half their 'keeper Harry Gregg was busier than me. He stopped a shot but as he was picking up the ball Nat Lofthouse barged him and the ball ended up in the net. It was like that then. Nat wouldn't have got away with that now. There was a bit of an argument but the goal stood and we won the cup!

At 5ft 9ins Hopkinson would maybe do well in the competition for the shortest goalkeeper ever to win an FA Cup winners medal.

Eddie had made five appearances for his country when, just before the World Cup in Sweden in 1958, England were humiliated 5-0 by Yugoslavia in Belgrade. He recalled:

> England had won every game I had played in up to that point and I'd kept three clean sheets. I was dropped and Colin McDonald, the Burnley 'keeper was chosen. I went with England to Sweden but never played. McDonald was injured the following year so I played against Brazil and Italy. In the end I got the blame for a 3-2 defeat by Sweden, they were World Cup finalists, at Wembley in 1960. The selectors went for Ron Springett, the Sheffield Wednesday 'keeper, after that.

Although his international career was over, Eddie continued to do well with Bolton. The side finished in the top six in England twice during the late 1950s and the secure hands of Hopkinson made a massive contribution to the club maintaining its status. He was a brave 'keeper, known for his skill in facing up to attacking players. He had a knack of spreading himself at the last moment in a star shape to maximise the probability of deflecting a shot.

Eddie recalled the first game in his team's fourth-round tie with Preston:

> Preston went two in front through Alex Dawson. He was a tall, strong man. Dave Hatton got injured in a run-in with Nobby Lawton and we had to pull Francis Lee back into defence.

Lee, then an England Youth International, would score ten goals for his country in twenty-seven games after moving to Manchester City. He got his first taste of League football earlier than most players. As a sixteen year old he made his debut for Bolton in 1960/61 and his right-wing partnership with the Trotters' Freddie Hill caught the attention of several First Division clubs.

Wanderers had no choice but to fight back; it was the cup and it was Preston. Eddie continued:

> Peter Deakin got two goals in five minutes to force a replay at Deepdale. If we could have won there we fancied our chances, as that would have meant a game against Carlisle who were a Fourth Division side at the time.

The replay took place at Deepdale on Monday 27 January 1964 and referee Mr D.A. Corbett of Essington (near Wolverhampton), in his initial season as a Football League referee, having started his Division One career the previous month at Burden Park when Sheffield Wednesday had been the visitors, started the game in front of 38,290 roaring supporters. Hopkinson remembered:

> The match was played at a terrific pace. Preston took every chance to shoot in the first part of the game. I managed to stop long-range shots from Holden and Wilson. At the other end Kelly kept out a hard shot from Lee and a twenty-five-yard drive from Freddie Hill.

Not long after this, Bryan Edwards, who had a good match at the centre of the Wanderers' defence, lost out in a tackle on Dawson, who at this point had scored fifty-five League goals in eighty outings for Preston. Alex did well to hold on to his balance and broke free. 'The Black Prince' produced a fine drive to beat Hopkinson. The Bolton 'keeper gave the big man credit:

> That Dawson goal that put North End in front was a fantastic effort. It was at least as good as his two headed goals in the first game. Not long after the first goal Wyn Davies missed a chance to put us level, he didn't get much of a look in after that. Then, almost straight away, Freddie Hill got his head to a Francis Lee cross, but the Preston 'keeper done well to turn it round the post.

Alan Kelly, the North End goalie, was kept on his toes for the remaining quarter of an hour of the first-half, making two superb saves from Lennard and Deakin. An effervescent, swiftly contended forty-five minutes was concluded by a Wyn Davies header that beat Kelly but ended up on top of the net.

Davies started his football with Caernarfon Boys' Club and Llanberis before joining Caernarfon Town in 1958. He had moved to Bolton from Wrexham in April 1960 for £20,000 plus a player exchange. This proved to be a good price, given that he went to Newcastle in March 1966 for £80,000.

The second half of the game saw Preston come out fighting, but although they were enthusiastic their shooting was below par. Hopkinson remembered:

> Dawson, Lawton, Spavin and Wilson all had chances but off target. Bryan Edwards got on the end of Gordon Taylor's left-wing corner, he was unmarked and he scored on the near post.

There were thirty-five minutes of the replay left to play when Gordon Taylor (the future Tsar of the Professional Footballers Association) enabled Edwards to make amends for his earlier mistake. According to Eddie Hopkinson this seemed to give his side new hope:

> We started to play a bit then and came close to taking the lead. If it hadn't have been for a good tackle by Singleton on Wyn Davies just as he was about to shoot from close in, we would have done.

Outstanding schoolboy performances brought Taylor to the attention of Manchester United and Arsenal but he opted to join Bolton, the club he had supported as a boy. He signed amateur forms in June 1960 and in January 1962 he became a professional with the club. Although he made his debut for the Wanderers in March 1963, it was not until January 1964 that he won a regular place on the left-wing. A diminutive, stocky flank-man who was equally at home on either side of the field, Taylor's powerful running and explosive shooting was a threat to any defence.

With a quarter of an hour to go, North End went ahead via a scrambled goal. Hopkinson lamented:

> Holden cut inside Dave Hatton and centred, Godfrey picked it up and passed to Wilson. His first-time cross caused a bit of a panic in our area. Lawton, Dave and me were all trying to sort it out. But Lawton got by Hatton and myself and forced the ball over the line from a few feet out. Hatton injured himself trying to stop it going in.
>
> In the last few seconds the ball was cleared off of the Preston goal line, but Preston hung on. It was a close game.

The Bolton XI that day had been a tough prospect for Preston – with Hopkinson in goal, Hatton, Farrimond, Rimmer, Edwards, Lennard, Hill, Deakin, Lee, Davis and Taylor, Bolton were no pushovers. Apart from the distinction brought to the side by Lee and Hopkinson, Freddy Hill had ten Under-23 and two full England caps, and Wyn Davies would make thirty-four appearances for Wales. Syd Farrimond had turned out for England Youth and Warwick Rimmer was a former English Schoolboy international. There was no doubt that North End had done well to match Bolton as the Wanderers pressed hard in the closing stages, and their reward was the knowledge that Wembley was only 270 minutes away!

Death of a Chairman

The death of the club chairman James Herbert Ingham just a few days after he had seen his North End side defeat Bolton in the Cup shattered the mood of hope that had engulfed Preston over the previous few months. Ingham, who had become

Preston's fifth chairman two years previously, had been a member of the board since 1945 and had held the post of vice-chair for fourteen years. He was an ambitious man with an adventurous, fighting spirit. Ingham could be tough, but was also a compassionate optimist who, despite his determination to pull the club back to the footballing heights where its supporters believed it belonged, never interfered with team affairs. This gained him a lot of respect from the players, as demonstrated when Alan Spavin, George Ross, Norbert Lawton, Tony Singleton, Alex Dawson and Willie Cunningham carried his coffin to his final resting place.

Ingham often repeated his beliefs that 'Good players would come to a good club if the prospects were bright', and 'If you are successful, you have money to buy'. This straightforward vision was becoming a reality during Ingham's brief stewardship. If he had been granted a longer tenure Preston North End would certainly have been a very different club today. Perhaps Deepdale could have acted as an exemplar in English football and given the game some resistance to the parasitical excreta of commercial capitalism that has purloined the spirit of England's great football clubs and alienated the supporters, the lifeblood of the game. When Jimmy Ingham died something in football passed with him.

The Black Prince

I bought Dawson to be Preston's power-punch; I wanted him to hit hard and fast, to knock out opponents. And you've got to admit, he did the job and looked the part.
Jimmy Milne – Preston North End

The signing of Alex Dawson from Manchester United in October 1961 for £20,000 was the start of manager Jimmy Milne's long-term plan. According to Milne, Dawson's recruitment,

> ...was due to United's manager, Mr Matt Busby, doing North End a favour.

Alex Downie Dawson was a man seemingly designed for aerial combat. From his first days with Preston he showed superb form, scoring thirteen goals in

Alex Dawson,
Preston's 'Black Prince'.

his first nine appearances. He was one of a dying breed of battleship centre forwards in the mould of Nat Lofthouse. The son of a Grimsby trawlerman, Dawson, although born on 21 February 1940 in Aberdeen, Scotland, played for Hull Schoolboys and gained six England caps at schoolboy level in 1954/55. He emerged from the junior ranks and signed professional forms for Manchester United shortly after his seventeenth birthday in May 1957. The previous November he had scored the winning goal in his League debut against Burnley at Old Trafford.

Alex had been a member of Manchester United's FA Youth Cup-winning side in 1956 and was also in the team that beat West Ham 8-2 in the 1957 final. Dawson had netted in each of the last three matches of that season, assisting United in clinching the League Championship.

Along with other United youngsters, Dawson was a regular in the first team after the Munich disaster. The bustling centre forward was one of the inspirations behind United's march to the 1958 FA Cup final. Not only did Alex score on his debut in the League, he also netted in his first League Cup and FA Cup games. In that term he scored five goals in six matches, including a hat-trick in the 5-3 cup semi-final replay win over Fulham at Highbury on 26 March 1958. That made him the youngest post-war player to score a hat-trick (he was eighteen years and thirty-three days) in the FA Cup and it took him and his side to Wembley. Dawson played outside right in the 1958 final; however the whole country (apart from Wanderers fans) was disappointed when Bolton won 2-0.

Strong and robust, with a direct approach, Dawson began to be pushed aside with the arrival of David Herd at Old Trafford in 1961. As such Alex moved to Preston in October 1961 for £18,000. During his five years with the Manchester Reds he put away fifty-four goals in ninety-three games.

Alex scored on his debut as North End shared four goals with Rotherham United at the Millmoor Ground. Dawson continued to be a regular goal-getter throughout his stay at Deepdale. His deadly finishing reminded many a Preston fan of their one-time dynamic leader, Tommy Roberts. Dawson showed himself to be the devastating spearhead in a well-balanced Preston side, but within this equilibrium power was the keynote. Alex was a fine header of the ball whilst possessing strength in both feet; the pairing of such gifts is rare. He was big, swift, strong and fearless, with the physique of a rugby player. Dawson had developed a goal-forcing technique built around the art of surprise, darting into the box with purpose. He had been Preston's top club scorer in the 1962/63 season with twenty-seven goals. He never stopped going forward.

Manchester United and England hard man Nobby Stiles called Dawson 'a wrecking ball of a player', tipping the scales at twelve stone eight pounds, packed into a 5ft 10in frame. His menacing demeanour, dark hair and complexion earned him the moniker of 'The Black Prince of Preston'.

3

The Fifth Round

Favourites don't always win. If they did, football, sport, wouldn't be worth watching.
Alec Ashworth – Preston North End

It was the summer of 1960. Floyd Patterson was the World Heavyweight Champion having just regained the title from Sweden's Ingemar Johansson. Sonny Liston was terrorising the division and was eager for a crack at the World crown, but Patterson's manager Cus D'Amato refused to allow his man to fight Liston due to the contender's criminal past. In fact the newspapers at the time were asking whether Liston should actually be allowed to fight for the championship. While all this was going on, despite his fear of flying, Light Heavyweight Cassius Clay was winning Olympic gold in Rome for the United States.

Patterson defended his title against the likes of Tom McNeeley, but Liston was beating far more credible fighters such as Cleveland Williams and Eddie Machen. As such, in 1962, Patterson felt obliged to give in to public pressure and defend against Liston. To the surprise of no one, Liston took the title, knocking out the champion in the first round. There was a rematch and Patterson had the satisfaction of lasting a few seconds longer.

Cassius Clay began his professional career not long after winning Olympic gold, defeating Tunney Hunsaker on points after six rounds. He continued his unbeaten path over the next three years defeating Archie Moore, Sonny Banks, Doug Jones and London's own British and European Champion, Henry Cooper. It was against Cooper that Clay suffered his first professional knockdown, courtesy of 'Henry's 'ammer' (left hook).

Brash, cocky and supremely handsome, the young Clay openly challenged and berated Sonny Liston for a chance to fight for the sport's richest prize. Most people thought Clay was a lunatic – he was effectively enraging a champion considered an invincible ring monster by most of the world. Everything about Liston was ominous. He was a hardened criminal and a big and powerful fighter, his thick build, his mean, narrow eyes, his two periods in jail and his alleged connections to the Mafia made him more than fearsome. Apart from his power shows against Patterson, Liston had knocked out other contenders such as Williams, Nino Valdes and Zora Folley. His only loss had come during the early 1950s and even then he had proved his toughness by lasting the distance despite suffering a broken jaw. Liston was as intimidating as any fighter in history.

The build-up to the fight got well into its stride around the time of the fifth round of the FA Cup in Britain and Clay's relentless taunting of Liston, describing him as a 'big, ugly bear' distracted the sports headlines away from football. Clay stalked the champion, even turning up uninvited at Liston's house one night with a bear net. Liston retorted by saying 'I think he should be arrested for impersonating a fighter'.

The tension around the fight had heightened when Sugar Ray Robinson took Clay's side before the fight, while heavyweight legend Joe Louis backed Liston. Clay summed up the situation by stating,

> Me and Sugar Ray are two pretty dancers – Joe Louis and Sonny Liston are flat-footed.

The fight took place on 25 February 1964 at Miami Beach. Most boxing writers gave Clay no chance saying it was cruel to let a pretty boy in the ring with an ex-convict, predicting that Liston's left hook would inflict huge damage on the challenger's chin. Clay was made a 7–1 underdog, leading Clay to repeatedly recite, 'If you wanna lose your money then bet on Sonny'.

At the weigh-in Clay was hysterical, prophesising that Liston would 'fall in eight'. He was fined $1,500 for his behaviour by the Miami Boxing Commission. Some witnesses interpreted Clay's performance as the actions of a frightened man, a theory apparently confirmed when his blood pressure was found to be high before the fight.

On the night of the fight the arena in Miami was half empty. People thought that the contest was going to be another swift decision for Liston. The fight started with Clay looking nothing like a loser, circling the ring making Liston appear ponderous. Clay did not dance as much as expected in the opening round, a three-minute period that showed the challenger had no qualms about standing in front of his opponent. The pair carried on fighting for seconds after the round ended with the noise in the arena drowning out the sound of the bell.

In round three, Clay opened a cut over Liston's eye with a left/right combination. The challenger was boxing beautifully and by the end of the fourth round Sonny Liston seemed substantially older than his supposed forty years. With the cut under one eye and swelling under the other, his legs growing weary, he was quickly running out of steam. As the round ended Clay snapped a right-hand lead off Liston's chin which rocked the champion.

However, Clay went back to his corner complaining that his eyes were burning. Although never proved, the general consensus was that an ointment had been applied to Liston's gloves with the intention of impeding Clay. It was subsequently passed off as being liniment from Liston's eye, but the pain it caused the challenger seems to indicate there had been an act of desperation in Liston's corner.

At the start of round five, Clay was partially blind. His trainer and corner-man Angelo Dundee could only instruct his fighter to run and dance and Clay spent the entire round back-pedalling, poking left-jabs into the champion's face. It was amazing but Clay was fighting one of the most feared heavyweight champions ever with impaired sight. But having got through the round Clay had weathered the storm and by round six Clay's eyes had cleared and he spent the round dictating the fight in emphatic style.

A weary Liston headed back to his corner. Before the start of the seventh round, the bloodied and tired champion told his corner he did not want to continue, citing an injured shoulder as his main reason. To the amazement of all involved he stayed on his stool at the start of round seven. Most people that night thought that Liston had just given up.

Clay began a mini version of what was to become the legendary 'Ali shuffle' in the centre of the ring, before hysteria took over as he told everyone in attendance how great he was, dancing around the ring he pointed to the press and hollered, 'I must be the greatest – I shook up the world'. Clay had beaten a champion who most people thought to be unbeatable, and began to stake his claim that he was indeed the best boxer the world had ever seen. Later he recalled:

> I don't have a mark on my face. I upset Sonny Liston and I just turned twenty-two years old – I must be the greatest.

During the fight, Clay refused to allow Liston to get off any big punches, and danced around the bigger fighter while landing lightening-fast combinations. This was to be the last ever fight for Cassius Clay. Within a month he had renounced his 'slave name' to become Muhammad Ali and a legend was born.

Ali and Liston would meet again for the title, once more in controversial circumstances.

Where is Swindon?

The last team anyone wants to play is Swindon. You can't win with 'em. Beat 'em and you've done no more than what you should do, get beaten by 'em and you are worse than them... although they've never really been a bad side... but people think because they are Swindon they must be bad...

Johnny Byrne – West Ham United and England

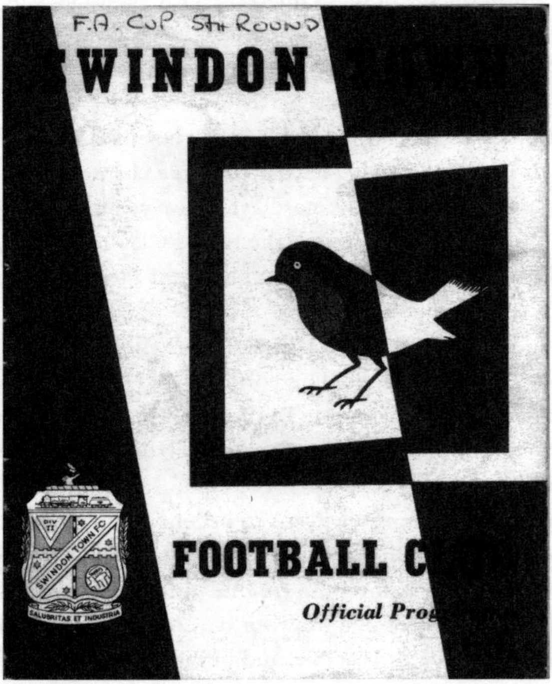

Swindon Town *v.* West Ham United, 15 February 1964 programme cover.

I've been to Swindon loads of times, but I'm still not sure where it is. I know it is on the way to Bristol, but every time I have to go to Swindon and I tell someone I'm going there they often seem to ask where it is. It sounds as if it should be 'up north', being essentially a railway town and being 'Swindon', but of course it's not. In fact it was founded in 1881 by Reverend William Pitt and became the first Wiltshire League club to gain entry to the Football League in the 1920/21 season, finishing fourth in the Third Division, just seven points behind Champions Crystal Palace. So now you know…

Railwaymen and Hammers

The pairing of West Ham United and Swindon Town in an FA Cup had only occurred once prior to 1964 and that was in the 1911/12 season. At that time both sides were members of the First Division of the Southern League (there were twenty clubs in that league and fourteen in the Second Division). Swindon Town had won the Championship in the preceding campaign with fifty-three points from thirty-eight games; the Hammers had ended up in fifth place with a points total of forty-five. Prior to that (as Thames Ironworks) the East Londoners had regularly met the Wiltshire side and the Irons *v.* the Railwaymen had developed an aura of rivalry; the railways were the biggest employer in the West Ham district before the turn of the twentieth century.

The Hammers' progress to the third round that year was due to a 2-1 home win against Midlanders Gainsborough Town, followed by the momentous dismissal of Middlesbrough (then members of the First Division of the Football League). West Ham had drawn 1-1 in the North-East and won the replay at Upton Park 2-1. Swindon had made it a double success for the Southern Leaguers over 'senior', Division One opposition by knocking out Notts County in the second round by two clear goals.

Twenty thousand turned up at Upton Park on Saturday, 24 February 1912 (receipts totalled £1,200). The Hammers' line-up comprised:

Joe Hughes, Bob Fairman, Vic Glover, George Redwood, Dan Woodards, Fred Blackburn, 'Tiddler' Ashton, Danny Shea, Fred Harrison, George Butcher and Tommy Caldwell.

The Irons were handicapped by the loss of Bill Kennedy, who had been crocked against Middlesbrough. That injury put an untimely end to his career, but Butcher did well as deputy, scoring the goal that enabled his side to gain a commendable 1-1 draw.

Unfortunately, Fred Harrison was ruled out of the replay at the County Ground and Joe Meillear (usually an outside right) was drafted in for what proved to be the last of his four appearances in the claret and blue.

It was too much for the Hammers, who were facing a team that had been leading scorers of the Southern League for four successive seasons. The 13,328 fans watched the home side net four without reply.

Swindon's next victims were Everton, who went under at the County Ground by 2-1 but finished Football League runners-up that season.

Barnsley greeted the Robins in the semi-final; the Colliers were then a Football League Second Division side. The tie ended goal-less, but Swindon departed from the competition through a single-goal defeat in the replay. Barnsley went on to win the cup, the goal-less final at Crystal Palace being followed by a 1-0 victory *v.* West Bromwich Albion at Bramall Lane.

We've been here before...

In what was the second FA Cup confrontation between the Hammers and the Robins West Ham found themselves facing Swindon Town for the third time that season. In the fourth round of the League Cup the Wiltshire men had forced a 3-3 draw and earned a replay, but at Upton Park the Irons had proved too strong, beating their visitors by 4-1.

Until that defeat in East London things had been going well for Swindon. A 1-0 victory over Sunderland (who would gain promotion that term) in the League and a 3-0 win against Chelsea of Division One in the League Cup had been part of a fine run of form. But then Northampton crushed the Reds 4-0 at the 'other' County Ground and from then on the Robins slipped out of the promotion race, narrow defeats leading to an apparent loss of confidence. What had seemed to be a good side looked more like a disorientated rabble as the club went 518 minutes without scoring.

However, the FA Cup seemed like a possible respite as the Swindon manager Bert Head took the club to their third appearance in the fifth round of the FA Cup since the war. Head, born in Midsomer Norton, was a fine example of West Country footballing tradition. He had been a centre half with his local side before signing for Torquay United in October 1936. He remained at Plainmoor until 1952 when he joined Bury. After making twenty-two League appearances for the Shakers, he became coach and later assistant manager at Gigg Lane.

In October 1955, Swindon Town offered him the manager's job. At the County Ground, Head persevered with the development of his young side and the club won promotion to the Second Division in 1962/63. Bert produced some fine young players, notably Mike Summerbee, Ernie Hunt, 'Bronco' Layne, Don Rogers and Rod Thomas.

Swindon reached the fifth round with a 2-1 victory over Manchester City, then a decent Second Division side, and then beat Aldershot by a similar margin. But the absence of Ernie Hunt, who had to have his tonsils removed, from the home encounter with West Ham was a blow for Swindon. For all that, the Hammers faced a very tough-looking side that included full-back John Trollope, who had made his debut for the Robins as a seventeen year old in the opening match of the 1960/61 season, a 1-1 home draw against Halifax Town, and Trowbridge-born wing-half Keith Morgan. He was playing for Westbury United when signed by Head in the summer of 1958. He made his debut for Swindon in a 3-1 win at Chesterfield on 27 September 1958. He then played in ten consecutive League games before losing his place in the side to Jack Fountain. Morgan regained his first-team place the following season when strong tackling and accurate passing were the main features of his play. Over the next five seasons, Morgan was ever-present.

Bobby Woodruff was another star of the Swindon side. Woodruff was a versatile player who made his debut in February 1959 at centre forward in a 2-1 defeat at home to Chesterfield. He also appeared at inside forward that season but it was in 1959/60 when he was switched to wing half that he established himself as a regular first-team member. The following season was his best in terms of goals scored; he netted thirteen in forty-four games including a hat-trick in a 6-0 home win over Port Vale.

Perhaps the man with the brightest future in Head's side was Mike Summerbee. A West Country boy from a footballing family, Summerbee's uncle George had been a professional with Chester, Preston and Barrow. When he left school, young Mike played for his home-town team Cheltenham until Swindon Town spotted his potential. He made his debut for the Robins in a 2-0 home win over Bournemouth in December 1959 and scored his first goal for the club in a 4-3 defeat of Colchester United in April 1960.

Blackburn-born winger Arnold Darcy played his early football for St Matthew's Youth Club before joining Accrington Stanley in March 1952. Over the next couple of seasons he made thirty-nine League appearances for the Peel Park club before drifting into non-League football with the then Lancashire Combination side, Wigan Athletic. His performances for the Latics, for whom he scored in the Lancashire Junior Cup final, prompted Bert Head to pay £1,000 for his services, with a further £500 due after Darcy had played in twelve first-team games. He made his first-team debut for Swindon in a 2-2 home draw against Coventry City in November 1956. Though not a top scorer, he netted a hat-trick in a 5-0 first-round FA Cup win over Aldershot in November 1958. Darcy was a provider of chances, his accurate crosses from both wings helping 'Bronco' Layne and Ernie Hunt to top the goal-scoring charts during his eight seasons at the County Ground. In 1962/63, Darcy appeared on both flanks, scoring five goals in twenty-six games.

One of the treasures of the Swindon side in the early sixties was perhaps the finest winger in the Football League. Don Rogers could have joined a more glamorous club but opted to spend his peak years with the Robins. He came to the County Ground on New Year's Eve 1960 and after impressing in the club's junior sides made his debut in November 1962 as Swindon beat Southend United 4-1. He played in just seven games that season, helping the club win promotion and scoring his first goal for the Robins in a 3-1 home win over Notts County. It was the beginning of the 1963/64 season when Rogers won a regular place in the Swindon first team. He not only scored seven goals in thirty-six games, but was also a member of the young Robins side to reach the final of the FA Youth Cup against Manchester United.

West Ham were greeted at the County Ground by a record crowd of 28,582 (the previous best had been 28,400, set against Stoke in 1952) and the receipts of £5,471 were over £1,000 up on the record set by the Everton cup-tie the previous year.

Rocking Robins

Geoff Hurst put the visitors ahead after just eleven minutes and the 7,000 fans that had made the trip from East London to the West Country prepared themselves for a repeat of the previous meeting between the combatants. But nine minutes before half-time Ken McPherson pulled the home side level. The big, bustling centre forward began his career alongside Tommy Lawton at Notts County. In 1953 McPherson moved to Middlesbrough for a fee of £15,000 but couldn't win a regular first-team place because of the fine form of Wilf Mannion and Charlie

Wayman. In November 1955 he joined Coventry City in the Third Division South and scored on his debut in a 3-0 win over Newport County. Though he only played in twenty-five League games that season, he was joint top scorer with eighteen goals. The following term he was the club's leading scorer with twenty-two goals, a total which included a hat-trick in a 4-2 home win over Bournemouth. At the end of the 1957/58 campaign, McPherson, who had scored forty goals in ninety-one games, was allowed to join Newport County. McPherson proved to be a prolific goalscorer for the Somerton Park club, netting fifty-one goals in 128 League games before leaving to end his League career with Swindon Town. Ken made his Swindon debut in a 3-1 home defeat at the hands of Portsmouth on the opening day of the 1961/62 season. After scoring two goals in just eight League appearances in that season, he converted to a centre half and replaced Maurice Owen early in the following term.

It seemed West Ham and Swindon were destined to require history to repeat itself with just over a quarter of an hour of the match remaining and a replay looming large. However, Byrne converted a Brabrook cross which forced the Robins to push forward looking for an equaliser. But this did little more than provide a happy hunting ground for 'space-finder' Hurst. He scored just four minutes after his striking partner, like Byrne, profiting from a Brabrook cross.

During the final thirteen minutes of the game, Swindon kept on trying but did not look like being able to get back into the match. However, just as the League Cup defeat at the hands of the Hammers late in 1963 had broken the momentum of the Robins early season form, so the demolition of 15 February 1964 seemed to jump start Swindon's League campaign and they were promoted to Division Two as runners-up to Northampton Town.

West Ham were now just two games from Wembley and their second FA Cup final – the first time East London had gone to the Twin Towers it had been for the inaugural Wembley cup final in 1923.

The Hammers' First Cup Final

At the start of the 1922/23 season, West Ham, at the time a Second Division club, sold their captain Billy Cope to Wrexham. He had been with the club since 1914. Bill had a kick like a mule, which was effective in more ways than one. The sale provided the finance to bring in Everton's Charlie Crossley, the former Wolves man Dick Richards and Billy Moore from Sunderland. Moore was an English amateur international. A small, slight inside left, he looked a bit lightweight, but he was to contribute much to the club and was selected to play for England at the end of the season.

George Kay took over the captaincy from Cope, but the sale of Syd Puddefoot to Falkirk was met with widespread disapproval from the Hammers supporters. He had been one of the club's top goalscorers, 104 in 172 appearances. Puddy was a local lad and had been with the club twenty years; he was an international player, and very much a favourite with the supporters. It seemed like a disaster, but the experience was something West Ham fans of later eras would come to recognise as being part of supporting the Hammers.

Syd King's lads had made the journey to Hull in the first round of the FA Cup a victorious pilgrimage. Billy Moore chalked up his tenth goal for the club at Boothferry Park while Vic Watson, the lad brought in to replace Puddy, put two away.

West Ham were drawn away again in the second round. Brighton were doing well in the Third Division (South), having lost just two times at home that season. The Hammers held them 1-1 at Goldstone. Jack Tresadern (at left half-back) played a blinder in the replay where Moore finally drove home the only goal of the game from a cannonball cross by Ruffell.

The third round allowed a Boleyn Ground match against old foes from the Southern League, Plymouth. The official attendance for the game was over 30,000, but it is likely that it was nearer 40,000. By this time the Hammers League record was beginning to look healthy. West Ham had netted four against Wolves at Molineux just before Christmas when Billy Brown hit the back of the net twice and was unlucky not to make a hat-trick. Watson got a hat-trick against Coventry at Highfield Road and the Irons put three past Port Vale, again away from home. Leicester were belted for six with no reply at Filbert Street nine days before the third-round game. Billy Henderson and Jack Young had shored up the defence and West Ham gained thirty points from a possible fifty-two. As such, the match against the Pilgrims went to form. The Hammers had a comfortable 2-0 win. Taff Richards and Moore did the honours.

Southampton at the Dell were the next obstacle. West Ham had lost there in the League the previous October. This was really a drawn-out affair. A dour struggle produced a 1-1 scoreline that brought the Saints to Upton Park. This was another battle. West Ham managed another 1-1 result, but only after Southampton had taken the lead. This meant a showdown at Villa Park. The last time the Irons had played at this venue in 1913 they had been slaughtered 5-0. However, a decade on West Ham managed the game well, and won quite easily, if just by the only goal of the game. A Dick Richards free-kick was put away by Bill Brown. Herbert Lock, the Saints 'keeper, didn't stand a chance. This set up a clash with Derby County at Stamford Bridge.

Watson had got both West Ham goals in the draws against Southampton, taking his cup tally to five in that season. Billy Moore had notched up three; Richards and Brown had grabbed one each. By the time the Hammers got to Stamford Bridge their League record showed that they had played thirty-one matches, won fourteen, drawn nine, and lost just eight. Goals 'for' had reached forty-four at a cost of twenty-nine goals conceded. West Ham had gone nine games without defeat and had lost just one game out of eighteen, winning eleven of these.

The crowd that gathered for the game in West London was impressive, almost 51,000. This was an all Second Division tie and it was a real cracker. The Rams had taken three points out of four from West Ham in the League, but that had been at the start of the season when the Irons were going through a bad patch, or 'settling-down period' as it had become known on the terraces. County had knocked out Bristol City, Sheffield Wednesday and First Division Spurs on their way to the semi – no mean feat. But more than this, they had kept a clean sheet in the process. As such, it was something of a surprise when just seven minutes into the game West Ham found themselves two goals to the good. The Hammers ended up taking the game 5-2. A truly splendid performance. The two Billies, Moore and Brown, scored twice each and Richards got the other. West Ham were only the third 'Cockney club' to reach the FA Cup final.

Bolton Wanderers, a good First Division side, awaited the Hammers at the new Empire Stadium at Wembley. There had been parades, rallies and celebrations all over the East End since the moment West Ham got through the semi-final. Everywhere houses, shops and streets were decorated in claret and blue. There was a great feeling of expectation and congratulation just for reaching the final.

Like West Ham, the Trotters had not got to the final by an easy route. Norwich, Leeds, two games against Huddersfield, and a quarter final at Charlton had proved a hard campaign. They had beaten Sheffield United in their semi at Old Trafford, a Davie Jack goal putting paid to the Blades' hopes.

The Wanderers had some masterful players: Ted Vizard, the long-time Welsh international, Jack, the smart and dangerous inside forward Joe Smith and in goal the stone wall himself, big Dick Pym. They scored nine goals on their way to the final and only let in two. On form, the Wanderers looked better in defence than the Hammers, who had conceded seven goals on the road to Wembley, but West Ham appeared to be stronger on the offensive, having netted fifteen times in cup games that season.

The Irons had eleven games to play in the six weeks prior to the final – something of a tall order. The Hammers had gone twenty-three games without defeat before losing at home to Barnsley, game number thirty-eight of the season. For some reason, Syd King played his strongest team for all the remaining games, giving no one a rest. As a consequence, in the week of the final there were doubts about the fitness of Ruffell, Watson, Young and Hufton. But they were all in the starting line-up for the game.

Wembley was a fantastic structure for the time. It had been completed just four days before the final. Although it still had some 'rough edges', it was the biggest and best stadium on Earth. The official programme said that it was 'incontestably the finest sports ground in the world' and that it was 'the largest in the world, the most comfortable, the best equipped'. It went on to claim that it could hold 'more than 125,000 people, and will accommodate 1,000 athletes'. In area it was said to equal the Biblical City of Jericho. 'The circuit of its walls is half a mile in length...'

After 1 p.m., people seemed to pour into the stadium from everywhere, through gates, over turnstiles and climbing walls. Most tickets were sold for five shillings, but ticket holders appeared to be in the minority. As the kick-off neared the situation was chaotic and frightening, with officials as helpless as everyone else. Kids were rolled down over the heads of the crowd like a waterfall, being placed over the barriers at the foot of the terraces. Not long afterwards the whole crowd followed, firstly onto the cinder track, and then onto the pitch itself. A solid mass now formed right across the park. By three o'clock, when the match was due to start, the whole place was choc-a-bloc. The pitch was covered with a seething mass of humanity in the middle of which the Grenadier and Irish Guards band played intermittently. As the King arrived they started bashing out *God Save the King*. They got through this pretty quickly; in fact, few could recall hearing it being played at such a pace. It was like a gallop. Before the last note died away the band were making a swift retreat, but at least everyone had stood motionless and quiet while the anthem was playing, so it had the effect of calming things a little.

After around three-quarters of an hour the pitch started to clear. At first this seemed to be simply because people had got fed up with milling about, but there were horses on the field of play. Soon everybody was at least behind the touch-lines, but only just. The pitch looked as if it was carved out of people.

There has been a lot written about the legendary 'White Horse', but this is in fact a myth. Press cameras had got a shot of a dirty grey creature out on its own at one point and it had come out white in development, but it was one of many equine stewards actually clearing the pitch. It had been a fine day up to about half-past two; the skies had clouded over about three o'clock, when His Majesty arrived. It then started to drizzle and it is likely that this affected the photo of the 'white' horse. In fact, it couldn't be identified after the game, but a look-alike was found and 'Billy' became a national hero.

The match finally started. Although at one point the authorities would have called the game off, they were frightened that it might cause a mass protest. The stadium had already been effectively stormed. Added to this it wouldn't have looked good with their Majesties up in the royal box.

The playing area was cordoned with people. This gave the initial moments of the game an eerie intensity. The pitch was darkened by the surrounding crowd and the players could quite tangibly feel the collective gaze of the throng. Every individual movement seemed to threaten an incursion onto the field of play, the crowd were that tightly packed together. Kay lost the toss so, of course, the Bolton skipper, Joe Smith, had West Ham play the first half against the wind and into the sun. The players seemed quite understandably intimidated by the heavy presence of the crowd. At first, both teams huddled around the middle of the pitch, keeping well away from the shifting, undulating perimeter. Many could hear the West Ham goalie, Ted Hufton, talking to supporters about his concern for his family in the stand. So when Davie Jack broke away after just three minutes, his way to goal was more or less clear. No one seemed to have much heart to chase him. It was as if the players had agreed that the game wouldn't go to full-time and decided to make a show, at least for the time they were on the field; 1-0 to Bolton. While all this was going on, West Ham had only ten players on the pitch. Tresadern, a keystone in the Hammers defence, had been stuck in the crowd after going in to retrieve the ball.

After a short while, the match was stopped for around ten minutes while the crowd were pushed from the edges of the pitch. The situation was now suffocating. Every time the ball was making the touchline below head height it was rebounding off the wall of spectators back into play. At the restart, things were not really much better, but King (Syd not George) must have said something to the team. They slung everything at the Wanderers. The pace was frantic. Then, West Ham won a corner. As with all the corners in that game Ruffell had to create a human alleyway, with the help of the police, to make his run at the ball. It was a beauty. Vic Watson closed in like a cobra, hitting an ironclad shot just over the bar. Hopes rose again as Richards bore down on the Bolton goal from the right wing, he teased past Billy Jennings and then, in close, feigned and twisted to avoid Alex Finney. Wanderers (and everybody else) expected him to centre the ball, but Dickie boy smacked in a low, rising shot, that tore through the concentrated atmosphere. The Bolton goalie, Pym, stuck out his right peg in desperation. He just about prevented the ball from entering the goal. Just as West Ham fans were bemoaning their luck at not being 2-1 up within forty minutes, Billy Butler, Bolton's outside right, sent in a tortuous cross that John Smith (their inside left), who had come haring towards the Hammers goal, managed to connect with. He barely got a toe to the ball. Hufton touched it, but could not stop the ball going into the net. The relief amongst the Irons supporters when the referee, Mr Asson, gave offside could be felt right through the vast host. They reacted as a single unit. This was not the usual comfortable feeling of being in a crowd. There was some menace here. Those present felt as if, at any time, the kind of quiet, lava-flow, insurgence that had taken place before the mass had settled was liable to reoccur. This had no connection to individual will. It was down to the instinct of the Leviathan crowd; the great, brainless, grunting beast that sagged around the touchline.

Half-time was a strange affair. The players decided to stay on the pitch. Or perhaps they didn't so much 'decide' but accepted that they were prisoners. There was nowhere for them to go. If they had attempted to go anywhere they would never have got back. The stare of the multitude was oppressive and seemed to cause them to cower. It was less than ten minutes before they decided that they might as well get on with things.

The second half started with everything to play for, and the situation looked good for West Ham early on. However, with less than ten minutes gone, Jack Smith, the Wanderers centre forward, the only Scotsman on the park, picked up a lovely, drifting pass from Vizard on his left. Smith anchored his leg to a thunderbolt and shot past Hufton. The ball rebounded off the people standing behind the net, as reticent as any of the players to dwell too long near the swarm. As it darted back to the relative safety of the field, it very nearly bonked Smith on the back of his head as he trotted back. The goal was met with a kind of muffled ripple of cheering and applause, which heightened the macabre, slightly unreal feeling the whole event had taken on. It all happened so fast that not many spectators knew that a second goal had been scored. After this the game petered out and Bolton won at a stroll. West Ham never really showed the ability they had demonstrated all season.

Charlie Paynter (the West Ham trainer) said afterwards that the pitch had been torn up badly by the crowd and the horses wandering over it. He was of the opinion that his wingers, Ruffell and Richards, were impeded by holes, divets and ruts that had been caused by the mass of boots and hooves. Billy Moore agreed. He saw the wings as an important consideration for the Hammers that had been effectively cut off. But captain Kay conceded that the better team had won and that West Ham had not been on form.

As the crowd disappeared, Wembley looked like a battle field. Entrances and turnstiles had been smashed down; the whole outer ring of the stadium was damaged in some way or another. It was quite shocking. This was the site of an attack; mass destruction. The media said nothing about this after the game, but what had taken place was a slow, insidious, magmatic, riot. The attendance was returned as 126,047 but it is likely that twice this many people had been in the stadium.

The day of the match and through to the next day there were celebrations right across the East End as the defeated Irons came home. The players were part of two parades through the streets of London's Docklands on consecutive days following the match. Hundreds of thousands of people lined the roads to see the team being carried along in a tram covered in electric light bulbs, blazing out the crossed irons and the motto 'Well Done Hammers'. Celebration of defeat seems somehow typical of East London.

Okay, where is fortune hiding?

The lads of '23 won promotion to the First Division, a decent enough compensation for what had been a farce of a final. But West Ham were (and probably still are) a club for whom the rainbow has always been just around the corner – 'Fortune's always hiding'. Upton Park has never lacked talent or players with technique but the history of the club has been premised on a lack of ambition. By 1964 the Hammers had not achieved anything apart from the Second Division Championship in 1958, a fine thing in itself, but hardly adequate compensation for forty years of loyal support from most of the East London population through times of war, poverty and hardship.

Including the match against Swindon, the West Ham side had stayed the same for ten of its previous eleven games and this would be the XI that would play in every round of the cup including the final. This selection pattern had started with the team's League win at Ewood Park, the last game of 1963, where Ron Greenwood had replaced Martin Peters with Eddie Bovington.

After 8 February 1964, West Ham had five successive League and Cup victories.

Young, Gifted and Claret

Up to 1964 West Ham had produced eighteen Youth internationals, who between them had won some eighty caps. The club had reached the final of the FA Youth Cup on three occasions, losing narrowly in the first two but winning the cup in 1963.

The tradition of producing fine players through employment on the ground staff had a long history even in the 1960s. Before the Second World War Ernie Gregory, Jack Wood and Ron Cater had come through to the first team via this route. The first post-war Youth international was Andy Malcolm, who was capped in 1948. In those days the England opportunities were more limited than would have been the case by the 1960s. Andy played for his country during the European Youth Tournament (a new venture for England at the time). Two of that tournament's games were played at Upton Park.

It was around 1956 that West Ham players really started to pick up junior international honours by the dozen. Bobby Moore played eighteen youth games in two years, giving him the record at that level.

The Hammers list of England youth internationals in 1964 was impressive:

Andy Malcolm (1948)	3
Dave Bickles (1961)	2
Ron Boyce (1960)	1
Martin Britt (1963)	3
John Cartwright (1957)	1
John Charles (1963)	1
Geoff Hurst (1959)	6
Joe Kirkup (1957)	1

John Lyall (1957)	1
Terry McDonald (1956)	1
Bobby Moore (1957–58)	18
Martin Peters (1961–62)	3
John Sissons (1962–63)	7
Peter Reader (1958–59)	11
Tony Scott (1957–58)	12
Andy Smillie (1958)	3
John Smith (1956)	1
Roy Walker (1957)	1
Derek Woodley (1959)	6

That's a total of eighty-two caps from nineteen players, only one of whom, Roy Walker, did not turn professional for the Irons. Of the eighteen professionals, again only one, Peter Reader, did not play for the West Ham first team.

Ten of the above players were active members of the Hammers playing staff in 1964, and another, John Lyall had only recently been forced to retire due to injury. West Ham could thus have fielded a full team of Youth internationals with first-team experience (apart from a goalkeeper, but Peters could have done that job pretty well at a push).

A.N. Other

Kirkup Peters

Charles Bickles Moore

Scott Boyce Britt Hurst Sissons

All these players turned out in the West Ham League side in the positions shown.

With the exceptions Johnny Byrne, Peter Brabrook and Jim Standen, the eleven players that West Ham fielded during their FA Cup run of 1964 had been Upton Park juniors. Most of these players had been discovered and brought to Upton Park by Wally St Pier.

Wally and Reg

Wally had joined West Ham as a centre half from Ilford in 1929 and in 1964 he was still on the Upton Park payroll. At fifty-seven years of age St Pier was already a legend at the club, having an almost magical propensity to discover talented young players. He had served as a player, assistant trainer and, since 1948, had been West Ham's 'Chief Representative' (head scout). Week in, week out he stood on the draughty touchlines or school playing fields, public parks or watching games on marsh grounds seeking the talent that kept West Ham's youth scheme flowing. St Pier's contribution to the development of West Ham United and English football is well known to those who have been involved with the Hammers at almost any level. However, few have heard of the man who informed Wally and the club about the talents of the likes of Hurst, Moore, Peters, Ken Brown and others too numerous to detail: a Plaistow man whose family by the mid-1960s had been unofficially talent spotting on the Irons' behalf for four generations. Reg Revins had devoted his life to searching out adolescent East End footballing aptitude. He had learnt the rudiments of his passion at his father's knee, who like his son never kicked a ball in competition (or otherwise) being, as he put it, 'a connoisseur of the game rather than a participant'. Reg once said, 'Some people make wine, take off their boots and socks, roll up their trousers and jump up and down on grapes. Others take out the cork, pour, drink and savour the stuff. The last one is me!' This was an interesting analogy given that like West Ham's founding father Arnold Hills, Reg was an ardent abstainer, even though he was often seen in the snug of the Boleyn Castle public house. This was (and is) the nearest hostelry to the Hammers' Upton Park home and the venue for the meetings of 'The West Ham Trolley Spotters' who, in the 1960s, had convened every second Tuesday of the month for decades. Revins was the chair, secretary and treasurer of this brave group of enthusiasts that included some of the county's leading exponents of the faceting of overhead-powered public road transportation (OPPRT) such as the all-England pairs champions 'Sir' Charlie Charles (whose forbear had played baseball for Thames Ironworks along with Revins' grandfather) and Harry H. Harold ('spotter to royalty'). Revins had inherited details of every trolley bus that had ever run from garages of the East London district from the first days of cable power and extending this encyclopaedic catalogue was second only to his quest to unearth youthful cockney footballing potential. The WHTS were recognised as committed imbibers, especially following a day out on a 'Sparky' (a trolley scout). But Reg would resist all temptations and be content to sip from his flagon of ginger beer, although he was to all intents and purposes addicted to Threadgold's Special Import Bangalore Rough Snuff.

The soccer discoveries of the Revins family went back to the first days of West Ham United at the turn of the twentieth century. Syd Puddefoot, Ted Hufton, Vic Watson, Jimmy Ruffle and Len Goulden had all, in the very first instance, been brought to the attention of the Hammers by a Revins. So often, as St Pier would be about to leave a schoolboy match, as if from nowhere, Reg would startle Wally by stepping into his path and 'nodding-the-wink' towards a budding player, invariably without speaking a word, the exaggerated one-eyed blink and head movement in the direction of a juvenile genius would be enough, as Reg would put it, 'to start the ball rolling'. However, the greatest of all the Revins finds never made the West Ham first team and has remained unsung: the gifted and wayward Nobby Strange. Strange came to Upton Park around the same time as Ernie Gregory. He was an attacking midfield genius who Ernie himself rated as one of the best players he ever saw. His story is long and complex and was always a source of remorse for the Revins family.

Revins, again like Hills, was a fundamentalist amateur and as such spurned any thought of becoming a professional scout (although the great man was never actually offered such a position). He was a devoted employee at the Cross and Blackwell's factory in Silvertown; being a 'master mixer' he was one of the few to be trusted with the exact recipe for that esteemed company's mustard pickle. Indeed, there are many who have memories of that epicurean delicacy that will swear it has 'not been the same since Revins'.

Unfortunately, Reg departed this world without propagating the observational genes of his tribe. The preparation of the finest piccalilli the world has known, the thankless and intricate classification of the infinite details of trolley propulsion, together with the seemingly endless, trudging search for soccer endowment around the inhospitable, frozen, grey, muddy playing fields of East London, never left this doyen of what he called 'the right-royal game of the proletariat' with the time or the room in his life for romance beyond the ball, cable and the jar. The demise of the lineage of the Plaistow tippers ended in tragic irony when Reg, whilst out on an all-night Sparky, was cut down in his prime by one of the last trolley buses to leave the East Ham garage in 1962. He was sent from this world almost instantly, being hit with some force. The very few people that knew Revins suspected that it would have been the way he would have wanted to go. Charlie Charles commented: 'He flew so high, nearly reached the sky.'

It can only be speculated how the Hammers of the twenty-first century might have triumphed if there had been a Revins progeny. However, working behind the eagle eye of St Pier, Reg had bestowed West Ham with a huge amount of potential that he sadly was unable to see come to full fruition.

A right bunch of Bs

West Ham had converted more local lads into first-team players than any other team in London. Nine of the team that would win the FA Cup for West Ham in 1964 were born in the Greater London area. One other, Geoff Hurst, had, like most of his other teammates, spent his formative years in East London within a few miles of Upton Park. Three, Eddie Bovington, Bobby Moore and Ken Brown, had played in the side that lost 2-1 on aggregate to Blackburn Rovers in the 1959 FA Youth Cup final.

In 1964 the West Ham side were all claret-and-blue to the bone, and all English. They would be only the second all-English finalists in thirty-three years to make the final and the last side to play only English players in every tie of the competition. Seven members of the team had surnames beginning, like 'Better', 'Best' and

'Beautiful', with the letter 'B' (Bond, Bovington, Boyce, Brabrook, Brown, Burkett and Byrne).

The Hammers of '64 were also one of the youngest sides to reach the cup final since 1945, with an average age of twenty-four. Just two players, John Bond and Ken Brown, had survived from the team that won the Second Division Championship in 1957/58. But this did not mean that they were inexperienced or naïve. Most of them had Football Association coaching badges.

Eddie the Bov

Eddie Bovington was a good team player; he'd work hard to get the ball and give it to you.
Bobby Moore – West Ham United and England

Both Eddie Bovington's parents were involved in the upholstery trade in Edmonton, where Eddie was born. An only child, he attended Croydon Road Junior School and Tollington Hill Grammar, Muswell Hill before arriving at Upton Park as a sixteen year old in 1957.

He was recommended to West Ham by the manager of a youth club side he played for and got a trial along with his friend Alan Durrant, who went to Bristol Rovers. Eddie then played against Fulham in an end-of-season South East Counties League game before being invited back to train with the Hammers and Malcolm Allison on Tuesdays and Thursdays. According to Eddie,

> West Ham was one of the best clubs a young player could go to. They were friendly, they played good football and they treated you well. The opportunities and the way the young players were looked after… it was a good place to be.

This said, Bovington lived in North London and his childhood football interests focused on Tottenham and Arsenal. His uncle took him to Highbury a few times. He recalled:

> I'd often go to White Hart Lane with my mates. West Ham were Second Division, so really I knew nothing about them.

Cars were not the everyday form of transport they are today when Eddie was a boy and he would travel to Upton Park from Edmonton by bus. There were four or five youngsters from the Edmonton area with West Ham at that time; Eddie remembered them:

> … Scotty, Micky Brookes, Bobby Keech, Jackie Burkett, we would meet up at Bridge Road.

Bovington had not been with the Hammers long when the club won promotion to the First Division. For Eddie,

> That put West Ham on the map. It was big for the players in the first team, but not so much for the juniors; you got nothing out of it yourself, except that you were part of a First Division club.

Bovington saw West Ham's lack of League success as the result of the side's over-adventurous style of play:

> We could always score goals but we gave away goals. You've got to get them, but there was a lot of good players there. They were good players because they knew how to play. They weren't coached as such; they came to the club that way.

According to Eddie, West Ham were the only team that wanted him at the start of his career. His starting salary was £4 a week. Bill Robinson, a coach at Upton Park during Bovington's early days, was a big influence on him. Bill was the first person to instruct Eddie in the ways of professional football. He trained Bovington and the other young Hammers and he picked the team. Eddie reflected on the kit he was provided with when he first came to the Boleyn Ground:

> For training we were given big, heavy, thick, dark-grey roll-neck jumpers and if you were lucky a pair of track bottoms.

Bovington was in the FA Youth Cup side that lost to Blackburn in 1959, but it was not a game that stood out for him. The most lasting memory of the match was the fact that he gave a penalty away. Looking back he saw himself as having a slight inferiority complex. In the youth team he was playing with the likes of Mickey Brooks, Johnny Cartwright, Bobby Keetch, Andy Smillie and Derek Woodley, most of whom were England Schoolboy internationals. Eddie felt the odd one out at times, although none of those individuals really made names for themselves at West Ham. For all this he recollected:

> But being at West Ham as a youngster was fun. We used to sweep the terraces and under the stands after training. There were so many old fag butts discarded under the old Chicken Run, it's a miracle it never burnt down.

Eddie signed professional in May 1959. Ted Fenton took him on at eighteen (seventeen was usual). For Eddie, Fenton

> ...was the governor and that was it. I just missed national service, but I would have been okay about that as most of the units had football teams.

The West Ham side used to get on the coach to go to training at Grange Farm, in Essex, then the property of Fairbairn House Boys Club in Canning Town. Eddie was in awe of the first-team players:

> Everyone thought Jackie Dick was great. He liked a gamble; he'd sneak out the back door at the ground on a Friday to avoid the bookies he owed money to. He and Noel Cantwell were outstanding players. When Vic Keeble arrived he was already a big name. He wore smart jumpers like Andy Williams and had been in the Newcastle cup final side. He also had a sports car. Nothing seemed to panic him, he was always very casual.

Eddie was a tough midfield battler, but although he struggled to break into the side for four-and-a-half seasons, he rejected a move to Southampton in 1962, showing his eagerness to make the West Ham first team. According to Bovington:

> I was an average club player, my strength was tackling. I wasn't the most skilful player.

He was compared with Andy Malcolm and Eddie always saw that as a fair assessment. He played to his own limitations. Greenwood mostly used him as a man-marker, although that was not really a way Ron liked to play.

The argument that Eddie Bovington was a similar type of player to Andy Malcolm is on the surface feasible, but anyone who was around to compare the two would see that Bovington, whilst a strong tackler, was much more in tune with the, 'movement and flux' football so important to Greenwood. He did not have the 'demolition' instincts possessed by Andy, needed by any side wishing to make an impression in the sixties and seventies. An inability to accept this fact was perhaps the most glaring weakness in the make-up of the England manager to be, and maybe the reason why West Ham never really developed the consistency to make an impact on the League until John Lyall took over. Greenwood had no Hunter, Giles, Bremner or Stiles. He could not call on a Tommy Smith, Maurice Setters or Jack Charlton. The potential that lay in Malcolm and later Harry Cripps was never honed, simply because it was not in Greenwood's personality to do this. Perhaps what is true is that Bovington was never given the chance to develop in this way at Upton Park. He made his first-team debut on 18 April 1960 in a 5-3 defeat at Old Trafford. According to Eddie:

> You always remember your first game. United have always been the biggest club around. It was a capacity crowd and I was playing against people I had only read about, Charlton, Violet. That is my first outstanding memory, that's something for every player.

But holding onto the number four shirt was always going to be difficult. Andy Malcolm reclaimed it for the rest of that season and Geoff Hurst (before he converted to an out-and-out striker's role) was coming up through the youth ranks. Bovington managed just seventeen first-team games up to the 1962/63 season, but in 1963 he married and he and his wife Pauline moved to Clayhall, Ilford in Essex. This was around the time that Bovington was becoming a fairly regular member of the West Ham first-team squad. He would share rooms with Bobby Moore on away trips and observed that despite his skipper's success, he remained unchanged. Eddie assessed his room-mate:

> Some said he was bit detached but he wasn't. He was always an ordinary, nice bloke.

Bovington was part of what he saw as the good social life at the club:

> I used to go about with Bobby, Johnny Byrne and Alan Sealey. We liked a drink. Geoff, Martin and Ronnie Boyce played cards.

Eddie could not recall the players ever arguing. He only drank about once a week and certainly not after a Monday unless the club were playing away, when the players might have had a few beers the night before a match. Eddie recalled:

> Ron Greenwood was okay with us drinking. Some overdid it at times though. We went to all games by train. In the buffet car on the way home, we'd have a meal and a few beers with the fans. Ron wasn't always happy with that and it was a bit much at times.

Bovington had a unique rapport with the Hammers' supporters:

> The thing was that even if we got beat at home, the fans would still come back because they were very loyal and knew they'd usually see a fair game. West Ham fans were all right, when they were on your side. They were good fans, West Ham have always been well supported. Win, lose or draw, they always come back.

However, Eddie's relationship with his manager was a complex one. While he acknowledged Ron's tactical influence and accepted he became a better ball-player under his tutelage, Eddie felt undervalued at times:

> I suppose because you're in and out of the side you blame the manager and think he should pick you. He had his reasons and that was that, but I wasn't afraid of seeing him and asking why I wasn't in the side. I stuck up for myself but the only thing you got back was: 'It's a better balanced side'.

Eddie respected Greenwood as a coach but his admiration was not always reflected in Bovington's assessment of his manager as a man. He was not sure Ron treated him completely fairly:

> Maybe if Martin Peters and Bobby Moore had not been at West Ham I'd have got more games, but as it was I played in the same position as two England players.

Ron changed the training methods when he came to Upton Park in 1961 and Eddie's play improved, mainly because Greenwood used the ball more in training. But the two never got on too well. Eddie reflected:

> I don't think he liked the way I played.

It is probably true that Greenwood put great emphasis on skill and that he liked the Martin Peters style – as Eddie was to say, Peters was 'more of a footballer' – but Bovington knew that sometimes you need more than that, as in the second League game against Blackburn in 1963.

Peters was always to feel frustrated about the decision to drop him, feeling that he had been singled out from the entire team that had conceded eight goals against Blackburn at Upton Park on Boxing Day 1963, saying 'I wasn't the only one to have a bad game'. But the rationale was impersonal.

Peters was much more to Greenwood's footballing taste than the pugnacious Bovington, who aligned with the Andy Malcolm tradition at Upton Park; belligerent, uncompromising and focused on destruction. Malcolm had been amongst the first to be 'shipped out' when Greenwood replaced Ted Fenton as West Ham manager, the 'way of the warrior' never being part of Ron's philosophy. But Greenwood knew that battles against lower-division clubs and even the lesser lights of the First Division required the presence of a terminator. His side had to achieve a balance that could respond to the opposition. With Byrne, Sissons, Brabrook, Boyce, Moore and to a lesser extent Burkett, there was more than enough 'art' in the side. The power came from Bond, Brown, Bovington and Hurst. Although Peters was often underestimated as a steely player, his selection would have compromised the Hammers armour in the context of the English attrition that was the FA Cup in the 1960s. West Ham's European adventures, that were to require more craft, cunning and subtlety, would see Peters used much more, but the warlike, dreadnought forwards of the likes of Burnley and Preston North End would have to face the menacing tackling persona, the intimidating, confrontational power of 'Eddie the Bov'.

It has become part of Boleyn Ground folklore that following the humiliation at the hands of Blackburn, Martin Peters was made the informal scapegoat of the West Ham side; he played no part in West Ham's FA Cup cause, 'Iron' Eddie Bovington being drafted in to replace him. However, Peters played in the first leg of the League Cup semi-final and continued to turn out for the Hammers in the League. Anyone who knows a little of the West Ham manager of the time's penchant for skill and subtlety over graft and muscle, and who attended or played in the games the Irons contested during the second half of the 1963/64 season will feel confident that Peters was not the subject of a Greenwood vendetta. Ron was, in the last analysis, a pragmatist. In fact, those who have studied the Greenwood mentality through the medium of the football he designed both with West Ham and England will recognise that his use of Peters betrayed not a taste for revenge or a want to attribute blame to a single player. Greenwood's selections reveal what he saw as the goals he was most likely to achieve, and he would have wanted to have realised them using Peters as a major element of his overall scheme, because more than any other West Ham player, Martin Peters personified what Ron Greenwood saw as football. Peters would have been an outstanding player in any era. He was precise, accomplished and could play in any position on the field (including goal). His complete mastery of the ball is exemplified by a story told to me by John Charles, West Ham's first black player and a colleague of Peters from their earliest days at Upton Park:

> We were practising crosses. Harry Redknapp sent over a cross to Peters. Martin heads it against the bar. He was about fifteen yards out. 'Unlucky,' shouts Harry. 'It wasn't unlucky,' says Peters, 'I was aiming for the bar.' 'Bollocks,' says Harry. 'Right then,' Martin says, 'I bet you ten quid that if you send over twenty crosses I'll put every one on the bar.' 'Okay,' says Harry. Well, he sent over twenty crosses and every one, all twenty, Martin bangs against the bar!

Peters, like so many other West Ham players of the 1960s, was a product of the Upton Park youth system. It is highly unlikely that Greenwood would have dismissed a player of his type or class on emotional grounds. However, there can be little doubt that Ron Greenwood knew the worth of players like Eddie Bovington, although this did not always translate to him using them. At times he seemed to want football to be something it was not, or set an example that others just would not be able to follow or even understand. For Bovington,

> Greenwood wanted the 'keeper to throw the ball out to a full-back. His idea was that if you had the ball, why kick it up the park and give yourself only a 50/50 chance of getting it back.

But, as Eddie understood, in the sixties teams had to have a ball-winner who would go through the back of players; defenders were allowed to tackle from behind and of course Bovington was good at that, although he was never considered to be a dirty player. Eddie was never booked or sent off during his career, but he admitted that a player had to do something relatively outrageous to get sent off and the manner in which the game was played could do some damage. He always regretted finishing Bryan Douglas' career. Douglas had congratulated Eddie after the match at Ewood Park in the last days of 1963. He had told Bovington that Eddie had not allowed him to touch the ball. But when the West Ham man had tackled Douglas from behind, the Rovers striker had torn cruciate knee ligaments. Bovington reflected,

> Bryan was a great player and a nice bloke.

Douglas did come back but was never the same player again. But, as Eddie saw things, it was a wonder there weren't more injuries. The West Ham side never warmed up. Bovington looked back with some incredulity:

> We might go into the gym underneath the main stand and do a few simple stretches or kick a ball about a bit. The thing I thought was a waste of time was coming back out again after the half-time break. I'd have sooner just changed ends and got on with it.

There Are No Songs About Carlisle

Football is a roller coaster of emotions but I'm glad I got on.
Alan Kendall – Preston North End

Preston's tie against the team that would be runners-up in the Fourth Division Championship that season looked like one of those games where sides of North End's ilk might come to grief. The Cumbrians had beaten Third Division Queens Park Rangers by a 2-0 margin and in front of Bedford's own fans handed out a 3-0 thrashing to the non-League side that had humiliated Newcastle at St James' Park. Preston's Jim Smith, who did not play in the fifth round, but who travelled north with his side, recollected:

> Carlisle had done well and had a run going. We decided to go there and be a bit careful. Of course Brunton Park was packed and they certainly thought they could go through. I think it was close in the end, only one goal decided it after all.

Jimmy Milne echoed Smith's view:

> We never took any side for granted. Carlisle had done well and were at home. How a team feels about itself can just override other considerations. But Preston was clearly the better side and had been on a good run as well.

Preston's starting line-up was the same XI that had faced Bolton in both the games with the Trotters and they proved solid enough to beat Carlisle United, who were playing in the fifth round for the first time in their history, at the first attempt, by the only goal of the game in a real battle of a match. For all that, the single was beautifully taken by the grafter of the Preston team, Alan Spavin. He sent his side through to the next round after finding an opening carved out of sheer chance, but executed with professional timing.

Preston and the Cup

Although Preston were playing their best football for years, the thought of reaching Wembley in 1964 would, by most of their supporters, have been dismissed as a dream. The club was founded in 1880 as an adjunct to the North End cricket club and originally had played their football to the code of rugby union. But the members turned to soccer after only twelve months.

Preston North End first participated in the FA Cup in December 1883, beating Great Lever 4-1. They would appear in seven finals, winning the trophy on two occasions. Early in their history, Preston won the record for the biggest win in the history of the FA Cup when they beat Hyde 26-0 in a first-round tie on 15 October 1887. They also boasted the second highest score after royally roasting Reading 18-0 in the first round in 1893/94.

North End were one of the twelve original members of the Football League in the 1888/89 season. They won their first FA Cup that term, defeating Wolverhampton Wanderers 3-0 at the Kennington Oval. Tommy Hunter, the Wolves outside right, hit the outside of the North End post before Fred Dewhurst opened the scoring for the Lilywhites. Jimmy Ross powered a shot against the Wolves crossbar but Dewhurst was on hand to convert from close range. Ross himself scored North End's second goal with a shot that Wolves 'keeper Jack Baynton couldn't hold. It was Ross who provided the cross from which Sam Thompson scored North End's third goal late in the second half. Preston had gone through every round without conceding a goal, a feat only equalled in 1903 by Bury. This was North End's second consecutive final, having lost 2-1 to West Bromwich Albion the previous term at the Kennington Oval. Preston fell behind after seventeen minutes when Jem Bayliss shot past Mills after bad defending by the Whites. Albion's 'keeper Ben Roberts was in fine form and denied North End an equalising goal until the fiftieth minute when John Goodall scored. Despite constant pressure, it was Albion who grabbed what turned out to be the winning goal when Woodall's volley hit a post before trickling over the goal-line.

North End were next seen at a cup final a third of a century later. On the Saturday prior to the 1922 FA Cup Final at Stamford Bridge, North End had lost 6-0 to their opponents for the final, Huddersfield Town, in a League match. The final itself was a rather dull affair and was settled by a very controversial goal. North End's Tommy Hamilton was penalised for a foul on Huddersfield's England winger Billy Smith and though a penalty was given, press and newsreel pictures showed the incident that prompted the award to have taken place at least a yard outside the box. This game was the last pre-Wembley final and of course the one before West Ham's first final appearance.

North End went into their first Wembley final in 1937 as clear favourites to beat Sunderland. Frank O'Donnell opened the scoring in the thirty-ninth minute to give Preston the lead, but the second half was a different story as Sunderland came back strongly. The Wearsiders, inspired by Raich Carter, scored three goals to win the trophy.

However, the Lilywhites came back to win in 1938, gaining revenge over Huddersfield, who had knocked out the cup holders. After a goal-less first half, inside right George Mutch hit the Huddersfield bar and Bob Hesford saved well from Bobby Beattie, but after ninety minutes, there was still no score. The game went into extra time and with just thirty seconds remaining Mutch was brought down inside the area. Having received attention from the Whites' trainer, George stepped up to the penalty spot and blasted the spot-kick into the net off the underside of the crossbar, bringing the FA Cup back to Preston for the first time in the twentieth century. North End had fielded the shortest forward line ever seen in a Wembley cup final: the average height of the five players was just under 5ft 6½in. But the victory was a fine conclusion to a season in which the Preston side had finished third in the First Division, just three points behind Champions Arsenal.

Preston had pioneered professionalism by luring Caledonian players south of the border from the earliest days, paving the way for big business football. By the 1937/38 season North End had almost become a Scottish side playing in England; sixty of their sixty-four First Division goals were claimed by nine Scots, the other four going to English-born outside right, Dickie Watmough.

In 1954, on their sixth final appearance, Preston came up against West Bromwich Albion. North End took the lead when Charlie Wayman, looking at least a couple of yards offside, raced clear to score – he had netted in every round of the competition. Albion threw everything into attack. The frantic charge culminated with Tommy Docherty bringing down John Nicholls in the penalty area. The referee pointed to the spot and Ron Allen brought the scores level. Albion's winner came courtesy of North End 'keeper George Thompson, who misjudged Frank Griffin's cross-shot, allowing the ball to drift over the line. The Baggies took the day by the odd goal of five, a scoreline that had some resonance following the first Saturday of May 1964.

The Captains

Mooro

I must have played with Bobby Moore more than anyone else. I often thought, 'he's gonna miss this', but he hardly ever did. He always wanted it on the edge of the box; that didn't always seem to make sense, but as the 'keeper got it to Bobby he was always in space.

Ken Brown – West Ham United and England

If you know anything of West Ham United, English football or even if your general knowledge might be classed as 'passable', you will already know something about Bobby Moore. So much has been written about his life and career after the early sixties, it is redundant to repeat it here, and I have written elsewhere of how he was ill used by football when he decided to hang up his boots. However, none of those who have written about Bobby, some who have claimed to have been his friend, really managed to portray the man authentically.

Bobby Moore was very much an ordinary person, who suffered, like many others whose only influence and experience in life revolves around football, from a type of social naïvety. You can see this from looking at any of the television interviews he gave from the mid-sixties to the mid-seventies. Those who tell you about spending a life in football from an early age often talk of how hard it is to 'do things for yourself' when they leave the game. This was brought home to me when chatting with one of West Ham's longest-serving members of staff, who went on to become a coach with the club after he retired from playing. We were talking about one of his colleagues from his early days with the club whom he had lost contact with. He asked me if I might be able to track him down, saying that 'the club must know where he is'. In truth, the Upton Park administration has few records of the whereabouts of former professionals and I told him this. 'No,' he replied, 'they must know.' It showed the reliance men who have been involved with football for a lifetime have on the club to meet their needs, particularly if they have played for mainly one team. When young men came to Upton Park at the age of fourteen, fifteen or sixteen, in the 1950s, the club made arrangements for everything in their adult lives, from housing to travel, training and even meals.

Some players, fans and journalists, certainly in the sixties and seventies, described Moore as being aloof. I heard fans say that he was, 'stuck up' or that he 'thinks he is better than us'. Along with many young boys, I hung around the ground after games, just to watch the players leaving. I spoke to Bobby many times as a lad, briefly as he left or arrived at the club or the Chadwell Heath training ground, the usual stuff: 'How'd it go Bob?'...'Alright Bob?' I was never an autograph hunter, so I think my greetings sitting on a fence or leaning up against a car would puzzle him a bit; I didn't want anything. Sometimes this would turn into a brief chat, especially when I was very small (I started going to West Ham when I was about four and was attending matches on my own at six) other times he'd ignore me completely. But rarely did I see Bob without a frown on his face. Even then I sensed that this had more to do with his shyness, maybe awkwardness with his profile, than any form of malice. Remember, he was something of a footballing enigma, as West Ham striker of the 1950s Vic Keeble, amongst others, has indicated:

> When Moore was on the way in, we thought he was a bit slow, but we knew he was going to be a good player.

Later, as a regular at the Black Lion in Plaistow, which in the late 1960s was a fashionable drinking place, or 'The Room at the Top' nightclub in Ilford, we would have slightly longer encounters, one or two times he bought me, and whatever girl I happened to be with at the time, a drink (particularly if she was pretty). I encountered Bobby three or four times after he left West Ham, only once 'officially' when he was managing Southend United. The last time we spoke he was working with Capital Radio. He was noticeably more relaxed then than at any other time we had met. But he remembered my name and asked firstly how my writing was going and secondly about one of the girls he had seen me with in Ilford. I did have a bit of a 'colourful' reputation in the East London area at the time, as did my family, but I was amazed he recalled these meetings and even these young women's names (most of the latter had long since deserted my memory banks).

Contacts of this sort, together with now literally hundreds of interactions with West Ham players from the 1930s to the early 1970s, leave me seeing Moore as not so much 'aloof' but as being detached or even isolated during his time at Upton Park. I think he felt this a bit too, although he might not have put it that way.

Those who did know Bob from an early age, the likes of his fellow apprentice at West Ham and cricketing teammate Eddie Presland, knew that, in essence, Bobby remained very much the East End boy, no matter how hard he or others might try to create a persona of something else. His simplicity endeared him to many of his long-term colleagues. His intuitive dislike of pomposity, at points, made his relationships with Ron Greenwood and Alf Ramsey a little difficult. As his long-time defensive colleague at West Ham Ken Brown recalled:

> One time he had ructions with Ron, but this was unusual.

This 'native' quality could bring its own problems. Each of us, from our backgrounds, bring aspects of our experience into our lives that are more or less hard to accept by others, things that seem more appropriate to one person than another might think, as Derek Woodley illustrated, looking back at a moment when working with Bob at Roots Hall:

> At Southend, the boys were swearing, the women were in an adjoining room. Bob's attention was brought to this. He went in and told the players to 'Stop fucking swearing as the fucking women were in the fucking next room'.

Robert Frederick Chelsea Moore was born on 12 April 1941. First Reg Revins and then Wally St Pier had seen Moore play during the early 1950s and it was the latter that had mentioned to Ted Fenton, the manager of West Ham United at that time, the boy's noticeable approach. In 1955 Fenton asked Jack Turner to take a look at Bobby in a cup-tie between Leyton and East Ham. Bobby didn't shine in the 3-3 draw and the scouting report reflected his performance saying that Moore was a hard worker but that there was nothing special about him. But Turner had spoken to a few people (including Revins) at that game and decided to give the boy another viewing. He turned up at the replay to see Moore score the winning goal and overall give an impressive display. Bobby looked strong and willing and Turner could see the influence he had on the boys around him. He was a big lad and already had good positional awareness and a certain presence.

Bob signed amateur forms for West Ham in August 1956 and made his debut for the colts side on 6 October that year. Almost exactly a year later on 2 October 1957 (Moore became a West Ham apprentice at the age of sixteen and was paid £7 per week) he made the first of his eighteen appearances (a record at the time) for the England Youth team, and two months later, on 2 December, he broke into the West Ham Reserves side. Before signing professional in May 1958 he had captained England Youth to the final of the European Youth Championships.

Moore made his debut for the West Ham first team at Upton Park on 8 September 1958. The Hammers beat Manchester United 3-2. He had a solid game in the number six shirt but few would have guessed his future from that showing. Bob won eight England Under-23 caps and made his debut in the FA Cup on 7 January 1961 in a third-round, Boleyn Ground, no-goal game against Stoke.

Moore was twenty-one when he was selected for the England squad to play under manager Walter Winterbottom in the World Cup in Chile. His first game for his country was an acclimatisation friendly against Peru on 20 May 1962, just before the tournament commenced. Most commentators were confident that Moore had been taken to South America to gain experience of being with the England team, but he played in all England's games during the tournament before Brazil defeated Winterbottom's team 3-1 in the quarter-final. On returning from Chile Bobby and Tina Dean were married on 30 June 1962.

After the game in Peru, Bobby became a regular in the England side. He is still, at the time of writing, the youngest ever player to have captained England when he skippered the side against Czechoslovakia on 20 May 1963, his twelfth appearance for his country. He would gain six more caps before the 1964 FA Cup final.

For one of his defensive partners of the 1960s, Jack Burkett:

> People said he was slow and couldn't tackle, but he was brilliant. He was good to play beside because wherever you were he could get you the ball. You wouldn't have to go fighting or looking for it, Bobby could find you with his eyes closed.
>
> People talk about yesteryear and would players be able to play in today's football? I'm sure we'd have coped. I would have done as a wing-back, because although I was defensively minded I was quick and liked to get forward.
>
> People like Denis Law and Jimmy Greaves would score goals now and no one would get the ball off George Best. Mooro would never have made a mistake because that's how he was.

And according to Ken Brown:

> I just spent my time covering for him. I was a defensive player – that was my job – and when balls used to come down to Mooro I always used to drop off and come around him but never once did he miss the bloody ball.
>
> He wasn't the quickest but he never got done and the secret was he knew what he could do with the ball before it came to him. He knew where people were instinctively.
>
> I used to feel for Mooro because he stood out in a crowd because of his blond, curly hair. He used to look forward to going abroad, especially to America, because nobody knew him and he could just relax.
>
> He could have a beer with the boys and that's what he wanted to do, just get away from everything and not be the centre of attention. He handled it brilliantly but if nobody paid him any attention he liked it better.

Bobby Moore's achievements in the first few years of his professional career were remarkable by any standards, but they are astounding when one remembers that he was born with very few advantages in terms of playing football. What he did have was a gift bestowed on many East End boys, the ability to endure and work hard; these were perhaps the advantages of his inheritance and birthright. However, he also had an insatiable desire to learn and did so, firstly from the older Hammers who trained him as a lad on Tuesdays and Thursdays, Malcolm Allison and Noel Cantwell, and then from Ron Greenwood and Alf Ramsey. Moore had no real pace so he was obliged to compensate by developing a radar-like positional sense. This came out of his ability to read a game and put himself in the right place at the right time, or even make where he was the right place at the right time. As a skipper of West Ham and England he was a subtle leader; his example and effort inspired those around him.

Noble Nobby

I still call Nobby Lawton 'Skipper'.
Howard Kendall – Preston North End

Nobby (known to his friends and colleagues as 'Bobby') Lawton was born in Newton Heath, Manchester on 25 March 1940. He joined Preston after spending three years with Manchester United. A probing, pushing right-half who could be a beautiful attacking player, Lawton was a product of Manchester Schools football and was a member of the 1955 Manchester Schoolboys side that ended West Ham Schoolboys' nine-year unbeaten run and reached the final of the English Schools Shield. Unfortunately they were beaten 4-3 on aggregate over two legs by Swansea Schoolboys.

Nobby, who represented Lancashire Schools, initially went to Old Trafford as an amateur, training two nights a week, turning professional at the age of eighteen and making his debut League appearance on 9 April 1960 against Luton Town. Lawton's best period at Old Trafford was the 1961/62 season when, looking bright and creative in a transitional team, he played in twenty matches and scored six goals, the highlight being his hat-trick from inside left in the 6-3 win against Nottingham Forest at Old Trafford on Boxing

North End Nobby.

Day 1961. However, in the following campaign he was not able to gain a regular place in the side, and when United paid £55,000 for Paddy Crerand, Lawton was allowed to leave, having played just four dozen games for the Red Devils.

One of his last appearances for United was against Tottenham in the FA Cup semi-final at Hillsborough. He was given the unenviable job of marking Danny Blanchflower. Nobby Stiles, one of Lawton's teammates that day, recalled:

> Nobby was a nice player, he passed the ball well, but he didn't have a lot of pace, which was a particular problem that day because Blanchflower was at his best, stretching us repeatedly with some beautiful passing.

In the second half Stiles felt obliged to take over the role of covering the Spurs skipper. This left John White, the man Stiles had been instructed by Matt Busby to look after, without a chaperone. The deadly Tottenham craftsman promptly finessed a pass to Cliff Jones, whose goal finished the match. It was directly after that game that Busby went to Glasgow to bring Scottish international Crerand to Old Trafford.

Preston were struggling in the lower reaches of the Second Division when the transfer deadline loomed large in the spring of 1963. Jimmy Milne signed Nobby from Manchester United for £11,500 on 19 March 1963. Lawton, standing just over 5ft 9ins in height, was not a big man, but he had a solid 11st 8lbs frame and he blossomed at Deepdale. He certainly had talent but this was sharpened by an aggressive streak. However he hardly ever pushed the boundaries of the laws of the game; he was always a gentleman in terms of his fellow professionals and was never a dirty player. His passion for football and his inspirational leadership qualities made him a tremendous asset to the North End cause. He was equally happy in attack or midfield and thrived on responsibility, a gift Milne swiftly noted and the Preston manager made Nobby skipper of his side.

During his time at Deepdale, Lawton became a vastly improved player and proved to be one of Preston's bargain buys of the decade.

4

The Sixth Round

Me and Bobby seemed to meet all the big stars at that time... just in the right place at the right time I suppose. The Ronettes were on tour and we went to one of the concerts and went backstage to have a chat with Mick Jagger. John Lennon was there too and Ronnie Bennett... don't know where the others were...

Johnny Byrne – West Ham United and England

Two days before the quarter-finals of the 1964 FA Cup, on 27 February, the Ronettes stood at number 11 in the British charts with *Baby I Love You*, a highpoint for this recording. Just behind the Ronettes, Ciff Richard lurked with *I'm the Lonely One* and one place ahead of the New York girls was *I'm the One,* by Scousers Jerry and the Pacemakers. It was the eighth consecutive week that the Ronettes had been in the top 40 and they would remain there for another month. The charts had been very much dominated by Liverpool. Apart from Gerry Marsden and his 'Fab Four' look-alikes, at that point Cilla Black was at number 1 with her version of *Anyone Who Had a Heart*, The Merseybeats were at 5 with *I Think of You* and Freddie and the Dreamers' *Over You* had just come in at number 20, whilst the Beatles had found what seemed like a permanent place in the record chats, having been hanging around for thirteen weeks with *I Want to Hold Your Hand* and in the top 30 with *She Loves You* for the better part of seven months!

The Ronettes had first entered the British best-selling list on 17 October the previous year with *Be My Baby,* reaching a high point of number 4 on 21 November that year. That record was to stay in the charts for ten weeks, which meant that the Ronettes were not amongst the best-selling recording artistes in the British market for just two weeks during a near six-month period and had become very much the ultra-sexy darlings of both Preston's and West Ham's cup runs. Indeed, their music had been a theme tune of the clubs' respective paths to Wembley. I was waiting with 36,550 others at the Boleyn Ground for the last-eight game with Burnley, having entered a good hour before the kick-off, and I recall singing along with the North Bank chorus:

> West Ham, we love you, West Ham, we love you, West Ham we love only you... woh-ol, woh-ol, woh-ol!

The Ronettes were perhaps the best remembered of the 'girl groups' of their era. They achieved their biggest success under producer Phil Spector. In towering, black beehive hairdos and dark eye makeup, the Ronettes were a classic mid-sixties girl group with a sultry twist – vulnerable but tough, sexy but sweet.

Veronica (Ronnie) Bennett (born 10 August 1943) her sister Estelle (born 22 July 1944) and their cousin Nedra Talley (born 17 January 1946) were all native New Yorkers and grew up in the city's Washington Heights/Spanish Harlem area avidly listening to rock and pop music, especially the 'doo wop' groups like 'Little Anthony and the Imperials' and 'Frankie Lymon and the Teenagers' who Ronnie cited as her earliest vocal influence.

Starting in 1959, the girls' grandmother would demand that the three stay in a room for an indefinite period and encouraged the three to harmonise. They called themselves the 'Darling' or the 'Dolly Sisters' (the former stuck the longest) and took their act to the famed Apollo theatre amateur talent contest. When they won, their grandmother started paying for singing lessons for them. Phillip Halikus heard the girls, saw their potential and became their manager. He started the three out with appearances at 'hops' and charity shows.

One night in 1961, the trio, dressed in tight skirts and with their hair piled high, went to Joey Dee's Peppermint Lounge, home of the twist craze, on New York's 45th Street. In the early 1960s the Peppermint Lounge in New York City was *the* place to be. The house band there was 'Joey Dee and the Starliters', whose *Peppermint Twist – Part I* became a number 1 song. While standing in line waiting to get in, the manager saw them and said 'girls, you're late', mistaking them for a singing trio that had failed to arrived. He took them inside and ushered them on stage and they belted out a version of Ray Charles' *What I Say*, even using the choreography they had been working on. The girls took the club by storm and were signed to appear regularly for $10 a night.

This slot quickly brought them to the notice of influential people in the music business and they appeared in a movie with disc jockey Clay Cole, *Twist Around the Clock*. The Twist was a dance sensation, and the Bennett sisters and their cousin could twist with the best of them. 'The Darling Sisters' were also booked to perform at the Miami Peppermint Lounge. There they were spotted by New York disc jockey Murray Kaufman, who converted them into 'Murray the K's Dancing Girls' for his touring company and his Brooklyn Fox Theatre Rock and Roll Revues. They also did duty with Clay Cole's *Twist-A-Rama* tour.

Meanwhile Phillip Halikus set up their first recording session through Stu Phillips at Colpix Records. Colpix renamed the threesome 'Ronnie and the Relatives' and issued their first single in the summer of 1961, written by Carole King, *I Want a Boy*. The next single, *I'm on the Wagon*, listed the girls as the 'Ronettes'. *Silhouettes* and *Good Girls* followed, but these songs were little more than local successes. They also recorded an LP's worth of material for Colpix/May, but it was not released until their glory days.

In early 1963 the Ronettes did an Exciter-styled rocker called *Good Girls*, which demonstrated their continuing recording maturity and a developing sound. Between their other activities, the girls found themselves backing artistes like Bobby Rydell, Del Shannon and Joey Dee on record. It was around this time that they met Phil Spector.

There are a number of conflicting stories about the way the Ronettes came into contact with Spector. One relates how Estelle, whilst dialling a phone number for confirmation of a recording session, dialled the wrong number and ended up talking to Phil Spector. One thing led to another and he supposedly asked the group to produce a demo for him. On hearing the girls he wanted to immediately produce a Ronettes record. Another, less romantic tale has it that a journalist from *16* magazine, Georgia Winters, introduced Spector to the girls while he was looking for talent in New York.

However, Spector had been a regular member of the audience at the Brooklyn Fox and had enjoyed the concerts there. He couldn't help but have noticed the reaction that many of these acts elicited from the young audience. He also noticed with no songs on the radio and no singles in the shops, the Ronettes still generated enthusiastic applause. One afternoon, Estelle and Ronnie were talking in their bedroom, discussing getting back into a recording studio and making records again. Eventually, Estelle got the idea to call Phil Spector, thinking that the man who had a number 1 hit with the Crystals could get them to the top of the charts as well. Estelle got the phone number for Philles Records and told the secretary she wanted to speak to Phil Spector himself. Amazingly, the secretary put the call through directly to Spector. Phil knew about the Ronettes from the Brooklyn Fox shows, and gladly offered them a chance to record for him.

Spector saw that he could mould the Ronettes to his specifications; he was already tiring of his association with the Crystals, substituting an outside singer, Darlene Love, on several records credited to them. He was taken with Ronnie's hard but sweet sound and saw the 'bad girls' in beehives as an act he could build an image around. Originally, Phil only wanted to sign Ronnie to a contract, but Grandma Beatrice Bennett said that the Ronettes were a package deal and that Spector needed to sign all three or none at all. So in 1962, Veronica Bennett, Estelle Bennett and Nedra Talley became part of Phil Spector's Philles Records. Up until that time girl groups rarely had an identity or even got their pictures on the sleeves of their 45s. That changed with the Ronettes. Spector gave them a more defined image than most female artistes of the time. They were still sweet and feminine, but they had hints of attitude; photographs of them were used to project their latent eroticism. Moreover, their songs dared to address the objects of their affection directly (*I love you* as opposed to *I love him*); they were, on something more than a subliminal level, seductive.

Before Phil Spector took them under his wing in the early '60s, the Ronettes were regionally successful. But the Spector-produced records are what everyone remembers, and for good reason; they featured some of his biggest, best productions along with equally impressive songs. The Ronettes arrived at a most opportune time – Phil Spector's artistes were benefiting from the 'Wall of Sound', a multi-tracked, overdubbed aural symphony Phil used as a musical smorgasbord to highlight his singers, with his 'wrecking crew' of session musicians like Hal Blaine on drums, Leon Russell on piano, and Glen Campbell on guitar. He also had a stable of writers including Jeff Barry, Ellie Greenwich, Barry Mann, Cynthia Weil, Pete Andreoli and Vinnie Poncia, who were among the top tunesmiths of their day.

After some time in New York, Spector left for the West Coast and took the Ronettes with him. He used his existing writers alongside other contacts Gerry Goffin, Carole King, Jeff Barry and others in the Brill Building (a place that was destined to enter into the mythology of popular music) to come up with some songs. Spector lavished all his attention on his new protégées, collaborating on material with some of the top Brill Building songwriting teams. The first single on Spector's Philles label in July 1963 was *Be My Baby*.

Be My Baby was co-written by Spector, Jeff Barry and Ellie Greenwich especially as a showcase for Ronnie Bennett. Right from the often-imitated drum kick that opened the song, *Be My Baby* announced itself as a pop classic; Spector's lush arrangement seemed to echo into infinity, while Ronnie's distinctive, sweetly vulnerable, seductive vocal delivery, along with her now legendary *woh-ol, woh-ol, woh-ol*, drove teenage boys wild, capturing their hearts and related organs enough to send the song to number 2 on the American pop charts in October 1963 and number 4 R&B. It became the all-time favourite record of Beach Boy Brian Wilson, who was directly inspired to emulate Spector's arsenal of production innovations; he also penned *Don't Worry Baby* for the Ronettes in tribute, but when Spector refused the song, the Beach Boys recorded it themselves and it was a decent-sized hit.

Everything about the Ronettes was BIG! Their hair, their eyes, their sound! In November 1963 they reiterated and emphasised all this with *Baby I Love You*. Its earth-shaking hand claps, thousand-pound drums and Leon Russell's insistent piano playing introduced the most powerful 'wall of sound' record yet, and the Ronettes held their own in a sea of orchestration, but not without some support. Spector, who added the backing voices of 'Darlene Love and the Blossoms', Ronnie herself, and the young Cher, overdubbing them until he had twenty to twenty-five voices, balancing out the dense instrumental tracks. *Baby I Love You* charted on 21 December 1963, though it only reached number 24 in America.

Other hits followed: *(The Best Part of) Breakin' Up*, *Do I Love You?*, *Walking in the Rain* and *Is this What I Get for Loving You?* These still rank as all-time girl-group classics; all were top-40 songs in 1964. All were recorded at Spector's favourite recording studio, Gold Star in Los Angeles. Spector usually put an instrumental on the B-side of his productions to deter disc jockeys from 'flipping' the record and taking attention from the A-side. However, this wasn't the case with the single *Is this What I*

Get, which was paired with *Oh I Love You*. This was the last number that Spector produced with the Ronettes before he married Ronnie in 1968.

With two hits in Britain, the group flew to the United Kingdom in February 1964 and toured with the Rolling Stones. While they were in the UK the Beatles sought them out, and they became friends. That same month the girls released *(The Best Part of) Breakin' Up*. It reached number 39 in the States and number 43 in Britain before Spector returned to high-powered teen rock with *Do I Love You?*, which had one of the most power-driven intros ever recorded. Despite only reaching number 34 in the US and 35 in Britain, *Do I Love You?* was one of their best records.

When the Ronettes returned to America, the Beatles were right behind them, Murray the K, the self-proclaimed fifth Beatle, met them because of the Ronettes. During 1964, Spector test-marketed Ronnie as a solo act, issuing two singles under the name 'Veronica' on his label. The first was a remake of the Students' classic ballad *I'm So Young* and the second a Barry/Greenwich/Spector composition *Why Don't They Let Us Fall in Love?* Each was backed by the Ronettes and each was pulled almost immediately after release.

In November 1964 the Ronettes joined 'Dick Clark's Caravan of Stars' and then returned to New York to record the memorable Christmas album, Spector's *A Christmas Gift for You*. The album's rise to greatness was halted by the assassination of President Kennedy. But around that time the Ronettes released *Walking in the Rain*, their most dramatic ballad. The Mann/Weil/Spector-written record reached number 23 in the US and won a Grammy for 'Best Sound Effects', the only Grammy Spector ever received. The Ronettes then appeared in the TAMI show.

In 1965 the Ronettes recorded *Born to be Together* and *Is This What I Get for Loving You*? These did not do well but were worthy of a greater response than they received. The energy that existed between Ronnie and Spector had provided the spark that made the Ronettes the success that they were. But by 1965 Phil had turned his attentions to promoting other acts such as the Righteous Brothers, and the Ronettes' record label became less viable. In fact, the Ronettes backed up the Righteous Brothers' classic ballad *You've Lost That Loving Feeling*. Their LP *Presenting the Fabulous Ronettes, featuring Veronica*, only reached number 96 in the American Album charts, though it was the best Philles album.

Although they were coming up with good material and still producing quality songs, as the mid-1960s wore on sales of Ronettes records declined. Although they remained an enormously popular act, they placed no more songs in the top 40. Ronnie's romantic relationship with Spector effectively forestalled her career and a three-year hiatus had followed *I Can Hear Music*.

In 1973, with her marriage almost over, Ronnie returned to performing. She appeared as Ronnie and the Ronettes at Richard Nader's Rock and Roll Revival show at Madison Square Garden. The new female trio included Denise Edwards and Chip Fields.

In the autumn of 1973, Ronnie worked with Stan Vincent to produce two singles of the new Ronettes over the 1973-74 period (neither charted) on the Buddha label, *Love, Love* and *I Wish I Never Saw the Sunshine,* which was a re-recording of a song the original Ronettes had recorded for Spector in 1965. Spector didn't release it until his 1976 *Rare Masters* LP came out in the UK.

Ronnie left her husband in 1973, and their divorce was finalised the following year; reportedly, Spector made a substantial alimony payment by sending Ronnie a truckload of dimes. In 1974, keeping Phil's name, Ronnie sang backup for Bruce Springsteen and appeared at his New York Palladium performance of 1976. This led to 'E Street Band' member Miami Steve Van Zant producing and arranging a 1977 single with Ronnie Spector and the E Street Band titled *Say Goodbye To Hollywood.* The song, written by Billy Joel, rocked with Ronnie's most inspired vocals since the early Spector days. Alas, it was not a success.

In 1978 Ronnie tried again with a song called *It's a Heartache.* The record was beaten to the charts by Bonnie Tyler's version that reached number 3 in the USA. Through the eighties Ronnie performed as one of the 'Legendary Ladies of Rock and Roll'. She also continued to make solo albums; including one called *Siren* in 1980 that was well received by her many fans. She has worked with artistes such as George Harrison, Southside Johnny and the Asbury Jukes, and Bruce Springsteen. It was in 1980 that the rock and roll mover and shaker Genya Ravan produced Ronnie on a fuzz-toned wall of sound rocker called *Darlin*, for her own Polish label. In 1986 she featured on rocker Eddie Money's *Take Me Home Tonight*, which put her back in the spotlight, as it reached number 4 in America. It incorporated Ronnie's singing of the lead line from *Be My Baby* and the following year Columbia issued a Ronnie Spector LP with the song *Dangerous*, backed up by the Bangles.

Ronnie Spector has the respect of a great many people in the music business, both for her talent as a performer and for her likable nature, and whilst the Ronettes were not to be the most commercially successful girl group of all time, their music was some of the most groundbreaking in the field and it endures and sells to this day. Anyone who thinks of themselves as having a knowledge of popular music will know and love half-a-dozen Ronettes songs.

In all, the Ronettes recorded twenty-eight songs from 1963 to 1967. While they were unique musically, the trio were also the first really erotically sensual girl group. Others before them seemed to be singing to their friends about the boys they desired (*Maybe*, the Chantels; *I Met Him on a Sunday*, the Shirelles; *He's So Fine*, the Chiffons). The Ronettes sang directly to the boys, *Be My Baby*, *Baby I Love You* and performer to audience relations have never been the same since. They were amongst the first of a new wave in pop music, as girl groups like the Angels, the Shangri-Las, the Chiffons and the Orlons followed, bringing female pop music harmony from its *I wish I had a boy who loved me* malaise into a lyrically tougher edge.

Only a few artistes in history have been capable of defining an entire era in pop music. Ronnie Spector is one of those artistes: the embodiment of the heart, soul, and passion of female rock and roll in the 1960s. No one has ever surpassed Ronnie's powerful trademark vocals, her gutsy attitude, her innocent but knowing sexuality. *Be My Baby* is widely regarded as one of the crowning achievements of Spector's oeuvre, and of girl-group pop in general. In fact, many critics have deemed it one of the most supremely romantic records of the rock-and-roll era; Spector's production frames the song's yearning lyrics and Ronnie Bennett's sweetly sultry vocals in a sweeping, near-symphonic level of emotion. Even though the Ronettes never managed another hit as big as *Be My Baby*, many of their subsequent singles boasted the same kind of creative synergy between Spector and Bennett. Although none of the Ronettes' other singles managed to make the American top 20, they continued to turn out high-quality work.

The Ronettes produced some very good, maybe even great rock-and-roll songs and are remembered as one of the premier girl groups of the 1960s. They changed the way female rock and roll looked and how it was performed. In a way, a bit like West Ham in football!

What Can You Say About Harry Potts?

You never knew what to expect from West Ham. But there's a limit to how much you should look at the other side to sort out what you are going to do, and we always fancied our chances if we could get them back to Turf Moor.
Harry Potts – Burnley

Burnley, Ron Greenwood's home-town club, came to Upton Park as West Ham's seventh opponent of February 1964. At that time there was not much to choose between the 'Cotton Town Kings' and the pride of East London in terms of League form. The Lancastrians were in eleventh place in Division One whilst West Ham were just a few points behind in fourteenth position. But the Irons faced a team with a proud tradition. Burnley had last won the FA Cup in the wartime season of 1913/14, but had been finalists in 1946/47 and as recently as 1962/63. They had been League Champions in 1920/21 and 1959/60 and finished as runners-up in 1919/20 and 1961/62 (a good but 'nearly' season for Burnley). The Clarets had been winners of Division Two in 1897/98 and took second place in 1912/13 and 1946/47.

Burnley had finished just one point behind 111-goal League runners-up Tottenham Hotspur in the 1962/63 season, and were greeted at Upton Park by an all-ticket crowd of 36,651 (including England manager Alf Ramsey) a club record at the time. After needing two games to beat Second Division Rotherham in the third round, the Clarets had disposed of Newport from the Fourth Division and Huddersfield from the Second Division to make the last eight.

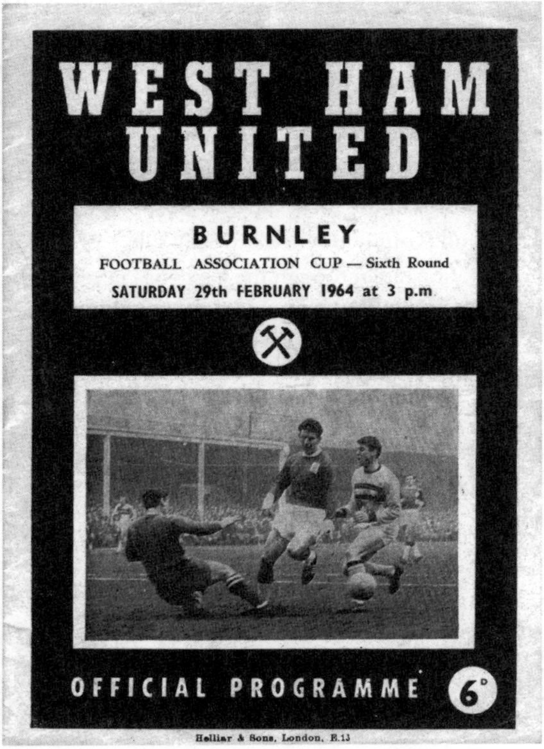

West Ham United *v.* Burnley, 29 February 1964 programme cover.

The Burnley manager had brought a distinguished side to East London. Harry Potts himself had been a product of Turf Moor's enlightened and ground-breaking youth policy. Born in Hetton-le-Hole in 1920, Potts had joined the Clarets as a professional in 1937. After breaking into the reserve side, the young Potts didn't get the opportunity to push his way into Second Division football before war broke out in 1939. Like many other promising players of the era, Harry's career stagnated during the first half of the 1940s, world conflict robbing him of nearly seven of his peak playing years. However, he made his Football League debut along with more than half the Burnley team on the opening day of the 1946/47 season. He was twenty-five years old and was one of the inspirations behind the Burnley side of that term. The defensive-minded Potts was the engine room of the Clarets' midfield. For four years Harry was hardly out of the starting line-up, working to establish Burnley as a First Division outfit. However, the Turf Moor crowd probably never saw the best of him. He became unsettled and slapped in a transfer request in the summer of 1950 and he moved to Everton for a record fee in October of that year. He had scored fifty goals in 181 games for the Clarets.

At the end of Potts' first season with the Toffees, the Merseysiders went tumbling into Division Two and after that Harry was never able to command a regular first-team place at Goodison Park. Eventually, in 1956, he joined Wolves as chief coach. After his spell at Molineux he became manager at Shrewsbury Town and took charge of Burnley in January 1958. He inherited expert backroom staff including Billy Dougall and Ray Bennion, two of the people he classed as having a huge influence on his own playing career, and the nucleus of a team that would become the most successful Burnley side in modern times.

At the end of his second full season as Burnley manager, Potts took Burnley to the First Division title. During his first years as manager Harry gave Gordon Harris and Alex Elder their debuts, spotted the potential of John Connelly and nurtured Brian Miller's move through the ranks. Those players blended with established professionals like Ray Pointer and Burnley clinched the title in the very last game of 1959/60. That meant that Potts would lead Burnley into their inaugural European campaign whilst taking them to the FA Cup final for the first time in fifteen years.

The Clarets at Upton Park

After losing Colin McDonald when he broke his ankle at Chelsea in December 1956, Adam Blacklaw played eight matches in Burnley's first team as a nineteen year old, but it wasn't until March 1959, when McDonald's League career came to an end, that Adam made the Burnley goalkeeper's shirt his own. His contribution to the League Championship campaign led to his first representative honours (two Scotland Under-23 caps). As the Clarets stormed to the title, Blacklaw missed just one match and his consistency over the following three years was exemplary. He won the first of his three full Scottish caps against Norway in Bergen in June 1963.

Perhaps the most famous picture of Adam Blacklaw is one of him being sent the wrong way by Danny Blanchflower from the penalty spot in the 1962 FA Cup final. Another undoubted low point was a last-minute incident at Anfield in February 1963, in the FA Cup fourth-round replay. With the seconds ticking away at the end of extra time, and the score 1-1, Blacklaw unaccountably kicked the ball against Ian St John and then had to pull the Scot down to prevent him scoring. Ronnie Moran stroked in the spot-kick, Liverpool were through and Burnley were out.

Blacklaw's father had been critically ill for some time before the match at Upton Park. Around twelve-thirty on the Sunday morning after arriving back in Lancashire from East London he drove to Aberdeen knowing that his father was declining rapidly. He reached the 'Granite City' just in time to see his father shortly before he passed away.

John Angus was a polished right-back. He signed for Burnley on amateur terms from the Amble Boys' Club in 1954 and became a professional on his seventeenth birthday the following year. Angus was an England Youth international and had represented the Football League. John was regarded as one of the very finest right-backs of his era. Many a Burnley fan has expressed the feeling that he should have won many more than his one full cap. Walter Winterbottom described his single England game, on 27 May 1961 against Austria in Vienna, as the best international debut he had ever seen, even though England lost 3-1. Angus was often seen as a better player than England's usual right-back of the time, Jimmy Armfield. He hardly ever seemed to get ruffled; it was not unknown for John to trap the ball on his own goal-line and dribble it out of his own area. He won a League Championship medal and an FA Cup runners-up medal with the Clarets.

Alex Elder was the only player to become established in the championship winning side of 1959/60 who made his debut during that memorable campaign. He arrived from Glentoran in January 1959 and soon impressed with his hard-tackling style and mastery of the long ball out of defence. He made his first Division One appearance in September 1959 in a difficult game at Preston. The young Elder was detailed to mark the legendary Tom Finney and, although the Clarets lost the game 1-0, Elder had done enough to make the left-back position his own for the foreseeable future. Still only eighteen, he made his full Northern Ireland debut against Wales in April 1960, going on to win thirty-four caps in his time at Turf Moor; oddly, he won his only Irish Under-23 cap in 1964, four years after making his first senior international appearance. A broken ankle kept Elder out of the side for more than half of the 1963/64 season.

Brian O'Neil was a hard-tackling, no-nonsense, never-say-die midfielder. The 'Bedlington Terrier' first arrived at Turf Moor as a junior in 1960 and made his first-team debut in April 1963, taking over the number four shirt from Jimmy Adamson. The contrast between the two players could not have been starker; Adamson was a silky mover and a great thinker; O'Neil was a non-stop player who concentrated on moving the ball from 'A' to 'B' as quickly as possible.

England Schoolboy international centre half, Oxford-born John Talbut, signed for Burnley in 1957, aged seventeen, and made his initial appearances in League football in two games against Leicester City over Christmas 1958. The competition for places in the middle of Burnley's defence was fierce at the time, Tommy Cummings and Brian Miller were always going to be difficult to supplant, and Talbut played in only seven League games in four years. But he displaced Cummings as first-choice centre half in 1962 and for three seasons his name was synonymous with the position, his dependable performances winning him seven England Under-23 caps in 1964.

One of a small number of locally born players to make the grade with Burnley, Brian Miller was born in Hapton in 1937 and joined the Clarets as a junior in February 1954. He made his first-team debut, deputising for Les Shannon during the FA Cup-tie marathon with Chelsea in 1956. Up against a formidable trio like Adamson, Seith and Shannon, and with the injured Tommy Cummings waiting to come back, Miller did well to force himself into the reckoning over the next few years with his solid hard-tackling style. He was ever-present in the League Championship season and won three England Under-23 caps in 1960. His consistency over the following seasons was a major factor in Burnley's success and should perhaps have earned him more than his solitary full England cap in Vienna in May 1961, the same match in which teammate John Angus also made his only appearance for his country; both men played out of position during that game, Angus at left-back and Miller at right-half.

Reputed to the first British footballer to have his own official fan club, Willie Morgan was the idol of many Burnley followers in the 1960s. A right-winger of the very highest order, Morgan was snapped up by Burnley scouts after being spotted in Glasgow (his place of birth). Willie became a seventeen-year-old apprentice at Turf Moor in October 1961. On the last day of the following season he made his first-team debut as a replacement for the legendary John Connelly. He ousted the club stalwart from the right-wing position the following campaign, when Connelly switched to the left flank.

Boasting a strike rate of more than one goal in every two games, Ray Pointer had one of the best goals-per-game ratios in the honourable history of Burnley Football Club. The 'blonde bombshell' failed a trial at Blackpool and returned to his native North East. It was from Dudley Welfare that the Cramlington-born goal-scorer joined the Clarets in 1957. England Under-23 honours and three full caps followed as Pointer became a vital component in the Burnley team that won the First Division title in 1959/60 and reached the FA Cup final two years later.

Andy Lochead was born in Millgie in 1941 and signed for Burnley in December 1958 from the Renfrew club in Paisley. He was amongst the goals when he deputised for Ray Pointer in 1960/61, but it was not until 1962/63 that he made the number nine shirt his own, Pointer moving to inside right. Following the departure of both Pointer and Jimmy Robson, Lochhead was to form a very effective partnership with Willie Irvine. His power in the air and his skill both on and off the ball had already won him a Scottish Under-23 cap in 1962, but the Scottish selectors chose to ignore him for full honours.

Gordon 'Bomber' Harris was a stocky, powerfully built 'engine-room' type of player who was deceptively quick. He was renowned at Turf Moor for the cannon-ball drives that regularly detonated from his left foot, possessing arguably the hardest shot of any Burnley player. He was born in Worksop in 1940 and was playing for a colliery team at nearby Firbeck when Burnley spotted his talents and brought him to Turf Moor in January 1958. In his first two years he played only occasionally but established himself in 1961 after Brian Pilkington had left for Bolton Wanderers.

John Connelly was born in St Helens, in the heart of Rugby League country, in 1938. He was serving his apprenticeship as a joiner whilst playing for St Helens Town when he joined the Clarets in November 1956. Connelly did not make an immediate impact in the first team (Billy Gray and Doug Newlands were vying for the right-wing position) and played only spasmodically in his first two seasons. He staked his claim to the number seven shirt during the 1958/59 season and finished his first campaign as a regular and second-highest scorer behind Ray Pointer. He went one better during the Championship season as Connelly, Pointer and Robson hit fifty-seven of the team's eighty-five goals. Injury forced John to miss the run-in to the title, his replacement, Trevor Meredith, scored the goal that clinched the championship in the final match. Of all the goals that John Connelly scored in his Burnley career, none was more memorable than his solo effort in the away leg of the European Cup-tie against Rheims. Picking up the ball in his own half, he rode a number of wild tackles and, letting fly from twenty-five yards, surprised the French 'keeper by sending the ball dipping into the net. The goal effectively won the tie for Burnley and set up an epic struggle against Hamburg in the third round.

Connelly won ten England caps in his time at Turf Moor, his first as early as 1959. He scored four goals for his country before his exciting wing play inevitably attracted the big clubs.

Claret and Blue v. Claret and Blue

After hearing the draw for the quarter-final, Harry Potts was asked what was going to be done about the clash of colours, both West Ham and Burnley traditionally wearing claret-and-blue strips. He replied:

> West Ham will wear claret with blue stripes and we will wear blue with claret stripes.

He recalled the clash at Upton Park:

> It's a game that sticks in my mind because it was one of those we should have won. We did well in the first half, one of the best of that season. I think it is fair to say we outplayed West Ham. John Connelly got a great individual goal to give us the lead at half-time. It was a bit like the goal he scored against Rheims in Paris when we played in the European Cup. He ran through three or four tackles and scored from about thirty-five yards out. He was a great player.
>
> We could have gone further ahead; Andy Lochhead and Gordon Harris had near misses with the West Ham goalkeeper beaten.

It was not long after coming out for the second half that Lochhead got a clear run, but was 'zealously curtailed' by Bovington. It was the twelfth minute after the break that West Ham struck back. Harry Potts recalled:

> Their outside left, Sissons, pulled the ball along the byline and, from a very sharp angle, sent it towards our goal. It rolled just over the line. Elder got it out but not before it was in.

The West Ham equaliser seemed to rock Burnley and the Hammers took advantage. Three minutes later Brabrook's centre was picked up by Byrne on the volley and sent over Blacklaw to put the home side into the lead for the first time. Byrne had achieved a new post-war scoring record of twenty-eight goals in a season.

Less than 500 seconds later the Irons seemed to secure the tie. Harry Potts saw it thus:

> I think Byrne was offside, but apart from that he pushed Brian Miller over before he scored. But that's the way it goes sometimes.

As soon as the Worcestershire referee Mr Jennings awarded the goal the Burnley players went into a frenzy that included Harris striking John Bond. For all this, Budgie's effort had been impressive, having overcome Miller and dribbled around Blacklaw.

The Burnley players rallied at what they saw as an injustice and were rewarded with hope. With just ten minutes of the match to go Pointer scored with a juicy shot. This provoked the visitors into a tremendous last effort to force a replay. Potts remembered:

> Connelly was brought down in the box but we didn't get the penalty. I think if that had gone in and we had got them back to Turf Moor we could have beaten them. We had the better of them for a lot of the time on their own ground!

But that was not to be. West Ham joined Preston, Manchester United and Swansea in the semi-finals. The Hammers had reached the last four of the FA Cup for the third time in the club's history (excluding the War Cup victory of 1940) and the first semi-final appearance (in peacetime) since 1933.

The League win at Ewood Park had been the season's turning point for West Ham, but the match against Burnley marked the moment when the Hammers came of age. The side demonstrated a ruthless determination that had often been lacking in their make-up. Byrne played wonderfully and his performance dominated the headlines of the morning papers the day after the match. He was, probably quite correctly, given the credit for taking West Ham into the last four. His alacrity and control on a problematical surface had indeed been the difference between the two sides.

Burnley got some recompense a few days later when in early March at Turf Moor they went into the break two up and made it three just after the half-time. A Byrne special came too late to save the Irons from defeat and Hurst's two strikes against the woodwork were consigned to the world of, 'what might have been'. However, Byrne had scored in six consecutive games and accrued nine goals in as many playing hours – a remarkable purple patch.

Budgie

Budgie was a good player to play with and you'd get good service off him. He'd take balls on his chest and ping them left or right with either foot. He had good movement…

Peter Brabrook – West Ham United and England

John Joseph Byrne was born in West Horsley in Surrey on 13 May 1939. Both John's parents were Irish and had migrated to Surrey from Dublin three years earlier in search of employment. Most of John's spare time in his youth was spent kicking balls about. He remembered:

> The kids used to traipse miles to a place called Sheeplease and we played long after dark. We used to plant torches in the ground so we could see what we were doing.

Thus the young Byrne refined the instinctive ability that made him one of the finest touch players to represent England in the post-war years.

As a talented twelve year old, John was noted by ex-schoolteacher Jim Blore as he watched Byrne play for the Howard Effingham School. Known also as Victor and Vincent, Blore had played for Crystal Palace and had turned out nine times for West Ham United during the 1935/36 season. He was to track John's development as he moved on to Epsom Town, play for Guildford City Juniors and appear for his county at youth level. Byrne was never to forget Blore as it was the one-time professional who introduced John to Crystal Palace manager, the former Tottenham goalkeeper Cyril Spiers, whose paternal approach helped the youthful Byrne feel at home at Selhurst Park.

Johnny had wept when he left school at the age of fifteen. He reflected:

> I don't know why because if I'd had a good education I wouldn't have been a footballer and that was the one thing I'd always wanted to do.

But his learning was just beginning. John told me:

> One of the best moments of my life was when Cyril Spiers offered me a trial with Palace. I'd left school at fifteen so I had to wait six months before the club

> could take me on. By that time I'd got a job as an apprentice toolmaker. I had four trials before finally being taken onto the ground staff. I think they were hoping that I would grow a few more inches between trials... I didn't of course.
>
> It was hard work. There were three lads on the ground staff (this was the days before apprenticeships) and we had to wash out the dressing rooms, clean players' boots, re-stud them and take bollockings from the players if they didn't think what we had done was up to scratch. I went home more than once having taken a wallop!
>
> We swept the stands and terraces, washed down walls and scrubbed floors. I got made senior ground staff member. In the end of course it was worth it for me, but the other two lads didn't make it.
>
> You couldn't call the professional players by their first names; it was always 'Mr'.

Early on in his career Johnny built a reputation as an entertaining player. By the conclusion of the 1956/57 season he had made fourteen appearances for Crystal Palace, moving from inside right to centre forward, scoring just one goal (he netted in his eighth game for the club). Byrne became a professional in 1957. Palace were fighting for survival in the lower echelons of the old Third Division South. However, by that time John had gained international recognition at Youth level, having been awarded five England caps (he had won the first of them whilst playing for Surrey). He looked back:

> I started off on £7 with an extra £3 bonus if we won and £1 for a draw. I was still in the Army, on National Service, when I got my first game as a pro. It was at Selhurst Park in October. It was a League game against Swindon Town. At half-time no one had scored and then again as the full-time time whistle went... it was 0-0 [John smiled].

It was around this time that John married a local girl, Margaret. He was halfway through his eighteenth year.

In his first professional season Byrne scored seven times in twenty-eight matches, gaining a regular place in the Place side. However, the Glaziers finished fourteenth, just below the dividing line that would have enabled them to become founder members of the new Third Division, which was created the following term. It was a poor second prize to be consigned to the newly formed Fourth Division, alongside the likes of Coventry City and Watford. Less than a week after the last game of the season Spiers lost his job: he was the first victim of the new Division. Byrne did not admire Spiers as a tactician but saw him, along with Blore, as one of the men who gave him a start.

Britain was rocked and the world of football shocked on 6 February 1958 when eight Manchester United players were among the twenty-one passengers killed in an air crash in West Germany. The United team had started their flight home to Manchester from Yugoslavia having fought out a draw with Red Star Belgrade to qualify for the last four of the European Cup. Their aircraft struck a fence as it took off from Munich's Rhiem airport. England lost Roger Byrne, Duncan Edwards and Tommy Taylor. United's manager, Matt Busby was seriously injured. What once had been a BEA Ambassador was reduced to a scrambled mass of shards and debris. The efforts of rescuers were made harder by the blizzard that blew across the airfield.

In June 1958, George Smith took over as manager of Crystal Palace. The first match Palace played under his leadership was the opening game of the club's inaugural season in the Fourth Division. On 23 August 1958, Crewe Alexandra came to Selhurst Park. The nineteen-year-old Byrne got his first hat-trick in the 6-2 win, demonstrating the kind of insight that would become his trademark. Smith's side finished in seventh place at the end of the term. Johnny claimed twenty-two goals in a club total of ninety-nine in all competitive matches.

Byrne's continued development was confirmed by his selection for the England Under-23 team, which made him the first ever Fourth Division player to win an England cap at that level. He was to make seven appearances for the Under-23s, scoring six goals. Playing with England's best young professionals opened Johnny's eyes and he saw that Selhurst Park, under the dubious leadership of George Smith, had taken him as far as it could; he asked to be placed on the transfer list. But John was still in the army and Palace put a price of £20,000 on his head. Not surprisingly, there were no takers. However, the arrival of the former West Ham and Brighton player Dave Sexton at Selhurst Park allowed John to continue his football education. Sexton, who would go on to manage a number of top-flight sides, including the great Chelsea team of the late 1960s and early 1970s, and to the time of writing was influential within English international football, was one of the founders of the Upton Park 'Academy', the informal think-tank that laid the ground for a new model of English football that would rule the world after 1966. In his brief spell with Palace Dave did much to help the young Byrne hone his game and tactical awareness. At the same time Sexton's wisdom confirmed Byrne's low opinion of George Smith, who had continued the habit of his successor of playing Byrne wide rather than at centre forward, the position John saw himself as being best suited to. As such, Byrne was not satisfied with the opportunities he was getting, seeing his twenty goals in fifty games in the 1958/59 term as evidence that his potential was being inhibited at a time when he was starting to draw the attention of bigger clubs.

In the 1959/60 season Byrne was his club's top scorer with nineteen League and cup goals but Palace could only manage eighth position, one lower than the previous term. Smith resigned and was replaced by Arthur Rowe in April 1960. During the 1930s Rowe had been club captain at Tottenham and an England international. In 1949 he became manager at White Hart Lane and in 1950 guided the North Londoners to the Second Division Championship. The following year Rowe had led Spurs to their first Division One Championship title. Rowe almost made it two consecutive titles for Tottenham in 1952 when the club finished runners-up to Manchester United. In the same season Tottenham reached the last four of the FA Cup. This was an unprecedented success story. Within the space of twenty months Tottenham Hotspur had moved from being something less than an ordinary Second Division side to a dominant force in English football.

It was Arthur Rowe who, whilst assistant manager at Palace under Smith, had convinced Byrne about his suitability for the centre forward role. Rowe recalled:

> He was playing at inside forward, a midfield 'kerfluffer' I called him. He'd had two great seasons for Palace. I said to him one day, 'Why don't you play up the front?' He said, 'I'm not big enough.' I told him that all the players I ever had trouble with in my career were little guys. He said he'd try it.
>
> It worked, and afterwards he said, 'It's not bad up there, I like it.' He was like Alan Ball, Eddie Bailey, all those small guys with bandy legs. He had a spark that could light fires! He had this tremendous skill, this ability to take people on. John was pigeon-toed, and it gave him four ways of dealing with a ball; the inside and outside of both feet. No ball ever gave him a problem.
>
> He was great at playing it away first time and moving off to a new position. He was so quick the defenders couldn't get near him. I would put him in the top four centre-forwards I ever came across. For two or three seasons he was fantastic.

John instantly respected his new boss. He once said of Rowe:

> To me he was football and he still is. He could tell me that black was white and I would still believe it. That's the kind of man he is.

Byrne's faith in Rowe was confirmed when, at the end of the 1960/61 season Palace finished just two points behind Champions Peterborough with 110 League goals and sixty-four points from forty-six games. Byrne was top scorer with thirty nets to his name. These figures gave Palace their first promotion in forty years.

Byrne completed his National Service during the 1960/61 term. He had played for 29 Company RAOC and helped his side win the Army Cup in the 1960/61 season, although the team had no credible form. John was always proud of this achievement:

> It was amazing really, probably equivalent to a Third or Fourth Division side winning the FA Cup. We really got together as a team and of course at the same time I was spreading the word according to Arthur Rowe.

Byrne skippered the British Army side in 1960/61 that included English internationals Alan Hodgkinson (Sheffield United), Bill Foulkes and the great Duncan Edwards (both of Manchester United). In one of his games for the Pongos John scored six goals.

Byrne started the 1961/62 term as he had finished the previous season and in November 1961 this resulted in him becoming the first Crystal Palace player to be capped by England since 1923, and one of the very few Third Division players to be picked for full England honours. It was during his first days with England that John picked up the nickname that would stay with him the rest of his days. Johnny Haynes recalled his first encounter with Byrne:

> The first time I met him was on an England tour – I was the captain at the time and Budgie stuck to me like a leech. Wherever I went Budgie was snapping at my heels, nightclubs, restaurants, boxing tournaments. He never stopped talking and it was then that I nicknamed him 'Budgie'.

The epithet stuck to the extent that later John even signed his autographs as 'Budgie Byrne'.

The England manager of the time, Walter Winterbottom, looked back on the start of Byrne's international career:

> John Byrne was the best young player of his generation. He had learnt a lot from Arthur Rowe, but the fact that he was an intelligent young man made this possible. There were few of his age that could match his talent, both to think about what he wanted to do and do it. Really, Byrne should have ended his career with a few dozen, maybe fifty English caps.

However, it was this prestigious talent that meant Byrne could not stay at Selhurst Park. Even today Johnny stands high in the list of Palace marksmen. In his relatively short career with the Glaziers he scored four hat-tricks and twice notched up four goals over ninety minutes. Until Ian Wright, Byrne was the highest post-Second World War goalscorer for Crystal Palace and was only pushed into third by Mark Bright in the early 1990s.

Budgie Flies East

The 1961/62 season was to be West Ham's fourth in the top flight of English football after a twenty-six-year absence. In their first term back amongst the elite the East Enders had finished in a very creditable sixth place, but positions of fourteenth and sixteenth in the previous two campaigns made them very much part of the 'also rans' of the old Division One. West Ham's manager, Ron Greenwood, had arrived at Upton Park in April 1961, replacing Ted Fenton, the ex-player who had led the Irons back to the First Division. Greenwood was the first West Ham manager not to have any previous links with the Boleyn Ground, but he presented strong credentials at Upton Park. He had given up the job of assistant manager at Arsenal and he had a good record managing the England Youth and Under-23 teams. Greenwood's father had worked at Wembley Stadium and as such Ron had been exposed to the best of football strategy from an early age. The young Greenwood had witnessed, first hand, the Hungarian demolition of England in 1953. At the time he was playing for Chelsea; he had been exposed to the coaching of Arthur Rowe, having, as a teenager, seen him play for Spurs and of course Greenwood the centre half (the same position as Rowe played) knew the Tottenham side of the early fifties well. Ron had also worked with Walter Winterbottom having turned out for the England 'B' side and had benefited from that great tactician's insight into the Hungarian style, although Greenwood had been one of the few Englishmen who recognised the way the East Europeans played that day in 1953. In fact, that November game, the last Harry Johnston (another centre half) would play for England, had been something of a dream made real for Greenwood. Puskas and his men were working according to his own vision of the game; seeing his personal insight literally played out in front of his eyes proved to be a motivating influence that would guide the rest of Greenwood's career in football.

Ron's knowledge of the young players available to England meant that Johnny Byrne had, for some time, certainly since Greenwood had become assistant manager at Highbury, been established in Ron's mind as a potentially great player. As such, from the moment he had taken over at West Ham, Greenwood had meant to bring Byrne to Upton Park and in March 1962 he did. West Ham paid £58,000 plus centre forward Ronnie Brett, who had come to the Boleyn Ground from Crystal Palace in 1959 and was valued at £7,500. It was a record signing for West Ham and the biggest deal ever done between two English clubs. Byrne's starting salary was £40 a week.

Johnny Di Stefano

It was Greenwood who was to dub Byrne the 'Di Stefano of British football', this 'twinning' with the Argentinean 'White Arrow' of Real Madrid, was to be repeated at various stages in the press, and there were strong likenesses, Johnny, being small (5ft 8in and 11 stone) for a centre forward, but able to play in any of the central attacking positions. Byrne also had an impressive turn of pace, tight ball control, a scorching shot and was a great passer. At that stage he had not reached his twenty-third year, but it was clear to anyone who watched him on the ball that he was an extremely skilful and artistic player. Byrne would often work deeper than a conventional striker and laid on as many goals for others as he scored himself. He added flair to a West Ham team already blessed with the likes of Bobby Moore and Ronnie Boyce, together with Geoff Hurst (who was breaking into the side), Martin Peters and John Sissons who were all developing fast.

In his first few games it looked as if Byrne wasn't making much of a difference to the Hammers. His debut match as an Iron, on 17 March 1962, was a goal-less draw at Hillsborough. Byrne's Upton Park initiation saw Manchester City come away having thrashed the home side 0-4. By the time John was in a winning West Ham side the Hammers had gone eleven games and almost nine weeks without a victory. Byrne's first two-pointer came from an encounter at the Hawthorns with West Bromwich Albion. Malcolm Musgrove scored the only goal of the game. At last, Budgie scored his first for the Hammers, the third in a 4-1 Upton Park defeat of Cardiff City on Good Friday. He recalled:

> It was a great relief. But I wouldn't have said it at the time. The crowd at Upton Park were right on top of you, the pitch went right up to the front of the stands and the fans, although they were great supporters, were always honest about their feelings. It's understandable, but we were trying something new for most of us. The way Ron wanted us to play did take a bit of getting used to… more for some than others though. And there were a few who expressed their doubts in no uncertain terms. But Ron's way was if you didn't want to play his way, you didn't have to and you got dropped. He was a gentle, calm man, but he could be ruthless if pushed. He wasn't one to do his nut and as far as I was concerned you kind of knew what he was going to do as far as the team was concerned. But if you didn't understand his ways he sometimes came across like a bit of an assassin…

According to West Ham manager-to-be John Lyall, who was still playing the occasional first-team game in the Hammers defence after John arrived at the Boleyn Ground,

> Budgie was like Jimmy Greaves, being confident, bright, full of humour and able to improvise, but in his first days at Upton Park he was trying too hard, attempting to take the lace out of the ball every time he got into the penalty area. He had to be taught to do the simple things. I watched Budgie wriggle past defenders, walk around the goalkeeper and then miss an empty net.

John had made eleven appearances for the Irons at the end of his first season at Upton Park. His side had scored ten and conceded seventeen goals in those games. Many were saying that the side had fared better when he had been absent from the staring eleven but from Byrne's arrival attendance at the Boleyn Ground had risen by an average of 4,000 and good early season form meant that the fans could point to a top-ten finish, just two points behind Aston Villa in seventh place, putting West Bromwich Albion below them on goal average and bettering Arsenal by one point and two places. In Greenwood's first complete term, West Ham had made an improvement of eight places on their First Division position of the previous season. Apart from Byrne, all the other big names of the 1964 campaign were already at the club when Ron arrived. John was the last piece in the jigsaw. According to Byrne:

> I was accurate in my passing and as such I was a good linkman. I was quick and could think fast. I was decent with both feet, that's very rare now. A 'swinger', a one-footed player, despite what Puskas said about a player who kicks with both feet falling on his arse, is limited in what he can do. So, if you think of it, I would have been wasted as an out-and-out attacking player. I wouldn't have been very good at it either. Not big enough!
>
> Games can depend on what happens between the centre forward and the opponent's centre half. If one gets the better of the other it often decides a result. If the centre forward is shut out of the game the entire forward line can just stop working. I always preferred playing at centre forward. I'd played on the wing and inside forward and in the middle but I liked that number nine shirt. Playing in other positions was helpful. I worked out on the wing at Palace, and that helped me learn how to make use of space and how I could, as a centre forward, work with the blokes playing wide. Playing inside forward, especially for England, helped too; switching position, interplay. Trouble a half back and he'll make a ricket. That's how me and Geoff Hurst played. You've got to have a bit of a brain to play in the way we did at West Ham. We kind of 'made' goals, crafted 'em if you like. I liked to pass the ball into the net. Playing centre forward allows you to be more than just a striker.
>
> In England everyone just used the far post as a target; not giving it a second thought, but this nearly always meant that the collecting attacker was faced with both the centre half and the goalkeeper to beat. But, with Hurst practising the late arrival into the box, the ball coming in to the near post often meant that he had a free pop at goal and given Geoff's power and accuracy this was deadly. West Ham were playing a very modern game compared to most of their opponents. It was quite complicated, and sometimes not all the players really understood what was going on and this was perhaps why we were not the most consistent of sides. However, when things fell together, when the team clicked and the system kicked in, we looked better than any side in Division One and could equal the best England and Europe had to offer and, from time to time, we'd beat them.

In the end West Ham settled for twelfth place in the League. It had turned out to be a rather pedestrian season for the Hammers; nevertheless Byrne was called up for the England squad along with Bobby Moore for the close-season tour of Europe.

Of course, after 1966 Geoff Hurst would be the name known throughout the world, but in 1963 it was Budgie who was the star of the West Ham side and Hurst the supporting act, the workhorse. John was a full and experienced international and, in the 1963/64 season, had led the Football League attack twice against the League of Ireland and the Scottish League.

For Greenwood, Byrne was the salmon and Hurst the chips of his side, but Geoff always acknowledged that playing alongside Budgie was one of the best things that could have happened to him. What Hurst gleaned from Byrne made Geoff a more complete, more modern striker. He commented:

> Playing behind Budgie and then playing up alongside him must have helped. That man was magic. Real touch, real class.

However, the best summing-up of Budgie I have ever heard came from the mouth of West Ham's 1960s centre half Ken Brown, who saw Byrne alongside Bobby Moore as the best of the best amongst the West Ham players:

> There was only one Johnny Byrne and the same can be said of Mooro. For his size, Budgie used to get whacked all over the park, but what a player! He could hold the ball, score goals and he loved his football. He always came up smiling and he loved life.
>
> I knew him ever since he came to West Ham when Ron asked me to room with him on away trips and 'look after him a bit'. I was proud Ron had asked me to do something like that but, bloody hell, he was a handful, Budgie. Lovely fella, but he was up to everything and always wanted to be doing something mischievous. We went to Ghana and places like that and Budgie and I were the only ones who never had stomach problems because we'd drink all the beer and keep the germs away!

Oxford with Honours

The one thing I learned from Matt Busby at Manchester United was never to bother about the opposition, just prepare meticulously and concentrate on your own strengths.
Nobby Lawton – Preston North End

The sixth round saw North End drawn away from Deepdale for the third time in their impressive cup campaign. The game against Fourth Division Oxford United was their fifth game in the competition but during their whole cup run, as the

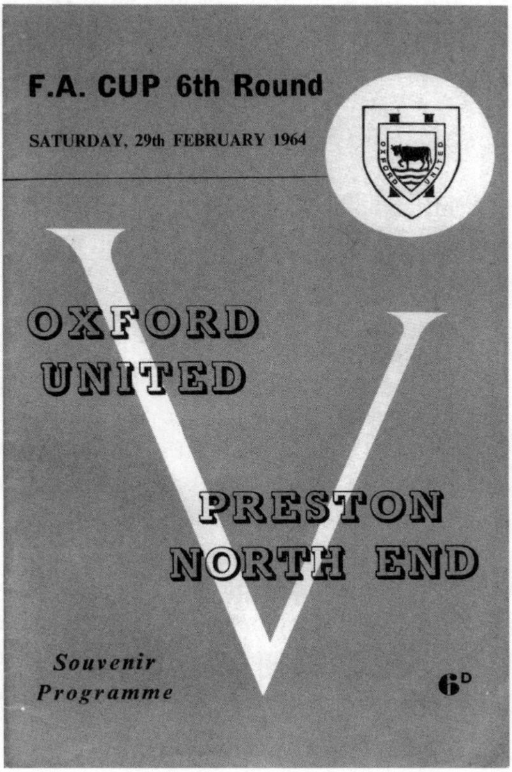

Oxford United *v.* Preston North End, 29 February 1964 programme cover.

semi-final would be played on neutral territory, their home fans saw them perform only once in the dour third-round replay with Nottingham Forest. Oxford were in their second season as a Football League club, having been elected to the League for the start of the previous season following the resignation of Accrington Stanley in 1962. They would have a few ups and downs during the next couple of decades. They were promoted to the Third Division in 1965 and to Division Two as Champions in 1968. In 1976 they went back down but were Champions for the second time in 1984 and went on to win the Second Division the following season. They finished eighteenth in Division One in 1986 and were unable to do any better than that before being relegated at the end of the 1987/88 term. By 1994 Oxford were back in Division Three, but were promoted again in 1996.

However, few clubs could approach the North End record in having been so much of a shuttlecock between the First and Second Divisions. They had descended six times and climbed back on five occasions. They changed four seasons running when they went down in 1912, up in 1913, down in 1914 and up in 1915. Up to 1964, Preston were the only club for which two players scored in all six big cup rounds in a season. Frank O'Donnell did so in 1936/37 and Charlie Wayman in 1953/54, but Preston lost at Wembley both times.

On their rush into the last eight, the first of only four Fourth Division Clubs to go so far in the cup, the U's had started by defeating Chesterfield 1-0. That had brought Third Division Brentford to the Manor Ground fresh from their 2-1 victory over Middlebrough of Division Two. After a 2-2 draw Oxford produced a terrific 2-1 win at Griffin Park, Bill Calder, who had been drawn from Bury to the U's colours for a relatively large fee, got both of Oxford's goals. Bill had been with Leicester City before joining Bury; he was a strong forceful centre forward who had the ability to upset defences.

First Division Blackburn were the next victims of the rampant Oxford boys. The 3-1 margin made the U's the giant killers of '64. At that point Rovers were placed second in the First Division and a record 21,700 Manor Ground crowd saw the likes of the legendary Brian Douglas, former England skipper Ronnie Clayton and international players Mike England (later of Spurs and Wales), Fred Pickering (Everton and England), Mick McGrath (Eire) and lethal marksman Andy McEvoy (Eire) humbled.

United took a thirteenth-minute lead through Tony Jones, who increased the margin soon after the break. Mike Ferguson pulled one back for Rovers in the sixty-eighth minute but Billy Calder cemented the shock of the season in the closing minutes. This was the only time that the U's had won through to the quarter-finals. The teams were:

Blackburn: Else, Bray, Joyce, Clayton, England, McGrath, Ferguson, McEvoy, Pickering, Douglas and Harrison.
Oxford: Harry Fearnley, Cyril Beavon, Pat Quartermain, Ron Atkinson, Maurice Kyle, John Shuker, Peter Knight, Arthur Longbottom (later switched his name to Langley), Bill Calder, Tony Jones and Colin Harrington.

Led by skipper Ronald Frederick Atkinson, who had been with Oxford over the past five seasons, these minnows were looking unstoppable. The Manchester United manager-to-be and non-PC TV pundit of the early twenty-first century was a strong, powerful, hard-working right-half. In fact he was one of the best half-backs in the Fourth Division when on top form. Ron had come to Oxford by way of Aston Villa in July 1959. His passion for the game came from his years as a Liverpool child. After moving to the Midlands, he started professional football with Wolves, but never got into the old-gold first team. He played for BSA Tools before moving to Villa Park in May 1956, where again he failed to get into the Football League side. For all that he was always ready with a quip, which would leave his audience rocking with laughter…

We were a very poor family. I had to go to school in a second-hand car.

However, the funniest thing I ever heard Atkinson say was not meant to be at all whimsical. It was during a documentary covering a groundbreaking West Bromwich Albion tour of China at the time when 'baggy' Ron was managing the Baggies. The team were given the chance to take a look at the Great Wall of China, amongst the few who were enthusiastic were Cyrille Regis, Brendon Batson and the greatest player who should have worn the claret and blue of the East End, Laurie Cunningham. As the programme was showing these three exploring the ancient wall with obvious fascination there was a flashback to Ron who had stayed at the hotel. He remarked: 'Seen one wall, seen 'em all.' It was hilarious, but summed up the man completely.

Ron was gifted to his engineer dad by a proud mum on 18 March 1939. He reflected, turning, as only he could, repetition into an art form:

> We always had a very happy home life. I've got to be honest and say I never had a time in my life that wasn't good. Never had a bad time in my life, a period that I haven't enjoyed. There might have been the odd season when things have not gone right but I have never ever been involved with a side that was really struggling. Mind you, I never set out to struggle. It might sound very obvious but it is very factual. I always believe that I will win every football match… I am the most surprised person around when we get beaten.

That sentence, 'It might sound very obvious but it is very factual' is a real humdinger of an 'Atkinsonism'; you can see why he was paid a king's ransom to commentate on games and act as a pundit in later years.

The Oxford programme on 29 February 1964 was full of bargain buys. For instance, you could have yourself an 'Imperial Good Companion' typewriter for £24 or, in the High Street, Oxford, a shockproof 'Ingersol '63' watch, with five jewels and golden finish was going for a mere 85/-.

The non-sporting entertainment for the quarter-final at the Manor Ground was breathtaking (literally) being supplied by the band and bugles of the 2nd Green Jackets. They were on for an hour before kick-off and at half-time and one or two in the crowd turned up especially to see them. They had recently returned from a tour of duty in British Guiana and by time they left the locals were well and truly convinced that as far as bugles were concerned the sun had yet to set on the British Empire.

North End approached the game with understandable caution. The club had long been notorious for their tendency to be knocked out of the cup by opponents in a lower grade than themselves, and they had suffered such a fate six times since the Second World War, their conquerors in every case being southern sides. They had also been eliminated from the cup in the sixth round twice in the previous four seasons, and seven times over the preceding thirty years. As such, recent history favoured Oxford who, together with skipper Atkinson, had a sturdy and experienced squad.

The goalkeeper, Harry Fearnley, signed from Huddersfield when Vic Rouse was injured. In the twenty-seven games in which he had played he had come out with a clean sheet in ten of them.

Cyril Beavon, the right-back was the first player to be signed by Arthur Turner when he took over as manager in 1959. Turner held the record for the highest number of appearances in the Oxford first team and had recently been presented with a £400 testimonial cheque. Cyril came from Wolverhampton Wanderers and made his mark with the U's as a reliable defender not averse to joining the attack, to good effect.

Pat Quartermain took over as the club's left-back after leaving the non-professional ranks in 1955. The local boy of the side, he started as a centre half and was coming up to his 200th first-team appearance.

At the centre of the U's defence was Maurice Kyle. Another former Wolverhampton Wanderers' player, he had amassed over 250 appearances in the Oxford cause and was an efficient, cool and controlled player.

John Shuker was the first-choice left-half. He had joined Oxford in 1961 as an outside left, and graduated from the 'A' team via the reserves, where he played in a number of different positions until settling into the first-team as a wing-half.

The outside right was Peter Knight. He had left Nottingham Forest to join Oxford in 1960, bringing much-needed pace to the side.

Arthur Longbottom was signed just before the start of the 1963/64 season from Queens Park Rangers. The inside right had also seen service with Port Vale and Millwall, and was the club's top marksman with sixteen goals to his credit – he had put four of those away in one game against Darlington.

Tony Jones covered the inside left position, although this was not his regular berth, having a preference to play wing half.

Colin Harrington had come to Oxford from Bicester but had previously been on the Wolves' books. What the outside left lacked in experience was countered by his excellent ball skills.

Inside left was Alan Willey. He had figured in several cup matches that season, scoring the goal that eliminated Chesterfield, and one of the two Oxford goals in the draw with Brentford.

As far as he could, Jimmy Milne stuck with the men who had taken Preston thus far in the cup, but Kendall was left out, allowing Davidson out of defence whilst John Donnelly played alongside Ross at the back.

The game was played on 'Leap Year Day' in front of an all-time record crowd at the Manor Ground (that stands to this day) of 22,750. Oxford made Preston work hard but goals from Godfrey and Dawson ended the U's giant-killing antics, giving North End a 2-1 victory and a place in the semi-final draw. Ron Atkinson was the most surprised person around…

The 'Keepers

Jimmy Andrews once said to me, 'look before you get the ball', and that always stuck with me. That was the best football advice I've ever got. If you think about it, it's not bad advice for life in general.
John Bond – West Ham United

Jim – in the way

Amongst the Hammers of '64 only Jim Standen would fail to gain international honours at some level. However, this was probably more to do with England's surfeit of fine goalkeepers at the time, starting of course with Gordon Banks. Standen was never a spectacular performer; there was nothing extravagant or flamboyant about his demeanour, but he was a solid, sound, sure-handed, agile athlete and for a time he was one of the best goalkeepers in the Britain.

Standen was born in Edmonton, something less then ten miles from Upton Park. In the early sixties, Jim was seen as having the cricketing potential to play for England at Test level. Indeed, he topped the county cricket bowling averages as a fast bowler for Worcestershire in 1964. He took sixty-four wickets at an average of just over thirteen, helping his county win the championship. He joined Worcestershire as a leg-spinner in 1958, but it was after switching to seam that he won his first county cap. It was through cricket that he got into football. As a boy he was on the Lord's ground staff. During the winter he played in goal for Rickmansworth Town. Harry Hibbs, the former Birmingham and England goalie, had seen Jim play and it was through Harry that Birmingham City showed interest in Standen as a 'keeper. However, Les Compton (the former Arsenal centre half and Middlesex cricketer) recommended Jim to his former club and Jim signed professional for the Gunners in April 1953 at the age of seventeen.

But at Highbury Jim was always in the shadow of Welsh international Jack Kelsey. He was with Kettering Town for a few months, but he went back to Arsenal and played thirteen League games in 1958/59 and in 1960 he moved to Luton Town.

However, again Standen found himself playing the part of an understudy, this time to international 'keeper Ron Baynham. In the Hatters reserve team and on the transfer list, he almost moved to non-League Hereford United. It was close to Worcester and Jim thought cricket was a better bet than football for him at that time. But Ron Greenwood saw something in Standen and brought him to Upton Park in November 1962 for £7,000, a paltry fee even then. Ron knew Jim from their time together at Arsenal and at first saw him as backup to Laurie Leslie; West Ham's Scottish international goalkeeper of the 1960s had broken a leg in a game against Bolton. On 24 November 1962 Jim got off to a good start, making his debut for the Irons in a 3-1 win at Hillsborough. In the 1962/63 season he played eighteen games for West Ham. But Standen managed to make the Hammers goal his territory by the start of the following term. At 5ft 11ins in height and weighing 11st 4lbs Jim was not a big 'keeper, but he gained a great deal from training alongside some great custodians of the net, the likes of Hibbs, Kelsey and Sam Bartram (who was manager at Luton during Jim's time at Kenilworth Road).

Standen always wore black shorts; even though the West Ham teams he played in never did (the Hammers nearly always donned white or light-blue shorts). He was also the only player in the Football League to wear a number on his back (number one). Many people thought this was just a matter of superstition or habit, but little about Jim's attitude to the game was not purposeful. He chose his garb in order that he might stand out from other players in goalmouth skirmishes and that his own defence could clearly see him, given the obscuring effects of an English winter; mud, grime, dark days, snow and even fog. Being a cricketer, his instinct was also to produce as dark a background to the ball as possible in relation to attacking players, making it just a degree harder, in the split second a striker sometimes has to make a decision, to define the parameters of the obstacle a goalkeeper presents.

Standen kept goal the way he kept a length in his bowling. He was a reliable guard of the West Ham goal for most of the sixties, standing firm behind the young Irons.

Alan James Alexander Kelly

Preston's Alan Kelly was born in Dublin on 5 July 1936 but grew up in Bray, Co. Wicklow where he attended the local St Peter's School. Early on his skills attracted the attention of scouts from many of England's leading clubs, but after leaving school he joined League of Ireland club Drumcondra with whom he won an FAI Cup winners medal when the Drums defeated Shamrock Rovers 2-0 in the 1957 Final. A year later, in April 1958, Alan became a Preston player. At 6ft tall and 12st 3lbs he was a powerful yet agile athlete.

Kelly made his international debut against West Germany. In May 1957 he played in the World Cup against England at Wembley but spent much of his time during that match picking the ball out of the back of the net. England trounced Eire 5-1, but blame for this result could not be laid at the door of the Irish 'keeper. However, Alan had to

Alan Kelly – Preston and Eire.

wait almost five years for his next cap. From then on, his inspired displays made him a regular in the international side.

Alan Kelly made his debut for North End in the FA Cup fourth-round tie at Swansea on 28 January 1961. The decision to play him came late following the illness of Fred Else. Alan had waited almost three seasons to take responsibility for the Preston goal – and he nearly missed the start of the game. Kelly got to the match just in time thanks to Jack Whalley, a Preston supporter, who gave him a lift to the Vetch Field. Four days later Kelly made his League debut in a 5-1 defeat at Sheffield Wednesday.

Kelly was full of the qualities that made the best of wardens of the posts. He was extremely courageous and quick to react, able to get down fast and come out boldly and confidently. He was a great bargain for the moderate fee North End paid to Drumcondra for his services.

5

The Semi-Finals

Brrrum, Brrruum...

1964 was a year of British speed. Donald Campbell captured land (403.10 mph) and water (276.33 mph) speed records in Australia and John Surtees became the only man to win world titles on both two and four wheels.

Surtees was born in Tatsfield, England on 11 February 1934, the son of a London motorcycle-and-sidecar racer and salesman. By the age of eleven he was working part-time as a mechanic for his father, before going on to join the Vincent HRD company as an apprentice engineer.

During 1949, despite being under-age, the youthful Surtees had started racing motorcycles. His first race was on a 500cc Excelsior B14, but he soon switched to a Triumph Tiger 70. At the age of twenty-one he had won almost 200 races. Surtees became British Champion and took MV Agusta to a plethora of victories, achieving in all seven World Championships, including the 1956 (500cc class), 1958, 1959 and 1960 (350 and 500), as well as winning six Tourist Trophy victories in the Isle of Man TT. His achievements were underlined in 1959 when he was awarded an MBE in the Queen's Birthday Honours list.

Driving an ex-Stirling Moss Aston DBR1 and the famed Vanwall Grand Prix car, in 1959 Surtees displayed the speed and confidence which had served him so well on two wheels to impress both Aston Martin team manager Reg Parnell and Vanwall boss Tony Vandervell. Surtees switched full-time to four wheels in 1960. A victory in Formula 500 for Ken Tyrrell at Goodwood confirmed his transferable talents and he made his F1 debut for Lotus in Monte Carlo. One race later, he finished second at Silverstone in the British Grand Prix, before taking pole position in Portugal.

In his first year in F1 Surtees did well enough, but in 1961 he signed with Yeoman Credit Cooper with whom he had a disappointing year. However, he helped develop the Lola Formula 1 car, finishing second in both the British and German Grand Prix, but winning at Mallory Park in England and at Longford in Tasmania, Australia.

Despite shows of prodigious speed by Surtees, this was the point at which Colin Chapman was forging his deep alliance with Jim Clark, and Surtees elected to move to pastures new just as the British team really began to establish itself. He was to have his most productive period with Ferrari, being able to speak Italian was a great help and he played a big part in transforming Ferrari into the power it is today. He drove for the Italian giant for three years and in 1964 won the Drivers World Championship title in his V-S Ferrari with stunning victories in Germany, at Syracuse, Italy and the Italians' home race at Monza, clinching the title in a dramatic Mexican Grand Prix, managing to hold off fellow Britain Graham Hill by just one point. An added bonus was the team win in the constructor's championship.

Surtees, now thirty years of age, continued to win numerous Formula 2 and sports car events, but a year after his four-wheel World Championship he was near-fatally injured when his CanAm Lola T70 crashed at Mosport Park in Ontario, Canada. It was a mark of the man that he astonished doctors with the speed of his recovery.

John left the Prancing Horse in the middle of the 1966 season having fallen out with the Ferrari director. This left Jack Brabham a clear run to the title. Surtees joined Cooper Masserati and was runner-up to Brabham in the World Championship. He recalled:

> That was costly to Ferrari and costly to me. I believe we lost one or two World Championships as a result.

He went on to drive for Honda and Lola and made the podium on a few occasions, but following the death of Jo Shlesser, Honda withdrew from racing in 1968.

After a dismal 1969 season Surtees left BRM to set up his own team, Surtees Racing Organisation, for 1970, just as BRM started winning again. The Surtees team was good but he never won the World Championship with it and his last win was in 1971 with the Oulton Park Gold Cup.

In 1978 due to ill health, resulting from his earlier crash in Canada, and major sponsorship difficulties, Surtees reluctantly closed down the racing operation. But he was a founder member of the Constructors Association and carried on to work closely with many of the major teams competing together and with Bernard Ecclestone, who he had known from his early days in motorcycling. He has kept a continuous interest in the development of the sport; although not being directly involved in recent years, through his many contacts John still participates.

At the time of writing Surtees drives for such companies as Mercedes Benz in historic demonstration events and does selected consultancy and promotional work in both the two- and four-wheel Grand Prix world. He is unique in that not only has he been a rider and driver who has competed with the world's best and beaten them, but he also has a knowledge of all the other facets of the sport from his involvement in the management of both his own team and also that of the Lola sports car programme and Honda F1 Grand Prix programme.

Looking back he reflects:

> ... the main thing I think is that whatever I've done, I've done from the heart. I have loved being involved, first building and riding motorcycles and then driving cars – but above all, competing.

At the start of the twenty-first century Surtees was concentrating on the slower-moving interests of property development, motorsport and engineering consultancy, and, when time permits, writing. He was a director of the British Racing Drivers' Club and a member of the Worshipful Company of Carmen. He lived in Surrey with his wife Jane and their three children Edwina (fourteen), Leonora (thirteen) and Henry John (eleven).

It is unlikely that anyone will ever emulate John Surtees' feat of being World Champion on two and four wheels. The ultimate professional, he had ruled the world on motorcycles, at Formula One level and the North American Can-Am Championship for sports cars. He was a racer who deserves a place in the Halls of Fame of both motorcycle and car racing. 'Big John' rarely won the accolades his success deserved. He is a quiet man and once said,

> I suffered perhaps from an excess of enthusiasm, of always wanting to get deeply involved with any project on which I was working.

By his own admission, he lacked the single-mindedness to seek out the most competitive drives that could well have brought him even greater F1 success:

> I feel fairly frustrated about my car-racing career... To fully justify my abilities as a driver I should have been just concentrating on getting in the best car at the time because time does not wait for you.

In a car, as on a bike, Surtees was a fearless, tough but fair competitor, as quick as the best without being wild. But where most of his rivals contented themselves with riding or driving, he had a deep interest in the workings of his machines. Some said he should have simply concentrated solely on racing, itself difficult enough, but he liked to tinker and probe in an unceasing quest for technical perfection. Resilience and determination were his abiding characteristics as a racer.

Swans in Birmingham

Teams win matches. It is easy to forget that in a game dominated by the idea of the hero, the 'star' player. But what football player ever won the cup or a championship on his own? It's about thinking in certain way. You can go the way of 'one strong man', everyone for himself and devil take the hindmost, but

teamwork is about doing things together, for each other: looking out for your mates and knowing that they will do the same for you.
Jimmy Milne – Preston North End

The meeting of Preston North End and Swansea Town (the municipality had not at that time been bequeathed the status of 'city') was the thirteenth time since the Second World War that Villa Park had hosted an FA Cup semi-final. The previous fixtures read like a roll of honour of the modern English game:

1932: Arsenal 1, Manchester City 0
1935: Burnley 0, Sheffield Wednesday 3
1946: Bolton Wanderers 0, Charlton Athletic 2
1948: Blackpool 3, Tottenham Hotspur 1
1953: Blackpool 2, Tottenham Hotspur 1

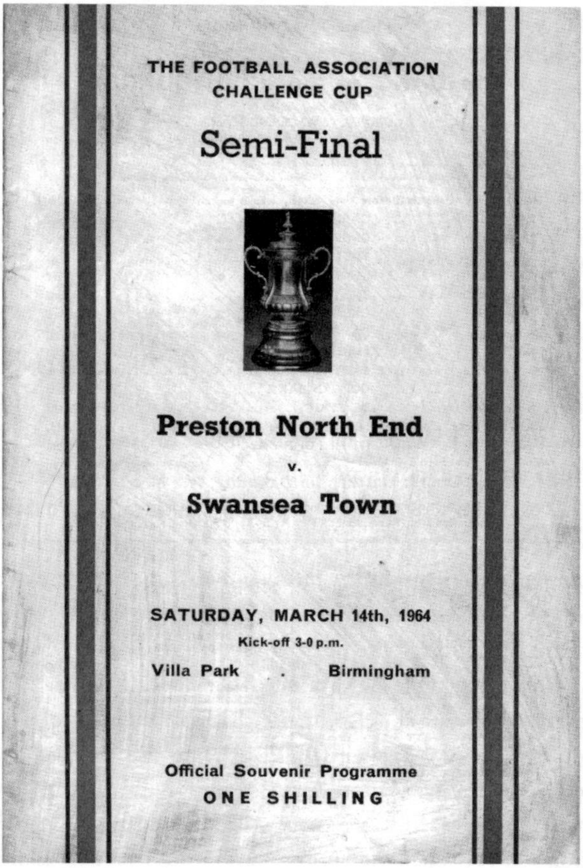

Preston North End *v.* Swansea Town, 14 March 1964 programme cover.

1954: West Bromwich Albion 2, Port Vale 1
1955: Manchester City 1, Sunderland 0
1956: Manchester City 1, Tottenham Hotspur 0
1958: Manchester United 2, Fulham 2
1961: Tottenham Hotspur 3, Burnley 0
1962: Burnley 1, Fulham 1
1963: Southampton 0, Manchester United 1

From 1932 six of the competing teams had gone on to become ultimate winners of the trophy. It was Preston's tenth appearance in the last four of the FA Cup. The other nine were:

West Bromwich Albion	5 March 1887
Crewe Alexandra	18 February 1888
West Bromwich Albion	16 March 1889
Everton	4 March, 16 March and 20 March 1893
Tottenham Hotspur	19 March 1921
Tottenham Hotspur	25 March 1922
West Bromwich Albion	10 April 1937
Aston Villa	26 March 1938
Sheffield Wednesday	27 March 1954

However, over the previous twenty-five years the Deepdale club had made thirteen visits to Villa Park and had only managed one win.

Swansea or Preston would be the first Second Division club to reach Wembley since Leicester City did so in 1949. Up to 1964, only four Second Division clubs had won the Cup: Notts County in 1894, Wolverhampton Wanderers in 1908, Barnsley in 1912 and West Bromwich Albion in 1931. In the future Sunderland would triumph over Leeds in 1973 and Southampton would take the cup back to Division Two in 1976. Of course, West Ham would join this club by defeating Arsenal 1-0 in 1980.

Founded in 1911, Swansea Town became one of the original members of Division Three in 1920. The club had produced a string of fine players, including a big favourite at Villa Park, Trefor Ford, as well as the Allchurch brothers, Mel Charles, Roy Paul, Cliff Jones and Terry Medwin. However, Swansea had only made the semi-final stage once before in 1926. Then, just as in 1964, the Swans were a Second Division club. The campaign had started with a 2-0 victory over Second Division Blackpool at Bloomfield Road. This was followed by a 6-3 home win over Stoke City, at the time another side from Division Two. A 1-0 win at The Den against Third Division Millwall was followed by a home draw and a breathtaking confrontation with Arsenal, the runners-up in the League Championship that season. The Gunners were beaten 2-1. However, First Division Bolton Wanderers, who would win the cup that year, put an end to Swansea's Twin Towers dream, knocking them out 3-0 at Tottenham in the semi-final.

As such the 1964 boys from Wales came to Birmingham with the intention of taking their club to Wembley for the first time, but they were also looking to be the second side since the FA Cup competition began in 1871 to take the trophy out of England, and emulate the achievement of Cardiff City in 1927. The Bluebirds, who had been runners-up to Sheffield United in 1925, defeated Arsenal 1-0 and made the Welsh mountains rock.

In the Swansea goal for the semi-final was former Hammer Noel Dwyer. Born in Dublin on 30 October 1934, Noel recalled his path to Upton Park:

> I played for Ormeau in the League of Ireland before I went to Wolves in August 1953. I made my League debut in the 1957/58 season. I turned out five times for them and my first game for the Republic as an Under-23 was while I was with Wolves.
>
> West Ham had just been promoted when Ted Fenton was looking for cover for Ernie Gregory and that was me! I signed in December 1958. I was twenty-three.
>
> At first I just got reserve-team games but got my first League game at the end of March. It was at Upton Park against Bolton. We won 4-3. John Bond played at centre forward and got a couple of goals. I did okay. Nat Lofthouse was playing for Bolton that day. Anyway, I made ten appearances that season and we finished in sixth place. That was good after promotion.
>
> The following season I got quite a few games and I did well enough to get my first full cap against Sweden at Dalymount Park on 1 November 1959. Noel Cantwell was the skipper and of course he was the West Ham club captain at the time. He had played more than a dozen international games by then.
>
> West Ham were doing good in the first part of the 1959/60 season. After a 3-2 win at Upton Park around the end of November, funnily enough against Wolverhampton, we found ourselves at the top of the First Division. But the next Saturday at Hillsborough we got beat 7-0 by Sheffield Wednesday. Before we'd been playing ten minutes they got three goals.

In fact those three goals went past Dwyer in the opening eight minutes of the game. A match report of the game concluded:

> The man who took the biggest sucker punch of all was Eire international goalkeeper Noel Dwyer. Dwyer just couldn't take or punch the ball clear as it came across from the wing. He was beaten through rank bad judgement.

That seems a harsh conclusion given that Wolves would finish the season as runners-up to Burnley, denied the Championship by a single point. Noel gained a further three international caps that season facing Czechoslovakia, West Germany and made another appearance against Sweden. After being drawn to face Second Division Huddersfield Town in the third round of the FA Cup, the Hammers came back to Upton Park for the replay on Wednesday, 13 January 1960 with high hopes of progressing to the next round. Noel remembered:

> The pitch was covered in snow and Denis Law, he was only about eighteen then, seemed to be the only player not sliding all over the place and they won 1-5. My last game for West Ham was in February. We were at home to Newcastle United and they beat us 3-5. We went three down again, before we'd played half an hour. But the lads fought back to make it level at half-time.

However, with goals after sixty and sixty-four minutes, The Magpies secured the points and Noel Dwyer's career in the claret and blue ended in defeat. He looked back on what happened next:

> I was back playing for the reserves for the rest of the season and knew it was just a matter of time before I moved on. I was a bit unlucky I think. Anyway, in August 1960 I went to Swansea. I'd played about three dozen games for West Ham. I was judged on a few bad defeats I think.

Swansea's road to Villa Park had been a tough one. Dwyer recollected:

> In the third round we beat Barrow 4-1 at the Vetch Field [Brian Evans, Roy Evans, no relation, Eddie Thomas and Herbie Williams were on the mark for the Swans]. Then we played three First Division sides.

At the home of Sheffield United a goal by Thomas forced the Blades to make the journey into Wales where the home side scored four times (Derek Draper 2, Jim McLaughlin and Thomas) without reply. The fifth round fated manager Morris and his men to more travel but with a brace from Keith Todd they dragged Stoke City to Swansea where goals from McLaughlin and Thomas plus a Dwyer clean sheet took the Swans to a quarter-final meeting with Liverpool. Noel remembered:

> Nearly everyone outside of Swansea thought the trip to Anfield would be our lot. But McLaughlin and Thomas got the goals that took us into the last four. In the end we were good value for the 2-1 win! Having beaten Liverpool we were confident we could beat Preston. By then I was rated as a useful goalkeeper, one of the best maybe, but having a bit of a European style I'm not sure everybody understood that. I was one of the most experienced players at Swansea at the time and I suppose that helped the younger players.

For all this, like Preston, Swansea had very few good results at Villa Park to look back on. In their four previous visits they had not managed a single win. But they had defeated the Lancashire team 2-1 in the fourth-round stage of the FA Cup two seasons previously. In more recent encounters, honours had been more or less even. During the opening weeks of the 1963/64 term the two sides had fought out a thrilling 3-3 draw at Deepdale and, although the December before that had seen Swansea trounce Preston 5-1 at the Vetch Field, ending a Preston run of eleven games without defeat, this was no more than revenge as Dwyer had been obliged to pick the ball out of his net six times at Deepdale in April 1963. However, overall, Preston had claimed thirteen wins and eight draws from their twenty-eight meetings with the Welsh side and as the teams arrived in Birmingham, Preston were making a bid for promotion whilst Swansea were doing all they could to avoid relegation.

Preston fans, except those who had paid their 12s 6d (67.5p!) for their season ticket, had queued all night for a ticket, and were greeted in Birmingham by torrential rain that transformed the home of the Villains' usually pristine pitch into a mire. In the hour before kick-off the rain-drenched crowd of 68,000 were treated to a musical programme that in itself was indicative, even in the mid-1960s, of the primal nature of football-ground-based entertainment. The fun started with *Caribbean Carnival*, *Gi-Gi* and, as the heavens opened, *The Happy Whistler.* Apropos of nothing, this triumphant was succeed by *Irish Salute*, *The Three Jets* and, in something right outside terrace fan taste, the title tune from the Rodgers musical *Oklahoma*. Given the truly non-Iberian conditions, the next serving must have felt like something of a piss-take to the dripping hordes trapped in the sodden stands, they were slapped with *Sambalita*, *El Radicario*, *Lady of Spain* and, for good Caribbean measure, *Copa Cabana*. There was a brief sign of consciousness of being in the throes of the swinging sixties with a rendition of *Telstar*, but the return to solid footballing values, always tinged with a touch of jingoism, was marked by way of the musical crescendo of *Lassie From Lancashire* and, of course, for the Welsh, *Men of Harlech*. The entire performance was a fine example of the kind of morbid eclectics that might be produced by a 1970s geography teacher that saw themselves as having a 'musical bent'.

Jimmy Milne called on ten of the XI who had defeated Oxford; the only change was Asworth for Godfrey. The Swansea manager, Trevor Morris had produced one of the youngest sides in the League to face a Preston team that was beginning to look like a solid and capable unit. But it looked like the pitch, which was dotted with small ponds and was reminiscent of a water meadow, would suit the side with the deepest reserves of will and physical force, whilst negating the finer subtleties of the game.

Both teams wore their 'changed kits' (there being no such thing as an 'away shirt' at that time). North End were in royal blue shirts and the Welsh side donned dazzling orange, a garish, migraine-inducing combination that would soon be neutralised by the addition of copious portions of mud. Some jocular Swansea supporters had placed an imitation swan on the centre spot and it certainly looked more at home than the players. Needless to say the icon was escorted to the stand by dripping police officers, probably reflecting on the ignominy of arresting a dummy duck.

As Preston skipper Nobby Lawton and his Swansea counterpart, right-half Mike Johnson, shook hands at the centre of the centre-circle, both knew this was a huge game in the histories of their respective clubs. Johnson had Swansea in his blood. He had been born in the town and had graduated through the teams of the club he had supported from his cradle days. With international recognition at Schoolboy, Youth and Under-23 levels he was a young captain and promising defender.

Dwyer looked back on the start of the match:

> As we kicked off it was a quagmire in places. We were the first to come close when our centre forward, Keith Todd, got a chance. He was a local boy, one of a few good youngsters produced by the youth scheme Trevor Morris had going at Swansea.

Todd had developed rapidly, gaining international recognition with selection for the Welsh Under-23 side. He flew past Lawton, seeming certain to test the poised Kelly, but Nobby caught him a yard outside the area with a blood-red tackle that sent Todd plummeting into the mud. Sheffield man Mr J.E. Towers, known to his fraternity as 'The Steel Referee', although lagging well behind the play, called a foul against Lawton and the Swansea left-half, boy from the valleys Herbie Williams, ex-Schoolboy, Youth and Under-23 international from the Swans nursery, stepped up to take the free-kick. Herbie, who was rated by many as a prospect the likes of which had not been seen since the great Welsh immortal Ivor Allchurch, blasted a cannonball of a shot through the well-constructed North End wall, but its flight took it just wide of the parameters of Kelly's domain.

As the game progressed, Swansea right-back Brian Hughes, another 'Morris Minor' with Welsh Under-23 international honours under his belt, alongside the rest of the Welshmen's defence, was kept on his toes by the aggressive Preston attack. Hughes was a tenacious defender, capable of playing in either full-back or half-back. Like the rest of the Swans' protective force he was exceptionally strong in the tackle and a tireless worker. However, North End forced their way past the strong back line and Noel Dwyer saved well from Dawson and Spavin.

Preston were nearly caught out when John Donnelly missed a long cross-field pass and the Swans' outside right Barrie Jones was able to pull clear. Jones was born in the Principality and had been nurtured by Swansea. He was a Youth, Under-23 and full international, consistently under surveillance by the giants of the First Division. Jones, a very clever player whose skill and confidence belied his youth, delivered a centre for Thomas. The forward's glancing header beat Kelly but luckily for North End the ball grazed the outside of his right-hand post.

North End's defence was looking exposed, trying to play their normal passing game with a ball that was, with every second, becoming more and more clogged with moisture and increasingly adhering to the sticky surface.

Noel Dwyer reminisced:

> Those were the days of heavy leather balls that soaked up water like a sponge and stuck like limpets to muddy pitches. Preston were probably the better footballing side, but the conditions, together with our determination to match Preston, equalled things up a bit.

This situation resulted in some exciting moments at both ends of the park. But the game was tortuously hard work. The Swans' inside right Derek Draper, who was hailed by the Vetch fans as 'the Didi of Wales', sent a savage header towards Kelly. It looked a definite opener but the Irishman just managed to get his fingertips to the ball. Draper, a fine ball player, was born in Swansea and having Youth international honours had been chosen as reserve to the Welsh Under-23 team.

The Preston reply seemed almost instant. Ashworth cracked a fierce drive that rebounded off of a Welsh defender for a North End corner.

Just before the interval, the Welsh side took the lead. Roy Evans, the Swans left-back, began a concerted attack on the Preston lines. Another of manager Trevor Morris's pipeline of local talent, after just eight Football League appearances Evans gained recognition by being chosen for the Welsh Under-23 side. He slammed the ball to Draper, who then squared inside to Lancastrian-born Eddie Thomas, the former Everton and Blackburn centre forward. Thomas evaded a challenge from Ross, before finding inside left Jimmy McLaughlin who hit a hard, low shot past Kelly. McLaughlin was a native of Londonderry. Before his time with Swansea he had played for Birmingham City and Shrewsbury Town. Jimmy, an Irish international, was a dangerous raider and prolific goalscorer.

In the second half, Preston attacked the Holte End. Within seven minutes of the restart Alex Dawson ran on to a lobbed pass from Lawton, but as Preston's Black Prince was shaping to shoot, Swansea's centre half Brian Purcell got in the way. A local lad, Purcell had been at the Vetch Field since his junior years. He was a shield of a player who possessed a devastatingly strong tackle and extremely swift recovery. His solidity at the heart of the Swans rearguard had been instrumental in the downfall of Liverpool. The Welsh reaper cut Dawson down like a chainsaw would an oak. It was a decisive stop but a definite penalty. Dwyer recalled the moment:

> Dawson had missed his last penalty at Derby, but he looked relaxed enough coming up to that kick. You have to make a choice with penalties, it's as simple as that and I went the wrong way.

That was Dawson's thirty-third goal of the season. The equaliser seemed to release a store of passion and self-belief in Jimmy Milne's side and both Ashworth and Wilson were only inches away from giving North End the lead. Playing with great confidence, the Lancastrians went 2-1 up in the seventy-first minute when Tony Singleton let fly with a thunderbolt. The ball sailed through the air and straight past a bemused Noel Dwyer who remembered:

> It went up like a rocket. The power he hit it with must have been phenomenal as at that time the ball must have weighed a ton!

It was Singleton's first goal for Preston. The Preston skipper, Nobby Lawton, who at the time of writing was in his sixty-fifth year, spoke with the alertness of youth when recalling that semi-final and the goal that sent his side to the Empire Stadium:

> Looking back, we were destined to go to Wembley that season. It was fate, I suppose. I'll never forget Tony Singleton's goal against Swansea in the semi-final. Tony just picked the ball up in front of me and launched it forty yards over the goalkeeper's head.

Singleton could have gone from hero to villain, for with just a few minutes to play, he conceded a free-kick ten yards outside the area. The initial missile was headed away by Dawson, but was returned into the box. Kelly was thankful to punch the ball clear just as it was about to make deadly contact with Todd's marauding knapper.

At last the whistle signalled the end of hostilities and the muddied warriors of North End were regaled with a gargantuan roar of relief and glorification from the Preston supporters, who could now dry off and begin preparations for the journey to Wembley that had been a decade in coming. George Ross had played with splendour in defence, and alongside Singleton, had created a blockade that restricted Swansea's potential in attack. Lawton had not stopped urging his troops on whilst setting the example of linking defence with midfield and attack. Davidson had given one of his best displays for the club and Dawson had not only pounded at a resolute barricade with continued attrition but had also found the time, strength and energy to contribute to Preston's security when needed. Holden played with magnificence and had shown a massive intelligence.

For Preston fans willing to read the runes, just as in 1926, a Lancastrian team had won their semi-final against Swansea. Bolton had gone on to beat fellow Lancastrians, Manchester City in the final. Another team in the last four in 1964 were Manchester United (but another was West Ham United).

Defending the Centre

The centre half in any side is the bolt on the door. The position is the fulcrum of the defence; it's where the balance is. Although no one position is more important than another, next to the goalkeeper the centre half is a crucial and specialised position on the field.
George Kay – West Ham United

Anthony Joseph Singleton

Tony Singleton first saw the light of day in Preston on 30 March 1936. Singleton had been recruited from local football. He was a tough, rugged, redhead (one journalist of the early 1960s called him 'rawboned' – the media employed a lot of ex-public-school boys in those days). Strong in the air and resolute in the tackle, he was courageous and an honest, down-to-earth, effective centre half.

Tony signed-on at Deepdale as a part-time professional in May 1955, turning full-time on leaving the Forces in June 1959. He had a six-year wait before he played his first senior (first-team) game for Preston; a Deepdale confrontation with Arsenal on 30 August 1960. Spavin, who scored one of Preston's two goals in the game, and Peter Thompson were also debutants that day as North End sent the North Londoners home pointless.

Singleton's inclusion in the Preston side was part of manager Cliff Britton's response to his team's fruitless efforts in their first three matches of what was to be Preston's relegation season. Britton had made two positional alterations and four changes in personnel. However, Singleton took a bash in the ribs in the course of the first half that called for X-rays and a lay-off, but he was to turn out for the Lilywhites thirty-seven times in the 1960/61 campaign.

Singleton was not dropped from that point up to North End's 1964 cup final. Standing 5ft 11ins, he was a beefy 12st 12lbs. In the early 1960s he was one of the outstanding young

Tony Singleton
– defending the centre.

pivots of the Second Division. Robust, but a scrupulously honest professional, Tony was the kingpin in the dependable Preston defence; a hard but fair stopper.

Topper Brown

Ken Brown might be seen to be typical of the home-grown East End player. Bobby Moore once said of him,

> Ken Brown was far from being everyone's ideal at centre half but he was right for us. He was powerful in the air and his priority was always to get the ball the hell out of the danger area. Sometimes he would whack it away when I thought we should capitalise on a situation and I'd say: 'Brownie, what are you doing?' He'd say: 'Don't worry; it's no trouble up there.' But he was always positive and it took a long while to replace him. He had a good understanding with John Bond.

Brown had been brought up in the style of play developed in the first few years of the West Ham 'Academy', but in other ways Ken was in the tradition of West Ham professionals. He was a favourite of the crowd from the beginning; his smile and ability to accept a mistake caused the fans and his teammates to warm to him, this was not unlike Dick Walker's (one of his illustrious predecessors at the heart of the Hammers defence) style, although Brown probably had greater ability than the former captain. Ken recalled:

> In my early days they didn't have squads; they had three teams. If someone wasn't playing well or they were injured, the reserve came straight in. I was in the 'A' team when both Malcolm Allison and Dick Walker were injured and I got three games on the trot, all draws.

Ken's debut took place in mid-February 1953, at Rotherham's Millmoor Ground, just five days after his nineteenth birthday whilst still undertaking his National Service:

> I was stationed at Aldershot when I was called up. When they issued jobs I was the last one left, but Ted Fenton had phoned and I was made the RSM's runner, which was RSM Bridger. I was in the office doing little jobs. I worked around the sergeant's mess and got a room to myself.
>
> In that first match Ernie Gregory was a bit hindered by the sun shining straight in his face from one side. He told me to cover all balls coming into the box from that direction. I've never headed the ball so many times. Anyway, I gave away a penalty, I felt terrible. The penalty was struck well and I knew that it was going in the top corner. Ernie literally flew and he tipped it over. I was

so pleased. I was jumping up and down and tried to grab him to congratulate him, but he pushed me and told me to, go away, every time I got near him. 'I should have caught it,' is all he said.

Gregory recalled the young Ken Brown as,

> … a big strong lad, solid and good in the air. He came into the first team and in his first three games he was up against the best centre forwards in the League. He didn't give them a kick! I used to give him a rollocking or two but he didn't mind. He used to say, 'You keep telling me Ernie, I will learn'. Ken could run all day. He was the sort of player they would pay a lot of money for these days… he was a good lad.

Although born not too far from the Boleyn Ground, Ken's family moved to Dagenham, where he became a pupil at Lymington Secondary Modern School. Although he grew up in Dagenham, staunch West Ham territory, he had not paid much attention to any professional club, and knew no more about West Ham than any other side. He started playing regular football at the age of twelve and was chosen for Dagenham Boys when he got to fifteen. He recalled:

> I went to live in Bonham Road, Dagenham. It was funny really because I never used to play football. I used to play cricket and wasn't interested in football but because all my friends used to bugger off and play, I eventually started playing and it went from there and we got into a situation with a street team called Neville United and eleven or twelve of us used to go round to Mr Flanders and do training in his little council house. The team was run by Bobby Flanders; we used to use his bathroom to clean up after games.
>
> Bonham Street produced many top-ranking professional footballers, including West Ham's Dick Walker and Terry Venables. Alf Ramsey and Jimmy Greaves were from the same neck of the woods.

Neville United played in a district league and with them Ken won a London Minor FA Myrtle (inter-league) Shield winners' medal. Ken met his first wife at a Neville United dance in Dagenham. He looked back on his Dagenham days:

> At school I played for Dagenham. I started playing seriously around fourteen or fifteen in the Dagenham League and one of the teams we used to play was West Ham's 'B' team and we used to beat them! After the match with them I was approached by Wally St Pier.
>
> We had a good team and had been together for a few years and Wally wanted me to join West Ham. I said, 'It's very nice of you but what would I want to

join your side for when my side keep beating you?' 'Oh no,' he said. 'You'll be playing higher football than this.' I said I'd think about it. Anyway, I went there eventually.

I'd started work at fifteen with my father. In two years I qualified to be a wood machinist but West Ham took me on as an amateur in the summer of 1951 and I played for West Ham in the London Mid-week League, at the Spotted Dog, Clapton's ground, an amateur club near to Upton Park. I liked playing a lot; I looked forward to the games. It was good because I got expenses and time off work.

Having completed an apprenticeship as a machinist, Ken had a good job with a solid future. West Ham were paying him for broken time. He was not yet eighteen.

The firm I was working for, 'Greves', was based between Bow and Stratford. I'd spent two years on the wood machine and all the time I wanted to be a footballer. Eventually they told me that I was having too much time off and that it was either football or work. By then I was a qualified cutter. I politely told them, 'You know what you can do with your job' and walked out. I thought that I would ask the Pratts [Reg Pratt had become chairman of West Ham United, after the death of W.J. Cearns. Reg's father had been F.R. Pratt, who was also on the West Ham board] for a job.

I was training at West Ham under Ted Fenton on Tuesday and Thursday evenings and, piling it on a bit, I asked him if he could help because I'd just been sacked. He said, 'You do your training son and I'll see you afterwards.' I saw Ted Fenton and piled it on a bit.

After everyone had gone he came down and said, 'Everything's fine, we're going to sign you on professional forms.' 'Pardon?' I said. 'Professional forms? What, to play football all the time? I don't have to work?' 'No,' he said. 'You play football all the time.' I couldn't believe that and I can remember it now. I more or less jogged and ran all the way back home to Dagenham. I didn't think about money, failure or anything like that. I hadn't expected that. I was that pleased, I could have been locked up! I told my Mum, but she didn't really understand, she said something like, 'that's good'.

Brown took a cut in wages from £12 to £9 a week for the chance to play football and made his debut in the Hammers 'A' team, at Norwich. The Canaries won 4-3 and in October that same year he made his first appearance in the Football Combination, again facing Norwich at Carrow Road, on Christmas Day, 1951. This time the Irons won 2-0. Ken played an important role in the Football Combination League success of the mid-1950s in the reserves and gained an LFA Cup-winners medal.

1. The Invincibles.

2. All the Hammers of '64.

3. West Ham's first cup final side.

4. Preston win in 1938. Bill Shankly (next to policeman) clutches his winners' medal. Andy Beattie looks up at Tom Smith holding the FA Cup. Frank Gallimore is far right.

5. Preston 1947/48.

6. Ernie Gregory, coach of the 1964 team, earning his wages during his playing days in goal for West Ham.

7. The Addicks of the '60s.

8. Noel Cantwell – Academy director.

9. Budgie before he was a Hammer.

10. Jim Standen – back at Highbury. Jack Burkett is on his knees. John Bond (obscured, left) and Alan Sealey (far right) look on. Ken Brown is the player obscured by the post.

11. Ron Boyce scores the second goal *v.* Blackburn Rovers at Ewood Park. This was West Ham's 'turnaround' game of 1963/64.

12. There's only one Bobby Moore.

13. John Surtees – the speed of '64.

14. Clay *v.* Liston – the other 'old *v.* new' battle of 1964

15. Ready for the semi, blood-red Pat Crerand.

16. John 'Muffin' Bond.

17. Geoff Hurst.

18. The Belfast boy.

19. Hammers *v.* United.

20. John Lyall. In 1964 everything ended and everything started for John.

21. Budgie on the ball.

22. Martin Peters – the man who was dropped.

23. Eras meet: Bobby Moore, cup finalist 1964, and Jimmy Ruffell, cup finalist 1923.

24. John Sissons nets the equaliser. 1–1!

25. Ronnie Boyce scores the winning goal. George Ross (2) takes it in.

26. Well done! In ascending order, Bobby Moore, Ken Brown, Johnny Byrne, Peter Brabrook, Eddie Bovington and Geoff Hurst.

27. Cup-kisser Moore.

28. West Ham's golden day.

29. Running round Wembley with the cup. From left to right, Johnny Sissons, Jack Burkett, Eddie Bovington, Ronnie Boyce and Geoff Hurst.

30. The cup comes to the East End.

Brown came out of the Army in 1954. He didn't turn out again in the Football League until August of that year, and got a run of twenty-three matches at the start of 1954/55 before Malcolm Allison returned to the centre half position. Ken played just one game in the 1955/56 season and only five the following term, but he was ever-present in the Championship year and the following three seasons.

For Ken, playing professional football in the first year at Upton Park was the highlight of his career in the fifties. He played his inaugural Division One game (his seventy-fifth League appearance) at Portsmouth, a 2-1 win for the Hammers on 23 August 1958. He had represented London in the same year in a match with Barcelona. His 100th League appearance was made on 31 January 1959 in the 5-3 defeat of Nottingham Forest at Upton Park. By the end of the 1958/59 term Ken had completed his first ever-present season in the First Division and he was elected 'Hammer of the Year'. The following September he was to receive his proudest accolade when on 18 November 1959 he stepped out at Wembley in an England shirt. England beat Northern Ireland 2-1. Joe Baker and Bolton's Ray Parry got England's goals with Billy Bingham scoring for the Ulster boys. Although Ken received a favourable press he was not selected again. Brown played in the Irons side that finished runners-up in the Southern Floodlight Cup in 1960.

Often described as 'cool' or 'calm', Ken was a consistent and commanding centre half. He assessed his own abilities:

> I could always head a ball, I never got ruffled. People say that I'm never miserable, but when you've worked in a factory, you realise how lucky you are to play football for a living. The game always has it's highs – my first goal for the club was a header, from a Peter Brabrook corner. In those days it was practically unheard of for a centre forward to go up.

That goal came in the 5-0 walloping of Birmingham City, at Upton Park on 6 October 1962, this was his 247th League game. He had to wait five months for his next glory moment; on 18 March 1963 he got his second Hammers goal in the 3-2 League defeat of Manchester United at Upton Park in his 263rd League game.

The early to mid-1960s were Brown's peak years as he played throughout West Ham's golden era. It was around this time that he got his nickname 'Topper'; he has no idea where it came from or why he got the tag but it may have come from rhyming slang – 'top hat and tails' = 'hard as nails' – or a derivative of 'Stopper'. Ken notched up his 300th League appearance on 18 January 1964; it was a 1-0 Boleyn Ground victory over Liverpool.

At 6ft and 13st 10lbs, Ken was a big, awesomely strong and dependable defender. Any flaws in his mobility were countered by unflagging zeal and unflinching courage. Ken was an all-round sportsman. Outside football, he played golf, squash and tennis, but he was also the comic of the side. However, he had a serious side. Alongside

John Bond he had taken over the reigns of player leadership at Upton Park after the departure of Noel Cantwell and Malcolm Allison. By the early 1960s the pair were, with Bobby Moore and Johnny Byrne, the architects of West Ham's style, much more working with Ron Greenwood than being managed by him. Indeed, there was a power struggle right through the 1960s and the tension between Moore and Greenwood was never far from the surface. Byrne was ever the diplomat, almost a go-between, especially after an example was made of the plain speaking John Bond in the first years of Ron's reign at Upton Park following Bond's long-term disappearance from the first team and near transfer to Queens Park Rangers. However, Brown's attitude was more ambiguous and measured than some of his comrades.

> As a coach, Ron Greenwood was second to none… He used to go and see the opposition and he'd come back and you felt as if you really knew who you were going to play against.
>
> Ron was excellent. He was a purist – too much of a purist really. He didn't like anybody tackling from behind and if anybody kicked anyone that was them finished. He didn't want to know that, he just loved football as football should be played.
>
> As a man, I had disagreements with Ron. Not verbal ones but I never felt that I was good enough. I never got a 'well done' or a 'well played' from him and I think he just saw me as a stopper. That used to hurt me… I prided myself on being good in the air and there weren't too many who could beat me…
>
> I see him now and I have great respect for him – always have done, always will do – but I never thought I was good enough.
>
> I remember playing at Ipswich and the ground was rock hard. I kept my balance, did my job and it went great, but after the match I got a bollocking from Ron for not doing more. Everyone else told me I'd had a blinder!
>
> I think Ron tried to replace me at one time with Tony Knapp from Southampton, but I was never going to leave West Ham after all those years.

Reds in Sheffield

By an interesting turn of fate, West Ham's last match before their FA Cup semi-final was a League game with Manchester United at Upton Park, the very side that stood between the East Enders and Wembley.

The match was just seven days after the quarter-final game with Burnley and a week before the semi-final match. Matt Busby rested star players Bobby Charlton, Denis Law, George Best, Maurice Setters and the longest-serving player on the Old Trafford books, having joined the club in 1949, Bill Foulkes. A survivor of the

West Ham United *v.* Manchester United, 7 March 1964 programme cover.

Munich disaster, Foulkes was born in St Helens where he had started his working life as a miner. A former right-back, in which position he was capped for England in 1955, he switched his 13st 2lb frame to centre half around 1960. He played in three cup finals for United but only got his winners' medal in 1963.

As a pre cup-tie indicator the League match at Upton Park was a non-event. The Hammers' performance was dire, but it looked as if the sides would go away from the Boleyn Ground with honours even before John Bond was punished for a poor back pass when it was picked up by David Sadler, who put the visitors ahead in the seventy-second minute. Four minutes from time, David Herd made it 2-0 as the Hammers pressed forward looking for a draw. Herd was to represent Scotland five times. He could play at outside right or centre forward. The son of Scottish international Alex Herd, of Manchester City fame, Dave was signed from Arsenal in July 1961. He was a 5ft 11in, a powerful 13st 2lb striker with a good shot with either foot. He began his career with Stockport County and went to Arsenal in 1954. Dave got a cup medal in 1963 to match his Dad's achievement of 1937.

Winning with what was almost a reserve side Busby might have been thought to have won the psychological battle. Indeed, many pundits thought that United's presence in the FA Cup final was a foregone conclusion.

Irons 2, United 1

The Hammers and United had only met in the FA Cup once, in 1911. The Irons had won 2-1 at Upton Park in a match that was described in *The Mail* of those days as a 'never-to-be-forgotten day for West Ham and all connected with the club'. The football editor of *The Sunday Pictorial* some years later recalled his comments in the *Daily Mirror* at the time of the match; he rated it among the best games he had seen.

United had been League Champions in 1907/08 and had won the cup the following year, defeating Bristol City 1-0. They were League Champions again at the end of the 1910/11 season just a few months after their meeting with the heroic Hammers in the cup. The West Ham XI on 25 February 1911 was: George Kitchen; Jim Rothwell, Aubrey Fairman; Bobby Whiteman, Frank Piercey, Tommy Randall; 'Tiddler' Ashton, Danny Shea, George W. Webb (an England international), George Butcher, Tommy Caldwell.

In those days the home team had to change if there was a colour clash, so, as stated at the time, 'West Ham played in all-white *costumes*'.

Among the visiting team were many notable names: goalkeeper Hugh Edmonds; full-back George Stacey; Dastardly Dick Duckworth at wing half; centre half Charlie Roberts; and a forward line consisting of Billy Meredith, Harold Halse, Sandy Turnbull, Enoch West and George Wall (a left-winger of repute). Roberts, Meredith, Halse and Wall were all internationals.

It was a third-round tie (corresponding to the present fifth round). United had defeated Blackpool 2-1 (the Tangerines conceded choice of ground) and Aston Villa at home by the same score. The Hammers had accounted for Nottingham Forest (2-1, Danny Shea got both goals) and First Division Preston North End (Webb scored a hat-trick without reply from the Whites).

The Manchester side were favourites, being top of the First Division; the Hammers held third place in the Southern League, so were understandably rated as underdogs. However, it was a game that caught the imagination, and the Boleyn Ground was packed with what was then a capacity 20,000 crowd.

In those days there was only one small West Stand, and apart from the east side 'Chicken Run' the remaining parts had no cover. So the fans who could not get into the ground occupied any vantage point they could outside. Panoramic pictures of the vicinity around Upton Park taken that day showed people perched on hoardings, telegraph poles and other vantage points available. But it was also a good-natured occasion with hardly a 'bobby' in sight and reports of the time remarked that 'the spectators got the best shilling's worth of their lives'. Well, the ones who paid did anyway.

George Kitchen was Hammers' star of the match, and it was from one of his clearances that George Webb gathered the ball to make headway; he drew Roberts

Manchester United *v.* West Ham United, 14 March 1964 programme cover.

out of position, passed to Shea, and the diminutive Danny beat Edmonds from just inside the penalty-box.

The visitors equalised before half-time from a corner; the goal was credited to Turnbull, but Kitchen later commented that the United centre forward had pushed him as he was about to clear the ball and used his elbow to score the goal. Apparently the referee, Mr 'Barty' Bamlett, did not have a good game as he disallowed a second-half penalty when Robert shoved Webb off the ball three yards from the goal-line.

With only two minutes remaining on the watch, Manchester United were kicking for touch and looking forward to a replay. These tactics were to lead to the checkmating of the Mancs. Ashton took a quick throw-in to Whiteman, and the left-half booted it across the field when the up-dashing Caldwell hit it first time to score the winner.

The Hammers victory over United in those early years was one of the highlights of the first days of West Ham's history and was just one of a number of stirring cup performances against teams of Football League status that earned West Ham United a nationwide reputation before becoming a League club themselves in 1919.

The disappointed United side were nevertheless effusive in their congratulations and expressed good wishes for West Ham's continuing success in the cup. Alas, it was not to be, and the Hammers fourth First Division opponents of that season, Blackburn Rovers, proved to be too much for the lads from the Southern League, beating West Ham at Upton Park; Butcher scored two and Rovers three.

The Manchester club's consolation was to win the twenty-club First Division with fifty-two points and to become League Champions yet again.

It never rains...

The second FA Cup meeting between the Hammers and United was the twelfth post-war semi-final to be staged at Hillsborough and the third in succession. The ground was being prepared for the 1966 World Cup; after the improvements it would be one of the finest football stadiums in Europe.

West Ham had never figured in a cup semi-final at Hillsborough. The last time the Hammers became semi-finalists was in 1933, when their progress was via: Corinthians, 2-0; West Bromwich Albion (who would finish fourth in the First Division that season), 2-0; from the Third Division South, Brighton and Hove Albion, 2-2 and then in the replay 1-0 (after extra time); and First Division Birmingham City, 4-0. They fell to Everton 2-1 in the semi-final at Wolverhampton. That season saw the Hammers in one of their fights for life in the League. They escaped relegation from the Second Division to the Southern Section by only one point. Unlucky Chesterfield went into the Northern Section with thirty-four points.

The 1964 semi-final was the only real focus for West Ham's young side. They had scored three goals against every club they had faced in the cup, two First and two Second Division sides. However, the team they confronted in the last four of the FA Cup at Hillsborough had caused many to wish that the club, founded in 1877 as Newton Heath, which as a result of bankruptcy failed to pay a gas bill of £6 and got their gas cut off, had not been saved by Mr John Davies, chairman of a Manchester brewery. Since the Second World War Manchester United had won the championship three times and been runners up on five occasions; they would be runners up again in 1964. In the 1963/64 season they had beaten both Tottenham Hotspur and Sporting Lisbon by a 4-1 margin in the European Cup-Winners' Cup. They were the FA Cup holders; they had got to the semi-final stage of the cup half a dozen times since the end of the Second World War and had been finalists on four occasions, last winning the tournament before the 1960s in 1948. West Ham's post-war FA Cup record showed that they had made the sixth round twice, in 1956 and 1963. Since 1946 sixteen Manchester United players had made over 180 England appearances. As they arrived at Hillsborough, West Ham were fourteenth in the League with thirty-two points from thirty-three games; they had scored forty-nine goals and let in forty-nine whilst winning eleven games, drawing ten and losing a dozen. United were in fifth place with forty points from thirty-two outings. They had eighteen victories to their credit, finished equal on four occasions and had experienced ten defeats. United had netted seventy-two times in those games and conceded forty-seven. Guess who were the favourites to get to Wembley in 1964?

Ken Brown recollected:

> In the semi-final we played Manchester United at Sheffield and they'd beaten us easily the week before at Upton Park with half their stars missing. But not in Sheffield, though all their big guns were in.

The entire range of the media agreed that West Ham would not be part of the final. It was thought by many that the Hammers were a team who enjoyed or could only play on firm pitches and as such the weather on the day of the semi-final seemed to confirm the Irons as underdogs. No one gave the East Enders a chance at Hillsborough, as the likes of Denis Law, Pat Crerand and Bobby Charlton were returning to the United side for the game after layoffs.

By 1964, Charlton had established himself as one of the best forwards in Britain and one of the most brilliant footballers in the world. Not only this but he was adaptable too – in the mid-sixties he preferred the centre forward role but had played at outside left for England. Charlton had tremendous speed off the mark, a baffling body swerve, and a deadly shot. Born at Ashington, he was signed by United in 1955. Bobby, a member of a well-known football family, made his senior debut in 1956. The previous season he had a long lay-off after an operation for a hernia but made a sound recovery and played in Manchester United's 1963 cup-winning side.

The game, being played at Hillsborough, was close to Manchester but in those days a long journey from East London. This merely iced the cake of pessimism as far as the Hammers' chances were concerned.

However, following the West Ham club policy of studying opponents, Johnny Byrne and Bobby Moore had been sent to watch United in their sixth-round replay against Sunderland, a side that would be promoted to Division One that year. The two friends told their teammates that they had not been impressed with Busby's side. According to the Irons' spies, the Manchester team performed well enough when they were in the lead, but gave every sign of being a side that might labour to come back in a match should the need arise. However, this was a strange prognosis given Manchester United's recovery in the dying minutes of the sixth-round battles with Sunderland at Old Trafford and Roker Park. When asked about this Byrne told me:

> We had to give the rest of the lads something. You couldn't let us go to Hillsborough thinking we had no chance.

For all this, both Moore and Byrne returned to London eulogising about the young Irish winger, George Best, who had stood out above every other player involved in the quarter-final. A seventeen-year-old Belfast boy, Best had only left home a couple of years earlier but was already being hailed as a genius. At the time he looked a frail waif of a lad and was noted for a disarming modesty, finding it hard to believe that he was the idol people were talking about. Matt Busby was partially right when he said at the time:

> This lad has everything. His temperament is perfect for the job and he has complete confidence. He still prefers to train with the juniors and Denis Law is like an uncle to him and George takes everything in.

This said, Budgie and Bobby were certain that West Ham could defeat the Reds of Manchester. Byrne advised:

> Don't give 'em any space, cut off their ability to run the game, make them follow us.

Eddie Bovington recalled the start of the day of the game:

> I remember waking up on the morning of the game thinking 'Christ almighty'. It hadn't stopped raining for two days!

Byrne recalled the morning of the game:

> I used to room with Ken Brown and I told him when we got up that it had been chucking it down all night. In fact that was the start of the second day of solid rain. On the route from the hotel to Hillsborough we were thinking that the match might be called off, it was pissing down. On the way we saw loads of West Ham supporters, most looking like drowned rats and you thought you had to do something for them. Seeing them motivated us.

Jack Burkett had similar thoughts:

> We were the underdogs and from the hotel to Hillsborough it was absolutely lashing down. We thought the game might be off but the whole route was lined with West Ham supporters and the rain didn't seem to bother them. There was mile after mile of claret-and-blue scarves and rosettes, so it was a case of: if they can do that, then we've got to work twice as hard to give them a result. It spurred everybody on.

Any United team is good, but this was one of the great sides to come out of Old Trafford. Their path to the last four had, on paper, been easier than West Ham's journey. Matt's men had disposed of two Second Division and two Third Division sides:

Southampton	(a)	3-2	Moore, Herd, Crerand
Bristol Rovers	(h)	4-1	Law 3, Herd
Barnsley	(a)	4-0	Best 2, Law, Herd
Sunderland	(h)	3-3	Hurley (og), Charlton, Best
Replay	(a)	2-2	Law, Charlton
Second Replay (at Huddersfield)		5-1	Law 3, Chisnall, Herd

However, the United side had been obliged to work hard to get to Hillsborough. Fierce duels with Sunderland – only ninety seconds of extra time remained when Herd centred into the Sunderland goal-mouth and Charlton headed the ball past Jim Montgomery to make the score 2-2 in the Roker Park replay. At Old Trafford it was a goal four minutes from time by George Best that enabled Manchester United to fight another day. That goal made the result 3-3. Apart from the cup the Reds had been committed to their assault on the League title and the European Cup-Winners' Cup (Manchester United were looking to complete a European Cup-Winners' Cup, FA Cup and Football League Championship treble). This might have been seen to have given West Ham the edge in terms of energy reserves, but United had scored twenty-one goals, better than 3.5 goals a game, on the way to the last four of the FA Cup, conceding just nine. The Hammers had let fewer in, just four, but had managed to score eight goals less than Busby's men. On top of this the Reds' defence looked ominous, including as it did Tony Dunne at left-back. Dunne had been amateur international for the Republic of Ireland before gaining full caps for his country. He was born in Dublin and joined Manchester United from Shelbourne FC in April 1960. Tipping the scales at 11st and standing at 5ft 10ins, Dunne was a neat ball-playing defender, quick to the tackle and skilful in distribution. He could play equally well on either flank. He moved into the senior side when former Hammer Noel Cantwell was ill two seasons before but played alongside Noel in the 1962 FA Cup semi-final and the final of 1963.

Dunne's defensive partner was the 5ft 10ins and 12st right-back Semus Brennan. He had been regarded as something of a utility man with special wing-half effectiveness but converted to defence under the tutelage of Matt Busby. Born in Manchester of Irish parents, Brennan joined the club's ground staff in 1955. He made his first-team debut as an outside left in a fifth-round cup game against Sheffield Wednesday a fortnight after the 1958 Munich air disaster. An Irish Under-19 defender, he was to become a fixture in the international side.

Perhaps most menacing of all the men in red was left half-back Maurice Setters. He was a tenacious, uncompromising wing half who was signed from West Bromwich

Albion in January 1960. Setters began his career with Exeter City and played for England Boys, England Youth and regularly for the England Under-23 team at wing half. He was a 5ft 7ins, 11st 6lbs sledgehammer of a player.

The United attack was perhaps even more threatening. Apart from Charlton, Law and Best, the Reds had Stretford-born Phil Chisnall. He was one of the youngsters Matt Busby had groomed for the Old Trafford side. He was brought into the first team unexpectedly for the quarter-final replay at Sunderland. Phil joined the club's ground staff at the age of fifteen. At 5ft 8ins and 12st 2lbs he was a chunky inside right and another English Under-23 international.

Thank you music lovers...

As the fans were deluged they could look forward to having their spirits raised not only by the promise of a dramatic footballing spectacle but also the half-time musical diversion that had been placed in the hands (or the lungs) of the Dannemora Steel Works Band, which seemed to give the Northerners even more of an advantage, but the pre-match entertainment was provided by the Dagenham Girl Pipers, so this probably evened things up. Johnny Byrne recalled:

> In the tunnel under the stand the United players were busy chatting up the girls in kilts… must have been their sporrans… the United lads didn't seem to care much about the game. I think that might have fired one or two of us up; they didn't seem to be taking us seriously. They were, I think, 3/1 on to beat us and we were 3/1 against to win!

Eddie Bovington saw things much the same way, though there was some disagreement about the odds:

> …when we got to Hillsborough the girl piper band was in the tunnel under the stand. The Man U lads were chatting to them instead of concentrating on the game and I think they thought it was a formality. They definitely took it lightly but nothing's a formality in football. They were something like 6-1 on to win; even we believed they'd beat us. But we did our best and they soon found out it wasn't going their way.

Underway, under water

Ken Brown recalled the conditions in understated fashion:

> … the pitch was really muddy… but you could still play.

According to Eddie Bovington,

> … the pitch was a bit of a joke… puddles and mud all over the place. How we finished and how the teams made it such a good game is a mystery really.

The rain that had been saturating Sheffield as the West Ham side had awoken that morning was still pelting down as the teams took to the field at Hillsborough and as the referee blew the wet out of his whistle for the start of the game the 65,000 supporters (West Ham and United had been allocated 20,000 tickets each) were more than thoroughly drenched, having paid from 5s to £2 6s a ticket for the privilege.

The Hammers' fans had made the pilgrimage from East London by car, train and twelve coaches that had left Upton Park at midnight the evening before the match. The coach convoy had arrived in Sheffield at 8 a.m. The passengers had seen very little more than flooded fields as dawn had broken through the dark clouds before they were expelled from their transport to get fully wet through in the day-long downpour, wandering like depressed ducks around the swampy 'Steel Town' streets. The rumour that persisted years after that many returned to London with webbed feet has never been substantiated.

There was no respite once in the stadium. The West Ham fans were at the Kop end, which was uncovered. Those who got in two hours before the kick-off (and there were many… I was one) were able to watch the on-field entertainment of the Hillsborough ground staff frantically forking the pitch in a desperate attempt to drain the playing area. But this had no more than a minimal effect as the sky continued to pour out a torrent, like a gigantic, relentless waterfall.

On the pitch the players were literally paddling in the liquid mud. There had been a brief let-up in the inundation just before the game started and this had persuaded the referee, Mr Ken 'I don't care what the weatherman says' Stokes, to allow the match to be played. Stokes, who hailed from Newark, was a foreman electrician at Ollerton Colliery. He had been in soccer all his life. Educated in Worksop, he had played football throughout his school career. On leaving the world of childhood learning Kenny entered into local competitive matches with enthusiasm, but an illness and an operation ended his playing days in 1947. However, within a year he was back in the game again as a referee, having passed his examination within the monastic-like brotherhood that was the Nottingham Football Association at the age of twenty-eight. Two years later he broke into the heady heights of the Class 1 refereeing inner sanctum. He steadily increased his status, graduating through the local minor Leagues, the Midland Counties Mid-week League, the Midland League and finally was appointed to the nomenclature of the Supplementary List of the Football League. That was in 1956. In 1963 he was placed on the 'Hekel' of the 'Full List', the Nirvana and Valhalla of refereeing practice. He had been in charge of the first-leg FA Youth Cup final at Chelsea in 1961. However, meteorology did not appear to be his strong point. Bobby Moore had the habit of putting Vaseline on his forehead, just above the eyebrows, to stop sweat running into his eyes, but before he and Denis Law had tossed-up the water was running down Moore's face in small torrents.

Just a few minutes into the match the twenty-two players on the Hillsborough pitch were covered in mud (it looked slightly worse on the 'Reds' who that day had started as 'the whites', the Hammers wore their light blue shirts with the two claret hoops around the chest). Manchester United, who many saw as a stronger and more physical side than the Irons, might have been seen to have been favoured by the conditions; the midfield especially would have been demanding for even the hardiest. Yet from the moment West Ham kicked off, playing towards the Leppings Lane end, they worked together with a great deal of confidence, playing above themselves, depriving the opposition of the ball. Johnny Byrne recalled:

> We liked to play football, we were a footballing side; the mud didn't make much difference to that. Bovington marked Charlton and Ken Brown was on Denis Law. Jim Standen was solid in goal whilst me and Geoff worked well up front.

The Hammers certainly adapted to the muddy conditions much better than their counterparts in the Manchester team. Bobby Moore was dominating the field, marshalling Bond, Bovington, Brown and Burkett to generate a resilient defence. John Bond told me:

> It was the kind of game where it was crucial to score the first goal. Bestie hit the crossbar from about twenty yards and early on both sides came close, but at half-time no one had scored…

Sissons was doing a great job against the intimidating Crerand, and Hurst brought a magnificent save from Dave Gaskill in the United goal. Gaskell, a native of Wigan, was not a big man for a goalkeeper (5ft 10ins and 12st 2lbs). He had blossomed out of the Old Trafford ground staff before becoming a professional at Old Trafford in 1957. A former England Schoolboy and Youth international, he made his League debut in November 1957. Over the previous two years Gaskell competed with Irish international Harry Gregg for the place between the United posts.

When the teams came out for the second forty-five minutes every player on the park seemed determined to break the stalemate, but it was the Irons' twenty-one-year-old inside right Ron Boyce who scored when, just over ten minutes into the second half he looked up to see the United 'keeper off his line. Ron knew of Gaskill's propensity to do this and from just over halfway inside the United half he lofted a shot past the stranded 'keeper into the top left-hand corner of the net.

Boyce recalled:

> The first was a shot from about twenty-five yards… I really got hold of it!

With Byrne looking the best centre forward in England, West Ham made it 2-0 when Sissons, seeing Jack Burkett running towards him, intended to cut a short corner back to the Hammers' full-back. The West Ham wing-man saw Pat Crerand coming back across the field to watch Jack.

Patrick Crerand was signed from Glasgow Celtic in February 1963 for £56,000. He was a Scottish international with fine ball control and excellent distribution skills, yet, at the same time, he was always strong in the tackle. He developed a great understanding with Denis Law. Crerand was at his best in an attacking role, but he also excelled in sweeping passes to the wings and the swift through pass. He was 5ft 10ins and 11st 10lbs. Sissons knew that if he let Crerand know what he was going to do the Scot would put a stop to it.

So the West Ham flanker shaped up as if he was about to take a conventional corner. Seeing this, Crerand moved back to the middle. Sisson recalled:

> Pat had to do that, he had to cover the corner, but I sent a short ball to Burkett.

Picking up the Sissons pass, 'Jack-the-lad' contrived a curling, shoulder-high centre, which was met, on the six-yard line, central to the goal, by the head of Boyce, who had expertly timed his run. The glancing contact went in just inside Gaskell's far post. Jack Burkett pulled the years back,

> I'd been marking David Herd and Willie Morgan, but I remember going up into the penalty area and laying on a chance for Ronnie Boyce to make it 2-0.

Boyce, who had netted just five in the League that season prior to the semi-final, reflected on the sweet irony of the moment:

> It was the only time I ever scored twice in a match! Even I couldn't believe it!

The goal had 'Made in Chadwell Heath' written all over it; it was a West Ham training ground special that delighted Ron Greenwood. In a seven-minute period during the first twenty minutes of the second half, West Ham had taken control. As his teammates slapped Boyce's soggy shirt after the second, Wembley seemed a certainty. Then United went into overdrive and laid siege to the West Ham goal. But the cockney boys defended like demons until, with only fifteen minutes to go, Jim Standen went face first into the mud as Law piled into the Hammers goal-warden with a two-footed tackle. Johnny Byrne recollected the moment:

> Jim was a bit dazed, the mud had got into his eyes. John Sissons got a bucket of water and he washed some of the mud away, but he still wasn't seeing straight when the game restarted.

By this time the pitch was a sea of slime. Ken Brown recalled the next critical move:

> I remember putting the ball on a mound for John Bond to take a free kick just outside our box and he just kicked right under it and they scored.

Bond had opted to take the kick to give the ailing Standen some recovery time. The wearying 'Muffin' as the Hammers veteran defender was known, was, as his nickname indicated, one of the most powerful strikers of the ball in the game, but one is not allowed mistakes. From the terraces it was clear that Bond knew, almost from the moment he struck the ball, that he had mis-hit it. In fact, his foot had made more of a connection with Brown's mud pie than the ball. Bond's face and shoulders dropped in a blast of disbelief, disappointment, embarrassment and sudden exhaustion as, in a trice, from a West Ham perspective, the worst person on the pitch to pick it up, was in possession of the ball. Without hesitation, Best passed to Phil Chisnall who sent over a cross that connected with the head of United's inside left Denis Law, for once free of Ken Brown's custodial presence. Law out-jumped the still dizzy Standen and, after seventy-eight minutes, United were back in the game. During much of the 1960s many believed Law to be the best inside forward in the world. United paid the Italian club Torino a British-record fee of £115,000 for him in July 1962. Dennis was not, at 5ft 10ins and 11st, intimidating physically, but he had a mean psychological streak that was propounded by his magnificence as a ball player, his superb marksmanship and natural opportunism. He had a maturity beyond his years, to such an extent that Busby made him captain of the team. Born at Aberdeen, Law joined Huddersfield Town as a sixteen year old and within a year was being heralded as a star of the future. He was transferred to Manchester City in March 1960, for a fee of £55,000, from whence he would move for his brief sojourn in Italy.

Johnny Byrne reflected on how United got back into the game:

> Jim hadn't even seen Best's cross coming in. Bondy had said 'leave it to me' and then gave the ball away. Poor old John got a right bollocking from everyone.

For Eddie Bovington:

> When Law scored with a header you thought they were going to come back.

The idea of extra time in the conditions would have been unthinkable. At the same time, if the game had gone to a replay it would have happened at St Andrews the following Wednesday at 7.30 p.m., and the pitch there was not a wholesome thought, given that the other semi-final at Villa Park had also been something of an aquatic event.

In the Hillsborough commentary box Wally Barnes, who was covering the match for radio was euphoric at the Reds' resurrection. Showing the usual media bias for Manchester United and against West Ham, at one point he threw any notion of impartiality to the wind saying, 'Man United will definitely get back into it now, West Ham look downhearted'.

But just seconds later a ball broke loose on the left, inside West Ham's half. It was near enough to the touchline for Pat Crerand to decide that Moore couldn't reach it in time, or, if he did, that Bobby would have no room to go past him. With the mud making quick changes of direction almost impossible, Crerand was too late to move when Moore got to the ball and hit it past the tough Caledonian right half on the outside and then running past him in a curve which took Moore over the touchline and back onto the field of play. Fending off two challenges, Moore somehow kept the ball live, the Hammer's skipper took it along the line for about thirty yards before hitting a perfect low pass into the gap vacated by the Manchester pivot, Bill Foulkes, who had moved wide to cover Moore's surge upfield, ahead of Geoff Hurst, who, as usual, had made himself space to run on to the ball. The big striker tore through the gap vacated by Foulkes to strike the ball low and hard, wide and right of Gaskell from the edge of the penalty area. Ronnie Boyce remembered the release of pressure as the ball crossed the line:

> I felt really relieved when Geoff scored his goal. It was a bit like the third goal he scored in the World Cup final.

It was still raining as Hurst was mobbed by his muddy colleagues. A minute later, with United giving everything to attack, Hurst nearly grabbed a fourth goal. Ken Brown looked back:

> Geoff had beaten Gaskill to the ball, but the mud was so heavy that it didn't have the legs to get over the line. It got stuck!

At last the final whistle shrieked through the wall of water signalling that West Ham had reached Wembley for the first time in forty-one years. At the same time the

Hammers had belied their reputation for being a team that could only play football on the firm, flat pitches of autumn and spring. Moore had been central to the whole affair, fending off attack after attack and making the last goal of the game. Boyce had seemingly covered every inch of the field. He did not score many. In all his 339 outings for West Ham he netted just twenty-nine times, but he had chosen the right first time to score two goals in a match in a major competition; he would never do it again. Eddie Bovington had shackled Charlton whilst Budgie had linked everything together and the West Ham fans went home sodden but delighted.

Have You Seen the Muffin Man?

John Bond was a wonderful kicker of the ball… he could find me with fifty-yard passes regularly. At times his dribbling skill was as good as any you could find. He was confident and strong, a great player to have on your side.
Johnny Byrne – West Ham United and England

John Bond signed professional with West Ham in March 1950, after a spell as an amateur at Upton Park. He had made more than 350 cup and League appearances up to the FA Cup final of 1964. He had toured South Africa with the FA in 1956 and had played for England 'B' and Football League sides. Bond had a kick like a donkey and could hit a dead-ball harder than any player one might care to nominate, hence his nickname 'Muffin'.

West Ham ran out at Highfield Road on 9 February 1952 with the nineteen-year-old John Bond in the centre of the defence in a tough-looking side that secured West Ham's second and last away win of the season. Jim Barrett and Bert Hawkins did the damage, giving West Ham a 2-1 victory, doing a Second Division double over Coventry City, who were bound for relegation. John Bond looked back at that, his first match for the Hammers:

> I played at left-back against a fella called Warner, a winger. One half of the pitch, straight down the length, was frozen over, so you couldn't stand up. The other half was soft; they had a big stand at Coventry that overshadowed one half of the pitch. We had to stand along the side of the pitch in great big roll-neck sweaters for a minute's silence, because the King had died.

On that day, a brief bulletin on the railings of Buckingham Palace announced that the King had died peacefully in his sleep. Britain now had a Queen. The young Princess Elizabeth and her husband the Duke of Edinburgh were on a tour of the Commonwealth, including Australia, when her father died. They had to cut their tour short immediately and return to Britain. She was twenty-five and had inherited one of the most demanding jobs in the world.

John told me about a communication he received following the game at Coventry:

> I've got a letter to this day from Ted Fenton (the West Ham manager at the time) saying, 'You must be absolutely delighted with the way you played. Harry Kinsell is fit and I'm bringing him back'!

Bond had been a student of football from his earliest days and had watched the giant-killers of his young days, Colchester United, train, which was when he first came to the notice of Ted Fenton, who had taken over as manager of the Essex boys after finishing up as a player with West Ham. John joined West Ham from Colchester Casuals as an amateur in 1950. He was the first of the successful 1960s side to arrive at Upton Park. John explained how his fifteen-year association with the Hammers began:

> Ted was an army bloke, he was interested in the cadet force. I didn't want to get into uniform, but you used to have to attend once a week to allow you to play for the army cadet force. Ted was involved and he saw me play whilst he was at Colchester, he asked me to sign up for them. When he went to West Ham he asked me to come and sign up there. I wasn't approached by anyone else; he was the only one who saw anything in me.

John came from a poor rural background, in the days when mid-Essex was still a long way from London. He carries an Essex country accent that is all but extinct. He went on:

> My parents never had a penny. I had to borrow my brother's overcoat to go and sign on. It was a big black thing with one of them tie-up belts. West Ham started me on £6 a week. On the Saturday my sister was getting married. I played in a five-a-side and got injured, I hurt me ankle. I asked Ted Fenton if I could go home for my sister's wedding. He said, 'I hope you don't make that bloody ankle an excuse. You can't play so you can go home to your sister's wedding.'

That was accusing John of lying, something few people would do today. John Bond could be accused of many things, but honesty and frankness are tangible qualities in the man. He continued:

> I never thought about it to years afterwards. How naïve I looked. Before I signed for West Ham Ted came round to my parents' house in a little place

called Stanway, just outside of Colchester. He told my mother and father what it would be like, 'we'll teach him to live in hotels', and all this business. Years after I understood all that. I'd never been in a hotel or lived away from home.

John said this with some incredulity in his voice:

My mother, in the summer, used to go apple picking, just down the end of our road. I went back on the Monday morning and she used to give me a bag of apples to take to Ted Fenton. I used to go into the ground and walk straight up into his office and give him this bag of apples. When I think back to that it makes me cringe. Can you imagine that happening today?

There were no cars, everybody had bikes. It was all very sparse. The first car I ever got was a 1937 Vauxhall, with a running board on it and everything. You thought you were the King of England in that. My dad worked in the sandpit, shovelling sand. He was as strong as an ox. He used to do that all day then come home and dig the garden. We had a massive big garden. Bless his heart; he died just before he was ninety.

I went to Stanway School. I'd go down the garden, pop under the hedge, and I was in the school. I played for the school. I played my first game for the school and of course, my mother couldn't afford a pair of football boots. I had to wear the boots I went to school in. It was raining and slippery as could be, I had no studs! Mr Gibbons was our teacher: he said, 'Bond would have been all right if he could have stood up, he kept sliding and slipping all over'.

My brother, Roland, was a big influence on me. He was brilliant. All the boys round where I lived didn't have 'thrappence' to their name and I was the only one who had a football, he bought that and my boots.

A few weeks before my dad died he gave my mum a hundred quid that he'd saved, that's as much as he'd ever saved in his life. It never done him an ounce of good. She used to get the money, gave him about two quid a week. He'd saved a hundred pounds! My mother died the day before her ninety-seventh birthday. She looked after herself right up until she died. Her sister died when she was 105. I have two brothers and a sister. My older brother played for Colchester Casuals too.

John looked back on the training facilities in his first years at Upton Park with the wonder the past brings to the present:

There was only two or three balls in the entire club. You got out for training about quarter past ten and run round and round the pitch, run a lap and walk a lap. I used to run with a little fella called Terry Woodgate. You'd be doing this

> for about three-quarters-of-an-hour and then you'd shout to Billy Moore to get the balls out. Billy would be standing at the entrance to the ground watching, with a fag in his mouth, that he never ever took out. He used to say, 'just do another one', then all of a sudden he'd come out and throw two balls out, and there'd be thirty or forty people there.

John met his wife Janet during 1951 in Oxford whilst he was in the army. They married in 1953. Later on, John did his bit in terms of bringing new ideas to West Ham and football in general. For example, the 'attacking full-back' that became the 'overlapping defender' and eventually metamorphosed into 'the wing-back' was not a continental import, according to John:

> We started the idea of raiding full-backs, Noel [Cantwell] and myself.

However, it wasn't all driven by innate genius:

> I didn't want to defend. I hated it. I was always keen to get forward. The hard point about the game from my point of view was running. I didn't like running really. If I could have stood still to play the game I'd have been a happy soul. It was always an effort. The ball wasn't a problem. If the ball came to me in the penalty area, it didn't matter if there were twenty people in there, I'd pull it down, and, without being big-headed, invariably I'd be able to do it. Sometimes you'd make a ricket. Ted Fenton, bless his heart, would accept all of that. I think, to an extent, he used to live off of it. He used to like it really. He liked seeing it. We were his boys. He brought Noel over from Ireland, me down from Colchester.

One person who, at times, didn't enjoy this type of play at all was the man who so often stood behind Cantwell and Bond, Ernie Gregory. Any spectator close enough to the West Ham goal might have heard some colourful language directed at the two full-backs as they skipped and danced around in his area. Gregory probably appreciated their skill but nevertheless never lost his goalkeeper's instinct to encourage his defenders to get the ball away.

John and Noel Cantwell would always be ready to test their skills in the forward line:

> When he got into trouble Ted used to put me up front. I scored a hat-trick against Chelsea. We were 2-0 down and ended up winning 4-2. A free kick, a penalty and a header. And I got two against Bolton. Ted was going to pull me off at Leicester and all of a sudden I blasted one into the top corner of the net.

Apart from his Division Two Championship medal of 1957/58, John had been part of the West Ham side to finish runners-up in the LFA Cup in 1958/59, and the winning Southern Floodlight Cup team of 1956 (he was also in the West Ham XI that finished runners-up in that competition in 1960).

A lot of West Ham supporters thought that John should have played for England. He must have been one of the best uncapped full-backs of his era. He was a quality defender with a devastating shot. However, John provided some insights into the situation:

> The press put other people forward, the likes of Jimmy Armfield and Don Howe and people like that played for England and I didn't. I went on an FA tour of South Africa in '55/56. The following year I went up to Manchester with the England squad, trained with Tom Finney, to do with the '58 World Cup. I played for a Football League team at Windsor Park; this included Ron Flowers and Johnny Haynes and all them. Bernard Joy wrote in the *Evening Standard*, 'John Bond secures his World Cup place'. I played well. I stayed at Bangor in Northern Ireland. After the game we went back to this hotel in Bangor, it was a time in English football when Joe Richards was top man, there used to be a committee of people going with the England set-up. We were having a drink and all of a sudden the bartender told us that we couldn't have any more drinks. That was only my first or second representative game, remember. I said, 'Can't we take some up to our room? Can't you get a crate of beer so we can have a few drinks in our room?' I was one of the newcomers in the side and all the committee people were sitting around there. The barman said, 'You can't do that'. I never played another representative game.
>
> Ron Greenwood was involved with the FA, with Walter Winterbottom, who was in charge of the team at that time. When Ron Greenwood came to West Ham he told me that story. He knew exactly what happened and exactly why I didn't play anymore. But I suppose it's like if people do things today, people step out of line, but perhaps they're a bit more lenient today.
>
> I knew I was good enough to play. I was every bit as good as Jimmy Armfield and Don Howe. I knew what I could and couldn't do. There was no point in me complaining or condemning anybody else. The only person to blame for all of that was me; one hundred per cent me.

John was a popular player at Upton Park, he knew the people well, living in the area and working in a local school:

> I used to do a bit of coaching at Stepney Green. Ron Greenwood said when he first come to the club that I was, what was the word?... something like an idol, at West Ham. It's in his book. That was because I got on famous with

the supporters. I used to do things like I'd dribble in me own area. I'd chip balls back over people's head into Ernie's arms in a crowded goalmouth. I'd go rampaging up, having shots at goal. I think that they liked that. They liked someone being free and easy and adventurous. I was naïve enough to think, 'Oh sod it. I'll keep doing it'. I got on well with the 'Chicken Run'. I remember one day that they were moaning and groaning, we weren't doing very well, and I just shouted to them, 'The lot of yer go home. Nobody asked you to come here. Why don't you go home if you don't like it? Piss off home!' They didn't give me any stick for saying that, they didn't say, 'f— off Bondy', or anything like that. They just laughed. That was them and us together again. That's how things used to be with us.

It wasn't all football though:

We used to have the odd session at the Central. The social life was pretty good. I was always good friends with Noel. Nothing got on my nerves. The club wasn't quite as big as Manchester United, Newcastle or Arsenal, but given the opportunity, given my time again, I'd still play for West Ham United Football Club. It was a good homely sort of club. I don't like using the word, because I wasn't interested in going to West Ham because it was homely, I was interested because I wanted to play football at the top level, but it was a homely, nice club. The people were good.

I was one of the foursome. I was one really who played with Ted Fenton all that time ago, with Malcolm Allison, with Noel and Jackie Dick, at the start of the Bobby Moore era. When they all went, I still remained at the club. Then I spent quite a few years with Mooro and Hursty and Peters. Martin Peters was the best player I played with. He was different class. Hursty was good but he was a run-of-the-mill wing half, he was a handful-and-a-half of a striker to play against.

John recalled the arrival of Ron Greenwood:

Our first game under Ron was a 1-1 draw with Manchester City at Upton Park. Then we went up to Burnley and drew two each. We stayed at Porthcawl for a couple of days and then we played at Cardiff on the Saturday, the last but one game of the season. That's where the confrontation started between Greenwood and meself. Phil Woosnam was also left out, he hadn't played at Burnley because he was injured. We were training on the Friday morning, prior to the Cardiff game on the Saturday, when Ron Greenwood pulled me over and said, 'I'm not playing you tomorrow.' I said, 'What do you mean you're not playing me?' He said, 'I'm going to leave you out.' I said, 'But I'm fit.' He said, 'I know that, but I'm the manager and I can do what I like. I'm not playing yer.' I said, 'You're playing Phil Woosnam.' He said, 'That's right, but I want to bring Phil Woosnam back and I don't want to bring you back.' So, I had all sorts of confrontations that year. They then wanted me to leave the football club. I could have gone to QPR. I'll always remember I stood in the roller-rink in Forest Gate on a Monday morning, when we were training there; he pulled me over and said, 'What yer doing? Are you going to QPR?' I said, 'No.' And he said, 'You'll have to take the consequences.' I said, 'I'm prepared to do that.'

So, I then played for eighteen months in the 'A' team. I was a senior player at the time. I had played more games than anybody else and I was just left out of the side. All the wives and all the players got took to America that summer. We got to the sixth round of the FA Cup against Liverpool. West Ham took all the wives up there, Janet and I didn't go. I used to play at the Isle of Sheppy and places like that. I'd played 300 odd games for West Ham. That was him saying, 'You're not going to start to get the better of me.'

One day, I walked down the passageway from Thorne Road, where I was living, and it just struck me, 'it's not Ron Greenwood who's at fault, it's you. Get yourself sorted out.' From then my approach to everything changed. I'd play in the 'A' team and I'd try for me life. I'd train, I never spoke to anybody about it, it was just me, and it was me who confronted it, and sorted it out. Sometime after that I was in the treatment room at West Ham with Bill Jenkins and Ron Greenwood came in and asked if I would like to come to Aston Villa. We won that game and I scored the goal. From there I never looked back. From there on in, I idolised the man. I keep wanting to and never do it, go down and see him. There are two people in my life that are real heroes. One is Lester Piggott and the other is Ron Greenwood. I'd love just to go down and talk to him because he stimulated my brain so much in terms of football, more than anybody. More than Malcolm Allison and Malcolm did a good job.

From being a thirty-one year old when he came to the football club and thinking I knew everything, I found I knew absolutely nothing. He taught me all about the game, about coaching. Ron sorted my life out in terms of my personality and things like that and how to behave and everything. A while ago I got a note from Mickey McGuire. He used to play for me at Norwich. He was writing in the Norwich programme, saying that John Bond was ahead of his times in terms of his coaching, but if I'd have never have met Ron Greenwood I wouldn't have known anything about it.

I was as good a kicker of the ball as you could find in English football, and they are not just my words. They used to call me 'Muffin' because of the way I kicked the ball.

John 'Muffin the Mule' Bond looked like the unyielding old-style full-back, but he didn't play like one. However, the gift to 'bang the ball' didn't mean that John lacked accuracy:

> I could also drop 'em where I wanted to drop 'em. But I didn't take hints. I didn't take things seriously enough at times and I didn't know what life was really all about. Therein lies my weakness. I was an old country boy.

According to Bond's long-time defensive partner Noel Cantwell:

> It is easy to see John Bond as a sort of 'rock-solid' right-back. But he was much more than this. He was one of the first defenders who would look to play his way out of his own penalty area rather than just booting the ball out of harm's way. He wanted to be creative.

And he was: up to the cup final of 1964 he had scored thirty-one goals in his West Ham career, sometimes playing as an emergency centre forward, to prove the point.

In Defence of Preston

One time defenders just defended; stopped attackers. But the modern game requires defenders to be the first part of the attack. When you see all things as one, stop breaking things up into separate parts, then you are onto something.
Jimmy Milne – Preston North End

The Preston defence during the cup run of 1964 was one of the keys to the side's success. Scotsman George Ross was a commanding influence in that protective carapace and alongside Nobby Lawton, Andy Singleton and Jimmy Smith there seemed to be no real chink in the Whites' armour. The latter made the final not having played in the FA Cup since Preston's third-round game with Nottingham Forest. He may not have had the tackling power of his defensive partner George Ross, but as a converted wing half during the 1963/64 season, he used the ball well. Jim was another versatile Scot, able to play half-back, left-back or centre half; in fact he played in five different positions for North End, including an inglorious trial at centre forward in the relegation season of 1960/61.

Jim was tall and good in the air, but the way he swept the ball accurately up-field stamped him as one of the modern breed of backs. He was a creator as well as a destroyer of attacks. Preston signed Jimmy in 1955 from Scottish Junior Club Arbroath Lads, his home-town side, for a nominal fee. He made his League debut at the age of twenty-one in the 4-3 home defeat by Manchester United on 13 December 1958.

Gordon Milne had been called up to play for the British Army in Paris and Frank O'Farrell switched to right half so that Smith could occupy his normal left half position.

Jim had played over 100 games in the first team by 1964. Whilst in the Forces he had been selected to play for the British Army both at centre half and wing half. He had made an almost miraculous recovery from a serious ankle injury sustained at Craven Cottage in 1961 that had caused him to miss thirty-one of the remaining thirty-two matches that season, leaving his future in doubt. He returned to the game as strong and as forceful a player has he had been prior to his lay-off.

Born in Inverness on 15 April 1943, full-back George Ross joined the Deepdale youth squad on 15 September 1958 after playing wing half for the Scottish juvenile team Hilton Athletic. He was one of the stars in the successful side that reached the final of the FA Youth Cup, only to lose over two legs to Chelsea. He made his League debut for North End in the First Division against Nottingham Forest at Deepdale on Boxing Day 1960. He matured swiftly and by the 1961/62 term he found himself a regular in the Preston first team and formed a fine partnership with fellow Scot Willie Cunningham. When Cunningham retired, Ross took over the number two shirt, although he was capable of covering either full-back role. By 1964 George had notched up more than 100 games in Preston colours and was on the fringes of the Scotland squad. At twenty-one Ross was swift for a back, a very fierce tackler and exceptionally clever in his positional play. In three years he had missed only five games.

Throughout their long history, Preston had produced many outstanding Scots: Peter McBride, Nick Ross, David McLean, Jack Gordon and Dave Russel were exceptional in the pre-Second World War period. Between the wars there was Bill (then called Will) Shankly, Andrew and Bobby Beattie, George Mutch, Jimmy Milne himself of course, Tom Smith and the immortal Alex James. Tommy Docherty, Joe Dunn, Willie Cunningham and Willie Forbes carried the tradition on after the Second World War. George Ross was to be another in this troop of tartan heroes.

John Donnelly came into the Preston side as a replacement for Ian Davidson in the quarter-final against Oxford. He was born in Broxburn on 17 December 1936 and had come to North End from Celtic. He was quick in the tackle and used the ball to good advantage. Donnelly kept his place for the semi-final against Swansea but was kept out of the final by Jimmy Smith.

George Ross.

The Time After Victory

The immediate moments after victory are precious and hard to recall. Exhaustion and elation are natural if ill-suited bedfellows, and different individuals and groups find their own way of dealing with and expressing that no man's land of time that spans the void between breaking through to a final and the playing of the same. Of course, for the vanquished the feelings are different. For Noel Dwyer, the Swansea Town goalkeeper, the defeat of his side had added significance:

> If we had won, and I think we could have done, it would have meant meeting with West Ham at Wembley. It would have been good to have met them in the semi, but even better in the final. If we had got to the final I think we might have beaten West Ham. But it was not to be.

Matt Busby was to say that the loss to West Ham was one of his greatest disappointments and biggest surprises.

Preston had shown huge strength and character at Villa Park, but the prospect of the FA Cup final seemed to distract them from the need to get out of Division Two. A disastrous 4-0 defeat at Sunderland brought North End down hard, but six points out of six at Easter put them back into the fight for promotion. Unfortunately, just one point from the next half-dozen matches left them in third place at the end of the Second Division campaign with fifty-six points, five behind Sunderland and seven behind Leeds United. Preston's points total would have seen them promoted in 1962 '63 '65 '66, and ten years later third place would have ensured promotion. It cannot be know'n how much this might have cost Preston, but cup final glory almost certainly robbed North End of years of sustained growth.

But Preston were the first Second Division side to make it to an FA Cup final for fifteen years. Their fortunes had been turned around by the events of 1963/64. After having reduced the playing staff by seventeen to cut costs to match what had become an almost breadline income, Jimmy Milne had bought wisely, blending experience with potential and achieved much more than anyone could have reasonably expected. Getting to the FA Cup final and being involved in the promotion race to the last ditch had resulted in a financial windfall for Deepdale to offset the deficit of over £30,000 from 1962/63. It is probably no exaggeration to say that Milne had saved the club. Every time I have visited Deepdale over the best part of the last forty years, I always feel that Preston North End should honour the memory of Jimmy Milne and what he did for the club. Liverpool and Leeds built statues in memory of Bill Shankly and Billy Bremner, respectively but with the greatest respect to these giants from different sides of the Pennines, who contributed so much to the clubs that are synonymous with their names, Milne did more for Preston. As such, it would be fitting for the rather anonymous 'Deepdale' to be placed aside for the sake of bringing the *Jimmy Milne Stadium* into existence. Unfortunately, as modern business interests kick in, it seems football stadiums will no longer be honouring the champions of the game; those responsible continue to sell the soul of the game, preferring the fickle sponsorship of spiritually inane corporate epithets, the likes of *Emirates*, *JJB* and *MacAlpine* to inspire them rather than names as large and as iconoclastically idiomatic as Jimmy Milne.

Straight after the victory over Swansea, in Preston the demand for cup final tickets began to be the town's obsession. As is always the way, those who wanted to go to Wembley far outnumbered the allocated number of tickets. Concern focusing the distribution of tickets was widespread.

All over bar the shouting

For Peter Brabrook,

> Having made the final, though, you suddenly start thinking 'Cor, we've got to win this now!' You think you won't have any pressure when you get to Wembley, but having come all that way we wanted to win and it was very hard.
>
> We were big favourites against Preston and after the semi-final the boot was firmly on the other foot.

Eddie Bovington recalled:

> I remember waking up the day after the semi and reading the papers in bed. I kept re-reading them because I still couldn't believe it!

Johnny Byrne recaptured the moment after the West Ham–Manchester United semi-final:

> We hardly believed we'd won. It was a great feeling. We'd made the final!

After the match with United, Ron Greenwood was verbose and emotional about his team:

> Look at them; this is the greatest day in their lives. I have been proud to be associated with this bunch of youngsters. Now the world and his friend will claim them. I accept that this must happen, but I will not let the leeches, hangers-on, glad-handers destroy what they have built for themselves. I will

> do everything I can to protect them from the wrong sort of reaction to this success.

The celebrations continued long after the game and well into Sunday. In the excitement, the team coach transporting the players had departed from Hillsborough for the short trip to Sheffield railway station without Ron Greenwood, who was involved in an interview with the BBC, but he met up again with his players for the journey back to St Pancras. However, the manager was the only one hoping to have a quiet meal on the train home. Ronnie Boyce remembered:

> The fans were as excited as us and a lot got into our carriage to join the party. There was a photo on the wall of Rob Jenkins [the club physio]'s clinic in Green Street, it's of us on the train coming back from Sheffield. I've got a cut lip! I've got no idea how that happened.

For Eddie Bovington,

> We had a marvellous trip back on the train. The fans were unbelievable and the train ride home was fantastic. It was like a party and in our wildest dreams we never believed it would happen. For me, it was an unbelievable feeling, but then you start thinking 'will you play in the final?'

Perhaps the most relieved man on the way home was John Frederick Bond. His one mistake had caused a lot of heart fluttering, but he had played as well as any West Ham player. Bond was a cavalier full-back as good as any defender in the League for the ten years up to the mid-1960s. At 6ft 2ins and 14st the claret-and-blue right-back was the longest-serving player in the West Ham side. John had almost left Upton Park in 1963 when he seemed destined for a move to Queens Park Rangers or Brentford. After West Ham's glorious semi-final victory he was heard to remark:

> Just think, it might have been Walsall, not Wembley.

And to Bond,

> The journey home that night was great. It was better than winning the final.

The West Ham party, who had been ensconced in their reserved dining carriage, celebrated hard and long with jubilant fans and officials. Johnny Byrne reflected:

> The cup meant more then I think. Well, it was probably the biggest competition in the world at that time. Not like now.

Eddie Bovington was also aware of the enormity of it all:

> When I was a kid at home kicking a ball against the wall, I always thought I'd love to play in a cup final. It was the only game they showed on TV then and I watched them all. It was such a big event.

So the celebrations were justified; Johnny Byrne continued:

> We were all in the restaurant car trying to eat, but it was packed with people. West Ham fans were always great. It wasn't about winning and losing. They laid into you at times, but they always gave you credit for trying.

Few Hammers' fans got home before one the next morning, some weren't seen for days, and one or two were never seen again!

The match had been a footballing success, despite the awful conditions, but it had also been a financial triumph. The gross receipts for the game were £32,680, the same as the previous year's semi-final between Liverpool and Leicester City that had been an English record for a match other than a cup final or international.

The Hillsborough semi-final had been a game won on and off the field. Ronnie Boyce recalled:

> No one gave us much chance of beating United when it came to the semi-final at Hillsborough.

But Ron Greenwood used the 'nothing to lose' ethos to transfer the weight of pressure to win on the mighty Reds. Boyce reflected:

> Ron didn't have to motivate us in the dressing room before the game. He was shrewd and good with tactics. He got us to see that with them having the talent that they had we couldn't give them space. He encouraged us to play when we got the ball. But the pitch was horrible. I don't think they would have played the game on a pitch like that nowadays. But we got on with it I suppose better than they did.

The best ever Hammers

That semi-final will always stand as one of West Ham's finest-ever ninety minutes. Beating Manchester United is a big event in the history of any team, but to knock them out of the FA Cup at the semi-final stage is a rare achievement for any English club, and not many West Ham players thought that it was possible. Johnny Byrne recalled the attitude:

> Most of the blokes thought that the draw against United was just the end of a good run, especially as they had beaten us the week before. But I never believed that we couldn't win. Greenwood has to take a lot of the credit. He'd tell us the obvious, like, 'When you're on the ball and space is not in front of you, it's behind you' – it seems a stupid thing to say, but it often takes a genius to see the simplest things. He was big on 'taking the ball on the half-turn'. If you could do that it gave you that split-second advantage. He liked to open sides up. He loved the game and was the best coach in England in his time – few have ever bettered him. He wasn't really like an English coach. He had much more in common with continental managers. He liked his sides to play the European sides and learn from them and he'd go through things we picked up at Chadwell Heath. We were doing things then that clubs like Arsenal and Chelsea have just started doing. Playing the 4-4-2 we were thought of as a European side. For Ron the most important things in his life were his family and football and that was part of the reason why I thought we could do United.

Everything after the Hillsborough triumph, maybe even the FA Cup final itself, was going to be an anti-climax for the Boleyn Boys.

West Ham got to fourteenth place in the League, finishing just above Fulham. Liverpool (from whom the Hammers took the full four League points that term) won the Championship and Manchester United were runners-up (of course the Irons had beaten them two times out of three that season – 4-3 to the cockney boys!). Hurst and Byrne were West Ham's goal providers. Together they scored fifty-eight of the 105 goals the Hammers scored in all competitions before the FA Cup final. Budgie was top scorer at the club with thirty-three goals. Unsurprisingly, Johnny was named 'Hammer of the Year' by the fans.

Both Byrne and Moore were picked for England's match against Scotland. This was the first time for forty-one years that two Hammers had played together for England at Hampden, Jack Tresadern and Vic Watson having helped fight out a 2-2 draw in 1923. Watson had scored in that fiftieth encounter with the 'auld enemy', but Tresadern, who would one day manage a Tottenham Hotspur team that included Arthur Rowe, had made a mistake that led to the first of the Scottish goals.

Retrospective analysis of the 1964 Hillsborough FA Cup semi-final demonstrates that West Ham swamped Manchester United. The Reds were unable to recover from the trauma and their season that had promised the richness of a treble ended with nothing.

The game had been a triumph of teamwork over individual ability. But all West Ham's skills were moulded rather than sacrificed, incorporated rather than curbed, into the one effective unit. The Hammers worked on the long-accepted principle that the team is always greater than the individual. Above all, this West

Ham United side was a cogent, watchful and intelligent group of young men, ever willing to learn, to try new ideas, to progress. Yet clearly their most admirable trait was their thoughtfulness. These combined attributes were telling soccer weapons.

West Ham United Football Club, as an entire entity, had been gearing to modern style and efficiency since the early 1950s. The Irons had been amongst the first to switch over to the lighter, more streamlined playing strip and footwear. Greenwood, and before him Malcolm Allison, had worked with the West Ham side to incorporate the innovative tactics used by the likes of Arthur Rowe's Tottenham in the early 1950s and taken on by the Hungarians and the Brazilians, and at the same time move towards the track-suited leadership and the organisational ethos engendered by a manager-coach. And, in between the wars, they were one of the first British clubs to tour extensively in Europe.

But there was more to West Ham's victory than history or innovation. Nobby Stiles, although one of the most disappointed of the United players on that rainy day in Sheffield, saw that West Ham had just got everything right. The diminutive (5ft 6ins, 11st 2lbs) inside right was from the Maurice Setters school in terms of build and tenacity. Born in Manchester, Nobby had played for Manchester City and England Schoolboys but joined the Old Trafford ground staff when he was fifteen and captained the Youth team before becoming a regular Central Leaguer. He made his League debut in 1960. His representative background meant that he knew many of the West Ham side better than most of his colleagues at Old Trafford. As a consequence, he was not surprised by what the Hammers had done, but nevertheless felt that his side should have been able to have taken the day. In the end, perhaps, United had been the victims of their own success. Confidence in self is a double-edged sword without adequate respect for the capacities of the other. According to John Bond:

> We were told not to bother to turn up.

Eddie Bovington confirmed the above,

> You start the run and never think you're going to get to the final. We had tough early games against Charlton, Orient and Swindon but, after beating Burnley in the sixth round, when we drew Manchester United in the semi we thought that was it.
>
> We thought that was the finish of it because the week before we'd played them at Upton Park and they'd put out a reserve side and beat us 2-0. That worked to our advantage, though, because they were so complacent. In the players' bar after they beat us at Upton Park we were having a laugh and they kept saying it wasn't worth us turning up in Sheffield!

> Even though it was thick mud and didn't stop raining all day, we just had one of those days when it all went right for us. Going in front 2-0, like we did, you thought we've got to have a chance and it worked to our advantage.
>
> They were a side of superstars really, but I marked Bobby Charlton, Ken Brown took Denis Law and we did well! We couldn't believe it and that was the best feeling of all, going in after that game and realising you'd made the final. It's not often you get to Wembley, and there are far better players than me who've never played in a cup final.

For Jack Burkett the semi-final was,

> ... a milestone in my reckoning because Manchester United were the team to beat then, as much as they are now, and winning it actually took us to Wembley.

It is hard to recall a United side so out-played, out-thought and out-fought in a game of such magnitude. History, for a change, has to give that one to the Hammers.

Geoffrey Charles Hurst

Geoff Hurst was a bloody cracker of a player.
Ken Brown – West Ham United and England

Geoff Hurst was born in Ashton-under-Lyne but was brought up in the Hammers' East London/West Essex homelands where he was spotted by West Ham playing for Chelmsford Boys (he had been recommended to the Irons by a family friend, Jack Redfern).

Geoff made his first appearance for a West Ham senior side against Fulham in a Floodlight Cup game in December 1958. He signed professional four months later. As a Hammer he won six England Youth caps and in 1959 a runners-up medal in the FA Youth Cup before making his League debut against Nottingham Forest in February 1960. His debut first-team goal for the club was scored in a 4-2 win over Wolves at Upton Park just a week before Christmas 1961, wearing the unfamiliar number four shirt. During the 1963/64 season he gained the first of his Under-23 caps. Hurst was a good learner and it was that, plus his exceptional physical and mental endurance, which enabled him to transform himself from an averagely good wing half into one of the world's most feared strikers. Geoff laboured to replicate the outstanding volleying ability of his strike partner, Johnny Byrne. He trained to gain something of the close control that

Budgie was so adept at and toiled to copy the way John cushioned passes on his chest and had the ball at his feet within fractions of a second, regardless of how hard it hit him.

Remembering his days as a half-back Hurst reflected:

> I was always attack conscious. I didn't seem able to acquire the discipline that you need in a defensive position.

Eventually, Geoff would fill the gap in the West Ham forward-line left by John Dick when the Scottish international was sold to Brentford.

In appearance Hurst was a strapping figure of a man, 5ft 11ins and 13st, filled with potential power as West Ham's inside left. But he was also a better-than-good cricketer and, like other Hammers of the time, could have concentrated on the summer game. He played professionally for Essex, making his county debut in 1962 and not a few thought he had the potential to make a Test-class batsman (he also 'converted' in cricket having started as a wicketkeeper). But Geoff's father, Charlie, had been a professional footballer with Oldham, Bristol Rovers and Rochdale. He had come south to play for Chelmsford City, so it is not surprising that the young Hurst always looked to 'the heroes of winter' as his inspiration.

On the field much of Hurst's running took him to where the ball would never arrive. He would pull defenders into false positions allowing his teammates time and room to operate. Geoff was a wholehearted, aggressive player. In his first season of striking partnership with Johnny Byrne they divided twenty-nine goals. In the 1963/64 season the pair claimed fifty-nine goals between them, Budgie leading the way with thirty-three in forty-five matches.

Ron Greenwood's successor and disciple, John Lyall, saw the partnership thus:

> Budgie had a great influence on the development of Geoff Hurst as a central striker. They formed a magnificent goal-scoring partnership. I think Geoff first realised the full value of controlling the ball with the chest, a hallmark of his game, when he watched Budgie doing it. Budgie would take the ball on his chest and, before it reached the ground, volley it out to the wings. Johnny had a wonderful sense of timing that enabled him to out-jump taller defenders and, although he was much taller, Budgie helped Geoff appreciate the importance of timing your jump.

From the moment Byrne had arrived at Upton Park there had been signs that the partnership with Hurst would be a dynamic one. Within a year they both knew where each other would be on the pitch at any given time. Hurst recalled Byrne as being,

Needle sharp and an incessant talker, he'd drive you mad in the dressing-room, but, once on the pitch, you just stood back and admired a rare talent.

In the penalty box he was as clever and cute as the Artful Dodger. He'd score goals and you'd scratch your head, wondering how he did it.

6

The Final

Whiplash!

The top ten television programmes of 1964 were:

Steptoe and Son (BBC)	Double Your Money (ITV)
Coronation Street (ITV)	Emergency Ward Ten (ITV)
Take Your Pick (ITV)	Around the Beatles (ITV)
Armchair Theatre (ITV)	The Avengers (ITV)
It's Tarbuck (ITV)	Miss World 1964 (ITV)

Few of these captured my imagination. I liked *The Avengers,* it was surreal and at times outlandish, with enough non-explanation to make it interesting. *Armchair Theatre* and *Steptoe and Son* were staples, and because of adult tastes *Double Your Money*, *Miss World* and *Emergency Ward Ten* were endured. But after coming home from an away match in Wolverhampton or Southampton you got home just in time for late evening repeats of such series as *Whiplash*.

This was one of the programmes that held my attention. It wasn't great, but for a nine/ten year old it was the right thing at the right time, especially as a distraction that could both wash over you and provide a sense of history after the Hammers had lost away from home yet again. It was a comforting fantasy based in reality; not unlike the experience of following the enigmatic Irons.

Whiplash was based on the true story of Cobb & Co., a stagecoach line that grew up in Australia in the Wells Fargo mould following the 1850s' gold rush. The boss of the company was Christopher Cobb, a handsome thirty-year-old Bostonian and son of Jeremiah Fulton Cobb, a transportation tycoon in the USA, with a sprawling railroad and stagecoach empire. The subsidiary company that they set up in Australia by 1870, Cobb & Co., was using 6,000 horses a day over incalculable miles a week of sometimes trackless outback. By 1880 they controlled over 4,000 miles of coach routes in Australia. Their 'Great Coach', with twelve horses, pulled some ninety or so passengers, but by far their biggest coach was the 'Leviathan', which was tugged by an equine regiment of twenty-two.

Whiplash was created by Michael Noonan and Michael Plant. It mainly concerned itself with standard Wild West type stories, with outlaws being replaced by bushrangers. The show got its title from the main character's preference for using a bullwhip rather than a gun. Cobb was portrayed by the American actor Peter Graves, who would later find fame as Jim Phelps in the 1960s spy thriller series *Mission Impossible* (he also directed part of that series).

Whiplash was a produced by the British ATV company and distributed by Incorporated Television Company Ltd (ITC – that was stewarded by Lew Grade) and filmed in Alice Springs, Australia. The backdrop of the series comprised locations like the MacDonnell Ranges, the Ormiston Gorge and Ayer's Rock. It had a good following and was rated as slightly above average television.

Graves was born 18 March 1926 in Minneapolis, Minnesota. His real name is Peter Arness. Graves is the brother to James Arness, who he directed as Marshall Matt Dillon in *Gunsmoke*, an American Western series that ran from the mid-1950s into the late 1960s and was very popular both in the USA and the UK, with characters like Miss Kitty and Chester (Dillon's sidekick) who provoked parody at the hands of nine-year-old boys (delivering, in a wildly exaggerated southern United States accent, a loud 'Hello Mr Dillon!' with an accompanying, very pronounced limp).

Peter Graves has combined an enormously successful film acting career, spanning the classic *Staglag 17* to the hilarious *Airplane II*, with an equally rewarding TV career encompassing more than a half-dozen series, several major mini-series and numerous movies for television. But he has worked behind the scenes on award-winning films like *Fargo* (1996) and *Dead Man Walking* (1995). Most recently he appeared in *Men in Black II* (2002).

There were thirty-nine episodes of *Whiplash* planned but only thirty-four half-hour plots were produced for 1960/61. It ran and re-ran well into the 1960s.

The *Whiplash* theme was sung by the Australian Frank Ifield, who had big hits in Britain including *I Remember You* and *Don't Blame Me*. For me, the lyrics, sung in Ifield's lilting style, and the rumbling music, evocative of a stage rolling across barren wastelands, was the most exciting and provocative thing about the programme:

Whiplash, Whiplash, Whiplash, Whiplash
In 1851 the Great Australian gold rush
The only law a gun, the only shelter wildbush
Whiplash, Whiplash
The Mulga woods and deserts, the stage thunders by
From Sydney to Camden and on to Gundagai
Whiplash, Whiplash, Whiplash, Whiplash
Hmmahmm, Hmmahnn

The song ended with a 'Yeeeahh!' and the sound of a whip cracking. I just loved it! It was going somewhere; a mysterious place, on and on. Nothing static, always moving; thundering through the woods and deserts, from Sydney to Camden… and on, yes on, to Gundagai.

The directors of *Whiplash* included some distinguished names of the future: Maurice Geraghty, John Meredyth Lucas, (who later worked on *Star Trek* and *Planet of the Apes*) and Peter Maxwell, who was involved with *The Invisible Man*.

Although *Whiplash* was made in the spirit of the western, it was faithful to its Australian location – Aborigines replacing 'Red Indians' (genuine Aborigines played Aborigines, whereas it was not unusual to cast white actors as Native Americans in many westerns) and production values were relatively high, premised on *The Lone Ranger*, and the kind of odd mix of values intrinsic to British television of the time. Episode 16 for example, 'The Canooba Incident', was about Chris Cobb and his sidekick Dan Ledward arriving in Canooba to set up a branch office for the Cobb stageline. But on arrival, they find that the town is, unthinkably, *run by women!*

On the other hand *Storm River* opened with the text:

> Although Australia has the second largest desert in the world – half the size of the Sahara – in the rainy season its rivers overflow and create vast swamps. It was one of these 'oceans' of reeds that discouraged explores from finding the source of Australia's great river system for nearly one hundred years.

It concentrated on Cobb battling his way through a violent storm with a lame horse and being subsequently felled by an unseen adversary. When he recovered consciousness he found himself on a bed in a room of a backwoods cabin – minus his money belt.

Episode 29, *The Haunted Valley,* made the point with the opening text:

> While the lawlessness of the American West has been exaggerated – the bush rangers who roamed the outback of Australia during the same period were among the most dangerous outlaws the world has ever known. Secret mountain passes and hidden valleys provided them with hideouts from which only an army of territorial police could dislodge them.

You can see the attempt to entertain and educate viewers. It was the perfect antidote or accompaniment to a day with West Ham, depending on results…'Yeeeahh!'

The Finalists Who Did and Didn't Make the Final

I loved Preston, the club and the people. They were always very good to me. I would have liked to manage Preston.

Howard Kendall – Preston North End

There was an official reprint of the cup final programme in the north of England, showing Preston's Howard Kendall at number six. Kendall replaced Ian Davidson, whose name appeared in the original copy. The programme for the final (which cost one shilling) named West Ham's John Sissons as the youngest player on the pitch, but Howard Kendall took that honour when he became a late inclusion in the Preston side.

Just before the cup final of 1964 the news got out that Ian Davidson, the Scotsman signed from Kilmarnock the previous year, having played in the first team in the run-up to the FA Cup final, including the semi-final, had been suspended by Preston. It seems that he had gone missing shortly before a 'rehearsal' for the final, a League match at Northampton, supposedly to attend a relative's funeral. Jimmy Milne discovered that this had been a ruse. The full facts of the matter have never come out but Wembley nerves were blamed at the time. However, this alibi was not substantiated by the actions of the Preston board who suspended the player for a fortnight, ensuring that he would miss the final.

A native East Lothian, Ian Davidson was another Milne bargain, coming to Deepdale for £15,150 in December 1962. Davidson was a 6ft, lean and rangy defender who could play wing half, left half, centre half or full-back. He and Jim Smith, who often played behind Davidson in the Preston defence, had a near-perfect understanding of one another's play. Davidson, a good tackler, was not likely to come surging through on attack like Nobby Lawton, but he did look effective taking a creative role, using the thirty-yard pass pumped through to his forward line with quite spectacular accuracy. The Deepdale crowd saw a similarity in the build and dour, tenacious, yet neat style of Davidson with the former Preston favourite Willie Forbes, and he was a player reminiscent of a certain Scottish tradition that fitted in well with what Milne was looking to cultivate at Preston.

It has never been clear quite why Davidson was kept out of the final but in an article he put his name to in January 1967, entitled *Idiot...! That's what I thought when I missed the cup final*, he wrote:

> One day I will tell the full story – maybe when I write a book. But not just yet. They say that notoriety is akin to fame, and my escapade in 1964 when Preston

Howard Kendall, Wembley star.

North End dropped me from the cup final side and suspended me for fourteen days 'for a breach of discipline' sent my name buzzing the length and breadth of the soccer world.

My misdemeanour brought fame also to the then seventeen-year-old Howard Kendall who took my place in the final, perhaps the only good thing that came of the event which led to my not re-signing for Preston during the close season. But I eventually came to terms with myself, and the club, for the 1964/65 season, and for sixteen games I was back in my old position, having been refused a transfer-request. Then, almost without warning, I found that I was on the list – resulting in my move to the North East. It was a sad ending to my spell in Lancashire.

I was born in Edinburgh. I started my soccer life as an inside forward at Ormiston Central School, in my home town, and when I left at fifteen I became an apprentice joiner, and played for a local team, Elviston Primrose. I joined Ormiston Juniors almost three seasons later. At eighteen I was offered professional terms by Kilmarnock. I accepted but still carried on my apprenticeship.

After half a season at inside forward, the club transferred Bobby Kennedy to Manchester City and I was asked to drop back to right half to fill the gap. I held the position with Killies for five or six seasons, but eventually lost my place to Pat O'Connor. Pat was in the Forces at the time and, of course, wasn't even in full training. But the club were flying him back from Germany every weekend, and I quickly felt that it was high time for me to move on. I asked for a transfer and was refused, but I kept pressing my case and was placed on the list. I had discussions with several clubs in November 1962, but chose Preston who were not doing well at that time, being in the lower reaches of the Second Division. I was able to help the club toward a more respectable position and by the end of the season I was a regular first choice. The following season came the great cup run, ending in Preston being beaten 3-2 by West Ham in the final. But without my aid.

It was a great pity, for until my unfortunate lapse a few days before the final it had been a great season for the club and for me. That magnificent cup run was certainly the highlight of my career and I have only myself to blame for the stupid circumstances that prevented me treading that famous Wembley turf. What I did was quite idiotic and completely indefensible. I deserved to be punished and was prepared to take it on the chin. I was full of regrets, but the suspension of fourteen days was a thing I could, and did accept. But I was very hurt by the fact that, even though many people thought my sentence justifiable, I was dropped from the cup final side.

I felt a complete idiot. Howard Kendall, after his cup success, played for the early matches of the following season, but I felt that I was playing as well as ever when I got my place back and had that sixteen-game run. It was, therefore, a bit of a shock when I was listed and moved to Ayresome Park.

So here I am… determined that this season we shall start the climb back to former glories, from the Third Division into which we were relegated at the end of last term.

I've changed a lot since I went north from Preston. I have much more self-discipline, much more control over myself. And I can promise you one thing – there will be no repetition of the senseless impulse that robbed me of that Wembley date, and possibly of a cup-winner's medal.

On the suspension of Davidson, seventeen-year-old Howard Kendall was promoted with Milne's full confidence. The lad was amazed:

I could not believe it anyway. My father said last night I should forget it, then I wouldn't be disappointed. Now it has happened, and I am too delighted for words… I don't think it will bother me all that much. I sincerely hope not!

Years later Kendall recalled how he became involved with North End:

I was playing for England Schoolboys at fourteen and Newcastle, Sunderland and Arsenal wanted me. But a Preston scout called Reg Keating said come and have a look at Preston. When I went down to Deepdale the club put my mum and dad up in the County Hotel near the railway station and they looked after us as if we were royalty.

I couldn't pick a fault with the club and Preston just felt right for me. I lived in digs on Lowthorpe Crescent and I was on £7 a week as an apprentice. North End used to give me rail vouchers to go back to the North East in the summer to play cricket and I still managed to save a £100 a week. It was a wonderful life and Preston always did right by me.

Preston had a smashing team – names like Alan Spavin, George Ross and Alex Dawson – and not for one second did I think I'd play in the cup final. There was little pre-match discussion then. I just walked in from a training session and there was the cup final team pinned up on the notice board in the Deepdale reception. It just read: H Kendall, number six. It was a complete surprise. I was stunned. Strangely, though, I had no nerves. I was protected from the hype by the older players. The plan was to give me the first touch from the kick-off at Wembley to settle my nerves. Of course the ball ballooned about twenty yards past me and the West Ham lads had a laugh.

Kendall, who had led the England Youth side to glory in the international tournament (the Youth European Championship of its day) in Holland the previous

Easter, was born in Ryton-on-Tyne on 22 May 1946. After turning out for England Schoolboys in a 7-3 win over Wales at Swansea, Kendall left Durham to become a Preston apprentice. He made his League debut in his native North East, eleven days before his seventeenth birthday in a 1963 2-2 draw with Newcastle. His first League goal came later that season at The Dell as Preston beat Southampton 5-4 in thriller of a match. He was one of Jimmy Milne's most important captures. He recalled:

> In August 1961 I went up to Chester-le-Street in the North East to watch a full-back, and Howard Kendall was playing in front of him. He took my eye, and after talking to his father we managed to sign him.

Kendall's selection at the age of 17 years 345 days made him, in 1964, the youngest player in the twentieth century to play in an FA Cup final, taking the record off of former Arsenal and England winger Cliff Bastin, who was at Wembley to witness his record being broken. It is perhaps slightly ironic that West Ham's Paul Allen would inherit this record when he played at Wembley for West Ham United in 1980.

The drama of the seventeen-year-old youth playing in a cup final stoked up the already burgeoning media interest and the game was extensively previewed on television. However, Kendall had a mature head on young shoulders and was not overawed by the prospect of playing on the biggest stage in the world and told reporters that (unlike Alan Spavin) he had slept well on the night before the final.

The drama surrounding Kendall and Davidson overshadowed the fact John Donnelly, after playing in the semi- and quarter-final games, was replaced by Jim Smith at Wembley. Apart from the first match with Nottingham Forest, Smith had not been involved in Preston's journey to the final.

Johnny Boy

John Sissons scored four goals in his first England Boys appearance, coming to the side from Middlesex Boys. He played international football at Youth level and was in England's Junior World Cup-winning side of 1963. Johnny was a member of the England team that won the International Youth Tournament for two seasons running. A glorious period for Sissons continued with his contribution to West Ham's FA Youth Cup victory of 1962/63.

The outside left, who could play as an inside forward, was born at Hayes, Middlesex. Sissons joined the Hammers on 29 July 1961 as an apprentice professional. He became a full professional on 2 October 1962 and made his League debut *v.* Blackburn Rovers on 4 May the same year. He had commanded a regular place in the Hammers side since Christmas 1963 and was one of key players in the club's magnificent cup run.

In the mid-sixties Johnny was hailed as the most impressive footballing find since Jimmy Greaves. His 5ft 6ins 10st 2lbs stature and deadly left foot caused many to liken Sissons to the great Ferenc Puskas of Hungary and Real Madrid. As such, he was considered to be a certainty for England's 1966 World Cup squad.

Sissons was a quiet and rather shy young man, but as the legendary manager of Wolverhampton Wanderers, Stan Cullis, said:

> Watching Sissons as a schoolboy, it was obvious that he would mature quickly.

It was the considerable talent that Sissons showed in the West Ham Youth, 'A' team and reserve matches that won him his early promotion to the first team on the left wing. The Hammers, who had lacked the power that comes with equilibrium, achieved that vital balance with the addition of Sissons. Progress was swift. As the daffodils heralded the coming of spring in 1964 Ron Greenwood observed that his young diamond was controlling the attack.

Sissons had tremendous instincts, but his control and astonishing left foot seemed to make him the complete left-winger.

Prelude

Having been denied a place in the League Cup final following the 2-0 Upton Park defeat at the hands of Leicester City in late March, the FA Cup was now even more of a prize for West Ham. For Eddie Bovington:

> The cup final was the biggest thing. I remember everyone was scared to tackle in our last game before the final, at Everton. Roy Vernon kicked John Bond and Bondy's gone: 'Oi, Roy, what are you doing?' Vernon's gone: 'Well, let us win and you won't get kicked!' We lost 2-0… psychologically, you're probably half-a-yard slower in the build-up matches.

Saturday 2 May 1964 was the day of the thirty-sixth FA Cup final at Wembley, and the eighty-third since the competition began. At that time it was seen as the major prize in English, perhaps world soccer.

The Whites and the Hammers

West Ham and Preston had met three times in the FA Cup before that day. The first encounter took place in 1911, the same year as the first FA Cup battle with

Manchester United (see above, pages 132-4). The visit of First Division Preston drew a gate of 12,500 (with receipts of £738). West Ham had fielded:

George Kitchen, Jim Rothwell, Bob Fairman, Tom Randall, Frank Piercy, Bob Whiteman, Herbie Ashton, Danny Shea, George Webb, George Butcher and Tom Caldwell.

Whilst North End put their faith in:

Peter McBride, Charlie McFayden, Tom Rodway, Edward Holdsworth, Joe McCall, Bill Wareing, John Thompson, James Bannister, David McLean, Arthur Mounteney and Arthur Winterhalder (who had started his professional career with West Ham).

'Tiddler' Ashton put the Hammers one up before the interval, but Scottish international Peter McBride kept the Irons at bay until only fifteen minutes remained on the clock. Then George Webb scored twice, and so impressed the England selectors that they bestowed two full caps upon him later that season. George played as an amateur throughout his lengthy career as a centre forward.

On 8 January 1938 at Deepdale Preston delivered a 3-0 knock-out blow to the Hammers at their first hurdle. The Preston side included several well-known names:

Harry Holdcroft, Frank Gullimore, Andy Beattie, Will Shankly, Tom Smith, Jimmy Milne, Dick Watmough, George Mutch, Jimmy Dougall, Bobby Beattie and Hugh O'Donnell.

The Hammers' side was:

Herman Conway, Charlie Bicknell, Charlie Walker, Ted Fenton, Richard Walker, Joe Cockcroft, Jack Kirkaldie, Tommy Green, Ron Williams, Len Goulden and John Morton.

The visitors did well until half-time, but Hugh O'Donnell and George Mutch turned the tables after the interval. To quote from West Ham's subsequent match programme:

> If our victors can reproduce that form they should be able to repeat or better their last season's success. They have our best wishes, for they gave us a good, clean and exciting game.

It turned out that way, as the Lancastrians went on to defeat Huddersfield Town in the 1938 final.

Eighteen years later there was a link between the second and third cup meetings between Preston and West Ham. Ted Fenton was the Hammers' manager; he had been on the losing side at Deepdale almost two decades previously. 7 January 1956 saw something of a war at the Boleyn Ground, but referee Arthur Ellis (who would go on to become a World Cup official and, more importantly, a referee of TV's *It's a Knock Out!*) maintained control, and West Ham took the day 5-2 thanks to North End conceding a number of free-kicks around their penalty area.

It was Albert Foan's most memorable game for the Hammers. He recalled:

> I was awarded the match ball for a hat-trick in the second half [forty-eight, sixty-six and eighty-three minutes] but at half-time we had been 1-2 down.

Tommy Thomson had put Preston ahead after only six minutes, but Billy Dare had equalled accounts just a dozen minutes later. The irrepressible Tom Finney got the Lilywhites second on stroke of the twenty-fifth minute with a cunningly hit penalty. But Dare finally killed off Preston with his second, five minutes from time.

The teams on that cold day in the winter of the fifties were:

West Ham: Ernie Gregory, John Bond, Noel Cantwell, Andy Malcolm, Malcolm Allison, Frank O'Farrell, Harry Hooper, Albert Foan, Billy Dare, John Dick and Ken Tucker.

North End: George Thompson, Willie Cunningham, Joe Walton, Tommy Docherty, Joe Dunn, Willie Forbes, Tom Finney, Tommy Thompson, Eddie Lewis (who later would become a Hammer himself – see above, pages 33-4), Jimmy Baxter and Sammy Taylor.

Before the fourth confrontation between the Hammers and North End Nobby Lawton looked forward to the event:

> The cup final at Wembley... 100,000 fans! The shouting. The colour. Barring accidents I shall be there, not looking-on... I can hardly believe it will happen to me! I still pinch myself to make certain I am not dreaming...
>
> When I was at Old Trafford I used to look around the dressing-room at stars such as Denis Law, Bobby Charlton... and I would think to myself: 'What on earth am I doing here? I'm not in their class.' I had always suffered from a lack of self-confidence. That, perhaps, is one reason why I always tried to the limit on the field of play. And perhaps it was trying too hard that gave me the reputation of being a rough player. This still worries me... I would never deliberately hurt anyone. That's not my nature. I had this inferiority complex when I was a schoolboy... I played inside forward. In 1956 I played in that position for Manchester Boys with Bert Lister (now with Oldham) and Roy Cheetham (Manchester City). I never thought I was as good as them, but we

had a fair season and reached the final of the English Schools' Shield... we were beaten by Swansea Boys! You can imagine my feelings when we were drawn against Swansea in this season's cup semi-final!

I left school at the end of that season and joined Manchester United as an amateur. I didn't think I would make the grade and so I took a good daytime job as a trainee manager for a firm of wholesale coal merchants. At the time it seemed to be the right decision, for everyone except me in the United Youth side (which included Alex Dawson and Mark Pearson) was asked to sign professional forms.

I was still an amateur inside forward at the time of the Munich disaster in 1958. Then I was asked to turn pro and decided to take a chance... I went to America with United and while we were waiting for Maurice Setters to join us from the Young England party I was given his spot at wing-half. I enjoyed playing in that position; it suited me more than the forward line. But the following season I was in front, and I played nearly thirty games for the League side at inside left. Then came 1962/63... my season of destiny. At the start of it I was given the right-half job and held it for ten games before being dropped. After that I was in and out of the team... I applied to be put on the transfer list and was asked to join Preston.

I didn't know what to do. They were struggling in the lower half of the Second Division. Friends advised me not to go there. But I wanted to play half-back and I wanted first-team football. So I said 'yes'. And I have not regretted it... when at the start of this season I was made skipper I was determined to justify the confidence placed in me. It was the turning point in my playing career. It gave me the confidence that had been lacking since I was a boy. I have no inferiority complex now. That's all in the past... I shout at, bully and cajole the boys on the field... I have been lucky, too, in that this season Alex Dawson has reached his peak. He has more devil... and he is scoring goals. Why? Because alongside him are people who are giving him the right passes. They are playing for the side not for themselves... manager Jimmy Milne has given confidence to the rest of the team... we have had a bit of luck but then no one gets to Wembley without a share of that.

The important thing is that we are there... or will be on May 2. If we don't win it won't be for the want of trying. Although West Ham are a First Division side we won't feel inferior...

Wembley Stadium, following the many alterations made during the winter of 1963 and 1964 in preparation for the 1966 World Cup, was one of the most imposing sporting arenas in the world. For the first time the crowd was completely covered.

Both West Ham and Preston had experienced tremendous support throughout their respective runs. The total attendance figure for the seven matches played by the Hammers in the competition was 333,934, an average of 47,705 per game. The total attendance figure for the three Upton Park games had been 106,199, which works out to 35,400 per game. The distribution of tickets for the final gave 3,970 to the FA, Preston and West Ham received 15,000 each but county associations were given 40,650, more than any other organisation. League clubs collectively got 21,040 tickets whilst other full-member clubs were allocated 2,260 tickets. The FA Council representatives and Wembley Stadium were provided with 2,080, so West Ham and Preston fans together made up (notionally) less than thirty-five per cent of the crowd! Before the game West Ham had expressed disappointment that accommodation could only be found for 15,000 of each of the finalists' supporters. Eddie Chapman, a former West Ham player and club secretary commented:

> The percentage of tickets allocated to finalists was extremely poor in those days. We allocated them by vouchers issued at a game at Upton Park. This particular game was not advertised as being one at which the 'lucky' vouchers would be given out. Different sections of the ground had their proportion of the vouchers and all in all it appeared to be a fair method of distribution. Of course, season ticket holders got tickets automatically. When it came to exchanging a 'lucky' voucher for the purchase of an actual cup final ticket our stewards and the police scrutinised those vouchers very carefully for forgeries to ensure everything was correct.
>
> The tickets arrived at Upton Park and they would normally have been put in the safe in my office, where other valuable items were held, but a week before that safe had been broken into by burglars. I didn't want to take the chance of another break-in and losing those tickets, they would have fetched a fortune. So I put the 15,000 tickets into the boot of my car and took them home and put them under my bed. I've thought many times since that it wasn't such a good idea. What if I'd have had an accident in the car? What if my house had been burgled? I wonder if anyone else has ever done that? Maybe someone has kept World Cup tickets in their coal bin?

The Gross receipts of the first Wembley final were £27,776, and the two clubs and the FA each received cheques for £6,365. The 1964 final notched up something close to £90,000. But even during that era the real financial prize was the promise of European football.

The FA Cup final of 1964 was West Ham's first Wembley appearance since the War Cup final of 1940. As a First Division side West Ham were favourites to beat Preston. The Hammers had scored three goals in every round of the competition. Some pundits were predicting that the Irons would score at least five goals or more, a tally that had never been reached in the history of Wembley FA Cup finals. The Lancastrians had finished third in the Second Division behind promoted sides Leeds and Sunderland, and were weakened (theoretically) by the absence of left half Ian

Davidson, and West Ham United were a quality side. Bobby Moore was England's skipper and 'Footballer of the Year', and England striker Johnny Byrne (who came fourth in the same poll) was in the best form of his life. But for all this, John confessed that like most of the other West Ham players, he had at times thought that the Hammers would never win anything. But sometime during 1964,

> Suddenly everything altered. We had become more confident. We thought, 'This is going to be our year.' There was a lot more interest in European competition. Win the FA Cup and you were in on that.
>
> West Ham stayed in a hotel in North London the night before the match. There wasn't much sign of nerves. Ron Greenwood had done his homework on Preston and we had all gone to see them play. Me and Kenny Brown kept the lads laughing.
>
> Our coach got to Empire Way about a half-an-hour before the kick-off. The West Ham fans were cheering, blowing horns and whirling rattles. Of course the Preston supporters were booing us.

Indeed, Preston had come to London on mass. The migration got underway on Friday night before the match. Thousands of cars, ninety-one coaches and the usual special trains were reported to be heading south. This was North End's first cup final run of the motorway age, and the town was almost emptied of cars. The morning of the match saw these vehicles surrounding Wembley full of sleeping fans. The Whites also had a temporary air force of around 100 who flew from Blackpool to Luton. On the way to Wembley the Preston players were comforted by the sight of thousands of fans wearing rosettes and dark-blue-and-white bowlers. But the supporters who could not make the pilgrimage to London were not forgotten. Arrangements had been made to rush a film of the final to local cinemas by Monday evening, a sobering thought in our era of instant satellite access.

Preston North End sounded like what they were; not 'Athletic', 'United', 'Rovers', 'Rangers', 'Town' or 'Academicals'. Like Accrington Stanley, Barnsley and Easington Colliery, there is a tough pragmatism suggested in the club title, a dour fortitude, steeped in a no-nonsense proletarian ethic; they were from Preston, the North End; a hard side, hard to beat, hard to play against. The intentions of Preston in attack were summed up firstly by the fact that Dawson, Ashworth and Wilson had scored fifty-five goals between them and secondly by Doug Holden, who had said before the final:

> I've not come to Wembley for a third time to lose.

For all this, North End were seen as the underdogs. The bookies and the newspapers had written off Preston, and according to the *Lancashire Evening Post*, even the local policemen gave the Lilywhites little chance. But looking at North End's side it is clear that they were a strong team, having a good combination of experience and youth. Nobby Lawton made the case for Preston eloquently when he reflected:

> The rest of the country thought it was humble little Preston going down to Wembley for a nice day out. Everybody had written us off, but as captain of that wonderful team I knew different. We were a fine football side, with a great blend of players like Dave Wilson, Tony Singleton, Alec Ashworth and that great striker Alex Dawson.
>
> Two months before the '64 final we had played Leeds at Deepdale. They won the Second Division title that season, with Johnny Giles, Norman Hunter, Billy Bremner and Jack Charlton in their side. It was the beginning of that great Leeds era, but we destroyed them at Deepdale 2–0. Leeds never got a kick, and that night I realised we were a great team. We played so well against Leeds I didn't want it to end.

Most North End supporters were confident that their side would bring the cup back to Lancashire. The focus on the final being seen as the main reason for missing out on promotion stimulated a belief that the fates had decreed that Preston should win the cup. However, the historical memory of Lilywhite fans was long and they protected themselves with a scepticism engendered out of a characteristic cultural pragmatism and the tribulations of being at one with a football team seemingly destined to continue a long decline.

But there is a strength that comes from being the underdog; it has long been something West Ham has relied on. The 1964 cup final stands alongside the 1975 cup final as a historical anomaly for the Hammers, it being a rare moment when the Irons are favourites to win anything. Johnny Byrne recalled:

> We were the favourites and I suppose this might have added to the tension. The neutrals always go for the unfancied side and the newspapers love a shock result. But if you look at the sides they were fairly equally matched; perhaps we had a bit more skill, but they had more experience in their side. Before the game Preston were being seen as 'brave underdogs', but we kept laughing.

Waiting

Byrne recalled the West Ham dressing room just before the final:

> People had ways of dealing with stress. Some players always seemed to be ready ages before a game. Eddie Bovington and Ron Boyce were like that. Kenny Brown always had a back massage. I never changed until just before kick-off. It was a long walk out to the pitch so we had plenty of time to think

> about what Ron Greenwood told us before we left the changing rooms. He said, 'All you've got to do is play your normal game... Just play football.' He just wanted us to relax and do what we did best. Ron also told us to start the game with Eddie Bovington playing deep to give us an extra marker. Bobby started the match as a sweeper. This seemed a bit dangerous as Dawson was a threat in the air and that wasn't Mooro's strong point, but Ron was thinking that there'd be plenty of knock-downs as much as anything else.

The combined bands of the Coldstream and Irish Guards blew away from 1.30 to 2.30 p.m. Their repertoire seemed in part to have been passed on from the Villa Park and Hillsborough semi-finals. They knocked out *Gigi*, *Telstar*, *World Without Love* (which was originally sung by 'Peter and Gordon'), *Can't Buy Me Love* and, surreally, *Maigret*. A rendition of *I'm Forever Blowing Bubbles* had been planned, and was included on the musical schedule in the match programme, but as Preston did not really have a song with the same resonance for their supporters it was thought the inclusion of *Bubbles* would have been 'invidious'. As such it was replaced by *Maybe It's Because I'm a Londoner* and *I'm a Lassie from Lancashire* was once again resuscitated as no one knew any songs about Lancashire or Preston. However, the appropriateness of the geographical reference was overridden by the fact that it was expected that the mostly male, stoutly 'northern' Preston supporters would be happy to claim to be *Lassies from Lancashire*. Those who did were of course subjected to some predictable rejoinders from the fans from East London. There were the usual boos from the Northerners as *Maybe It's Because I'm a Londoner* was played but the stadium was at one when the rendition of *Abide With Me* was offered – many of the East London fans were of an age to recall how this song was often used when the Blitz was at its height and the Docklands burned under Nazi fire.

Coming close to the traditional 3 p.m. kick-off, in front of 100,000 people the waiting continued. North End had sent their players to the Isle of Man for a break and to escape the mounting excitement in the town, and moved to a hotel in Weybridge a few days before the final. Manager Jimmy Milne had told the press that there could be changes to his starting line-up for the final that might involve Howard Kendall being drafted into the side. The team arrived at Wembley from their Surrey retreat full of high spirits. They were certainly not going to roll over and let West Ham walk away with the cup. The Preston captain, Nobby Lawton, had commented before the final that,

> West Ham are a team who enjoy their game the same as we do. If both teams go into the match as I believe they will this could be a classic cup final, like that of 1948 between Manchester United and Blackpool. We want the cup and believe we can win it and do Preston proud.

Nobby was to be at least partly right.

Jimmy Milne and Ron Greenwood led out their teams and they were introduced to the Earl of Harewood (the new president of the FA) who was accompanied by Joe Mears, outgoing president of the FA. Johnny Byrne, who was right behind Bobby Moore, the first West Ham player out of the tunnel, remembered the moment:

> We lined up opposite Preston, sizing them up and being sized up as the Earl of Harewood, who looked like a James Bond villain, was introduced to the teams. It had been raining in the morning and I noticed that the top of the pitch was quite slippery. Both 'keepers were wearing gloves.

At the age of twenty-four, in an era when twenty-four was much younger than it is today, Preston's skipper had walked behind his manager out onto the Wembley turf. He would become probably North End's finest post-war captain; certainly his inspirational qualities had played a huge part in taking Preston to their first Wembley final in a decade and their last for something in excess of forty years. Looking back, he recollected that point in time:

> All of a sudden the wave of punishing noise from the 100,000 crowd just ebbed away, and the band struck up the first verse of 'Abide with Me'. I'd held on to the emotion and nerves until then, but I was a bit overcome at that moment, close to tears in fact. I looked over my shoulder and the rest of the lads were coming down the tunnel in those famous white shirts, with the PP crest of Preston on them. It was an unbelievable moment for a young lad.
>
> When I was a kid at Manchester United I used to watch the Busby Babes train, legends like Duncan Edwards and Tommy Taylor, and I thought if these blokes are the professionals then I've no chance. I was never fiercely ambitious, and deep down I didn't think I'd make it. But there I was at Wembley, captain of the famous Preston North End and I felt on top of the world. I never thought anything like that would happen to me.

The christening of Prince Edward prevented the Queen from attending Wembley (HRH was never to fully forgive hubby Phil for organising the event for that Saturday, her being a lifelong supporter of the Hammers).

The Ref

Referee Arthur Holland presided over the toss. Asking who would call, Moore gave the privilege to Lawton. Nobby won and the teams stayed where they were. Holland, a Barnsley miner, rose every day at 4.45 a.m. to start his early shift at the colliery. But in his football persona he had officiated all over the world. On cup final day 1964 Arthur became the first cup final referee ever to have been sent off as a player.

As a goalkeeper for Barnsley General Post Office he was ordered from the field for speaking out of turn to a referee. I suppose you could say 'that was him sorted', the referee having 'stamped' his authority on the game and 'delivered' his decision.

The son of a local referee, Arthur was almost born to the life of an arbiter, but this side of his life blossomed when he realised that he did not have the qualities to make the grade as a professional player and, at the age of twenty-two, Holland took up refereeing. That was before the Second World War, but by the mid-1950s Holland had gained a reputation as a stringent disciplinarian. Known as 'The Iron Man of Soccer', he admitted to being tough when in charge of a match, but he was also composed, and he was liked and respected by players who knew what to expect from him. In some 2,000 games, played out across the globe, he never abandoned a fixture, and sent just six players from the field of play.

Holland had been placed on the FIFA list in 1959. In the same year he refereed the Amateur Cup final and hehad been in charge of the European Cup final between Milan and Benfica at Wembley in 1963. He had been a top-class official for fifteen years. Arthur had two daughters and two sons. One of the latter, in taking up the whistle, created a third generation of Holland referees.

The West Ham–Preston cup final marked the time when Holland, being in his forty-seventh year, had to be taken off the Football League list. But after the biggest game of his life he continued to take games in local leagues and promised, 'As long as I can keep up with it I shall be out there in the middle.' Arthur also continued with his other officiating role as a cricket umpire.

When questioned about the seriousness of the game that was to be his swan-song at the highest level, he reflected, 'All games come the same to me, they are all important.' This was emphasised by him choosing to be awarded a gold medal for his Wembley contribution in preference to a ten guinea fee, saying, 'Money is not everything and I would not dream of taking it. It's the medal for me.'

Holland confirmed his linesmen's readiness, Mr S.B. Stokes of Nottinghamshire with the Orange flag, and Devon's Mr F.J. Bricknell in possession of the flame-coloured pennant. He looked for the signal from the Royal box, checked his watch and blew his whistle. The 1964 cup final had begun.

The Heart of North End

Alan Spavin, at twenty-two years of age, was North End's dynamo. He came into this world in Lancaster, attended school there and played for Carnforth Rangers as a junior before coming to Deepdale at the age of fifteen in August 1959.

Spavin was in the Preston FA Youth Cup final team that lost to Chelsea in 1960, and scored on his first-team debut against Arsenal in August of the same year. A clever

Alan Spavin.

ball player and natural inside forward or midfield player, Spavin picked up plenty of good experience playing inside to Peter Thompson, who moved from Preston to become a Liverpool and England Under-23 winger. Alan was a much underrated, hard-working midfielder but he also possessed fine ball skills and created many more goals than he scored. He was one of those unobtrusive players, going about his craft relatively quietly and without show. In fact it was easy to miss his real worth to the side, but he was the brain of the resourceful North End attack. He worked hard in linking up the Whites' defence with their offensive potential and was very much the fuse to the dash of Ashworth and Dawson. In 1964, Alan was nearing his century of League appearances. He was to Preston what Ronnie Boyce was to West Ham – the team's beating heart; its throbbing engine.

Inside forwards Alec Ashworth and Brian Godfrey came to Deepdale in 1963, the same year as Nobby Lawton. Alec was born in Southport on 1 October 1939 and started his football career at Everton, where he made his League debut against Sheffield Wednesday in the First Division. After three seasons at Goodison, he moved on to Luton Town in a double-player exchange deal that took Billy Bingham to Everton. In July 1962 Alec signed for Northampton Town where he soon attracted the scouts after scoring twenty-five goals in thirty League appearances for the Cobblers, becoming their top scorer that season and helping them win the Third Division Championship in 1963. He signed for Preston in June 1963 for a fee of £15,000, making his debut against Leyton Orient at Brisbane Road in the opening game of the 1963/64 term.

Peter Thompson – the one that got away, moving from Preston to Liverpool.

During his first season with the Lilywhites, Ashworth formed an effective partnership with Alex Dawson; the two of them scored forty-four League goals. Alec, a big, powerful, seemingly tireless grafter, finished the season with a total of fourteen goals in thirty-one appearances, including a hat-trick in a 3-0 win over Bury.

Brian Godfrey, Welsh terrier.

Brian Cameron Godfrey, a creative midfielder who could play inside or wing forward, always seemed able to find openings for his colleagues, but was never slow to burst through from the middle to shoot for goal. Born in Flint on May Day 1940, he had started his career with his hometown club, Flint Alexandra. Brian was a relatively inexpensive £9,750 October buy from Scunthorpe United in October 1963. At first he deputised for the injured Ashworth, showing much of his teammate's zest for work. A Welsh Under-23 international, he had moved from Flint to Goodison Park, but played just a single League fixture for the Toffees. Although, at 5ft 8ins and 11st 2lbs, Godfrey was hardly an imposing figure, he proved to be a versatile member of the Preston squad and a prolific scorer.

From a bright display against Wigan at Deepdale in the FA Youth Cup when he was sixteen years old, born on Christmas Eve 1942 in Nelson, England Schoolboy international David Charles 'Tug' Wilson kept on impressing all the way through the tournament to the final, wherein North End played Chelsea. The youthful Whites managed a 1-1 draw in the first leg at Stamford Bridge. The second leg at Deepdale was played in front of a crowd of 27,764. Chelsea put on an excellent display, defeating the home side 4-1 on the night and so achieved a 5-2 aggregate win. Other members of that young North End side included future stars such as George Ross, Tony Singleton, Alan Spavin and Peter Thompson.

Originally an inside forward, Wilson's conversion to a flanker left him overshadowed at Preston by the huge talent of Peter Thompson until the latter moved to Liverpool. Wilson went on to gain honours, seven caps at Under-23 level and for a time was seen as Terry Paine's deputy in the England side. He showed himself to be a graceful and adept ball player as North End's outside right. After scoring a splendid hat-trick against Cardiff City on Boxing Day 1963 he inherited the hopes that had been laid on Thompson, being hailed as a reincarnation of 'Saint Tom of Deepdale'.

Manchester-born Albert Douglas Holden had made the first of his 419 appearances for Bolton Wanderers in the 1951/52 season as a seventeen year old against Liverpool in a 1-1 draw during November 1951. An England Youth international, he was swift to demonstrate that he had the character for the big occasion. He had chalked up just a dozen Central League games before turning out for the Trotters' senior side. Holden, although starting out as a left-winger for Bolton, made his mark for the club on the right flank and went on to play in a Football League XI and then win five England caps in 1959, which included facing a powerful Italian side at Wembley and the then World Champions Brazil in Rio de Janeiro.

Before 1964 Doug had played in two FA Cup finals. In 1953 he went away with a losers' medal, Bolton having been narrowly beaten, 4-3, by Blackpool (after being 3-1 up with twenty minutes to play). This was the 'Matthews Final', the game in which Stanley Matthews finally received the winners' medal he had been denied on two previous occasions. Five years later, Holden, reverting to the left wing, was part of the victorious Wanderers side that beat the Munich-ravaged Manchester United 2-0. Holden's Preston teammate Alex Dawson had played for the Reds in that final. Holden and Nat Lofthouse were the only Bolton players to appear in both the 1953 and 1958 cup finals.

Doug left Burnden Park with a credit balance of forty goals. In the autumn of his career, Holden's pace at outside left served Preston well. He was a fast, skilful player and fitted in perfectly with the role Jimmy Milne had paid a bargain £8,000 for him to play.

Jackie Burkett

Jack Burkett missed just two games in the 1963/64 season, playing in fifty-four matches before going on to play throughout the summer in defence of the American glory West Ham had won the previous year, which he had also made a massive contribution to. In the months between May 1963 and June 1964, he made close to eighty appearances for the Hammers.

The blonde, clear-complexioned Jack Burkett, at 5ft 11ins and 12st 9lbs, was the 'pin-up' of West Ham, with a legion of female fans who screamed in Beatles fashion whenever they saw him. West Ham's left-back played schoolboy soccer for Tottenham and watched the home games of Spurs and Arsenal as a lad.

Born in Bow but raised in Edmonton, North London, Jack played in the FA Youth Cup runners-up side in 1959 and for England Youth. Burkett made his debut for the Hammers' First XI against Colchester United in the Pearson Cup on 4 May 1960.

Although a modest (he summed up his contribution in 1964 with the statement, 'I am still a learner in the game') and unspectacular player, Burkett delighted supporters of the Hammers with his coltish style. He proved a worthy successor to that Upton Park favourite Noel Cantwell. Jack matured during West Ham's American tour of the summer of 1963 when the side won the International Soccer League, played in the final of the American Challenge Cup and emerged as a confident and aggressive defender.

Burkett was a forward thinker, who was heavily influenced by Ron Greenwood. He was offered the chance to join the Hammers at fourteen, in 1957, after legendary scout Wally St Pier spotted him playing in a schoolboy match for Tottenham. Despite the horror of watching his brother tip a cup of boiling tea over Ted Fenton's trousers when the Hammers' boss came round to talk to his parents, Jack was invited to train at Upton Park.

Eire's Noel Cantwell, the man who Jack succeeded as West Ham's left-back in 1960, and great Brazilian, Nilton Santos, were both, in different ways, inspirational figures for Jack at a time when foreign football was unfamiliar to most Britons. He reflected:

> The future of West Ham, player-wise, might have been built with Bondy, Malcolm, Noel and Malcolm Musgrove at Cassettari's Café in the '50s with their forward thinking.
>
> The first night I went to Upton Park training, they had us on the pitch with the ball and that made my mind up straight away.
>
> They were learning then to become coaches and we were the guinea pigs, both in Cassettari's and on the training pitch. It did us a favour because it made us better players. I modelled myself on Noel – the way I ran with my arms up. He was the first foreign-style full-back and he was a tremendous person who used to give us all the help under the sun. We used to talk over lunch in Cassettari's and he was a good influence on me.
>
> My bedroom walls in Tottenham were filled with pictures of foreign players. I wanted to be like Nilton Santos because, apart from Noel, he was the first continental person who influenced me. With the Brazilians being such a force in the '50s and '60s, he was someone to look up to.

According to Jack, the spirit that led the Hammers to the cup success was injected during some unusual training sessions under Ted Fenton, and he also learned some tricks of the trade from his first manager:

> We had one training session when we played rugby and we grew up more in that than at any other time. It was playing a different game but, also, the older players and the younger ones were in it together, and despite a few cuts and bruises we started to gel.

> We used to go round Pudding Lane (Chigwell) on road runs and it seemed unusual that, being the younger, fitter ones, we'd always come last. That was because the experienced ones would cut across country, or get on buses.

Despite the technical knowhow of his colleagues, it wasn't until Ron Greenwood took over from Fenton in 1961 that the side developed the tactical awareness that would make them feared opponents both at home and abroad. Jack speaks in almost reverential terms about Greenwood, a coach way ahead of his time who he rates as the best English manager ever.

> In Ron, we had the best coach in England – the best coach there's ever been in my opinion – and, despite us all being English, we were more continental than British. Ron always wanted us to be together as a group and we would always go to Germany pre-season. We had trips to Africa and America and Ron liked us to play against foreign opposition in preparation for European football. We played against the cream of football abroad and Ron would pick up things from that to go into training.
>
> We looked at the way we'd been playing and felt we possibly could have won the cup the year before when we got beat 1-0 at Liverpool in the last five minutes of the quarter-final. The majority of the side was young, with Bondy and Kenny Brown to provide experience, and with Johnny Byrne and Peter Brabrook coming in it came good.
>
> I had a great relationship with the fans. Luckily, by being young and having come through the youth system I had a special liaison with them and I came through at a time when you could see there was going to be a change in our future.

Jack made his Football League debut in the last game of the 1962/63 season (at Upton Park, against Fulham). He came into the Hammers side at the start of the following term as part of an effort to stop the terrible early season run. In his first game of the season, Wolves were held to a goal-less draw at Molineux. However, the Irons lost to newly promoted Orient, 2-0, at Brisbane Road in their next game.

Burkett was a left-back of the sixties, tenacious, quick-tackling and not averse to buccaneering forward on wing raids. Fans were no longer at risk of a heart attack if they saw a defender moving into the opponents' half, as long as teammates were covering. Jack was a swift, studious defender, able to join the attack and combine with John Sissons, but could swiftly get back into defence. He was to be a key player in the first part of the sixties at West Ham.

North End v. East End

The 1964 cup final was brilliant. We were expected to beat Preston easily but it didn't work out that way. Never does, does it?
Ken Brown – West Ham United and England

We really thought we could beat West Ham at Wembley, and we nearly did!
Alec Ashworth – Preston North End

The 1964 cup final started with both sides refusing to appear intimidated, but it was Preston that seemed more focused and concentrated in the early stages. Both teams were supposed to start the match by playing in 4-2-4 formations, Moore and Kendall covering their respective centre halves, but in fact West Ham shaped up in more of a 4-3-3 shape, with a loose defence, avoiding a flat back four.

Preston looked every inch a mature, professional outfit that knew just what they wanted to do and how to do it. These energetic pragmatics were unnerving for the Hammers, who seemed, from the start, not really to know what to expect from North End. The first attacking cross came from Spavin after just sixty seconds.

Within minutes of the kick-off, Kendall, looking composed and confident, justified his shock selection in the North End XI. His ingenuity started the attack that could have led to the opening goal. Alec Ashworth recalled:

> Howard pushed the ball to Nobby Lawton who placed it between Bond and Moore, for me to pick up. Jim Standen dived at my feet and just got to the ball. I should have hit it just a tiny bit earlier...

Almost straight after that Kelly emulated Standen, robbing Hurst of a chance to shoot from a low Sissons cross, Johnny having evaded the North End defence. With less than five minutes gone, Sissons, from a Moore pass, got in a dangerous cross that was skilfully cut out by Kelly. Shortly after this, Burkett, looking to impose himself on Wilson, was lucky to escape a booking following a late tackle but, undeterred, was at 'Tug' again just a few minutes later.

Johnny Byrne was fearful for young Jack:

> From the start we didn't play that well. I thought Jack Burkett was going to be sent off in the first ten minutes; he fouled their winger, Wilson, about three times and the ref told him he'd kick him off if he kept kicking.

Dave Wilson was doing well against Burkett, but in truth Jack's treatment of Wilson was no more than 'over rigorous' for the times, even though watching recordings of

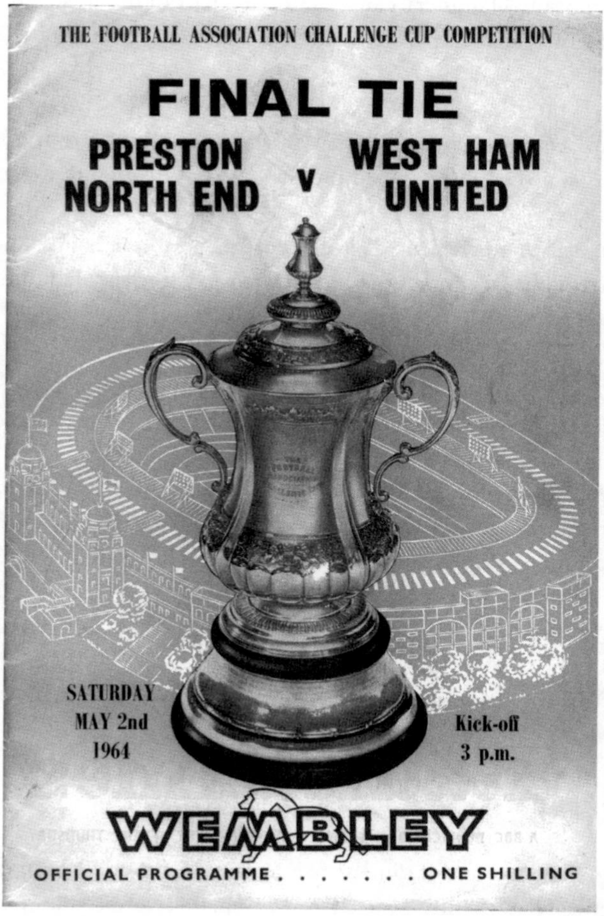

THE FOOTBALL ASSOCIATION CHALLENGE CUP COMPETITION
FINAL TIE
PRESTON NORTH END
v
WEST HAM UNITED
SATURDAY MAY 2nd 1964
Kick-off 3 p.m.
WEMBLEY
OFFICIAL PROGRAMME . . . . ONE SHILLING

Preston North End *v.* West Ham United, 2 May 1964 programme cover.

the game, at points, one can't help but feel for the Preston winger. Jack was certainly intent on limiting him, which of course was the highest form of flattery for Wilson.

But according to Burkett,

> I could have been the first player to be sent off in a cup final. It might have been nerves but I fouled the Preston winger, Wilson, three times in the first ten minutes and I always remember the referee running by, telling me to calm down or I could be the first man to be sent off.

As the first half wore on it was clear that the cultured Irons were unable to collect themselves, being disallowed any chance to establish their rhythm. It had been expected that the Lancastrians would favour long-ball tactics, but in fact this was more a feature of the Hammers' game in the first part of the final and Preston were posing West Ham a range of problems, not least in terms of sheer physicality. Nobby Lawton recollected:

> I recall running up and down like a whirling dervish before the kick-off at Wembley. I was incredibly hyped up, and in the first minute I clattered into Ronnie Boyce.
>
> It was a really hard challenge. We just got up and shook hands. The final was like that, hard but fair. When the kids come to visit us, my lad often puts the 1964 video on and says, 'let's see that tackle again, dad'.

Spavin, who was beginning to be a real problem for the Hammers' defence, showed his ability, tricking his way past a couple of defenders before whipping a cross into the box that Bobby Moore was obliged to thump clear, high into the grey London skies. A delightful flick from Howard Kendall found Lawton who played the ball through to Alex Dawson but Standen dived at the forward's feet to gather. The seventeen year old was justifying Jimmy Milne's faith in him and Kenneth Wolstenholme, commentating for the BBC, was correct and at his most passionate when describing Howard Kendall's performance:

> He wasn't in the team on Monday and now he is sensationally having the game of his life!

Byrne looked back at that those first minutes:

> West Ham had lost four of our last five League games and I suppose we were a bit careful. That's hardly ever a good thing. We were a side that counter-attacked; we'd liked teams to come at us and relied on moving fast out of defence and getting the ball up to players like myself, who could hold the ball up until someone else ran forward into the clear. At Wembley we couldn't get the counterattacks going. The Preston skipper, their right half, Nobby Lawton, and their inside left, Alan Spavin, kept Preston pressing forward. That was really the way to play West Ham in those days.

This strategy bore fruit when after just nine minutes Ashworth shot wide from only six yards. A minute later Kendall passed to the powerful, muscular Dawson who sent a left-foot shot from the edge of the penalty area with not inconsiderable clout. Standen, whose nerves had been tested from the opening whistle, got down to the shot but was unable to hold on to the ball and Doug Holden took swift advantage, having to do no more than stroke the ball home. This was not a disaster, but it felt like it to me and the other West Ham supporters watching in the stands. The last thing any team wanted playing on the energy-sapping Wembley turf was to go a goal down early on in a game. It was now vital for the Hammers to respond.

The inspired northerners, with their ambition to be the first Division Two team for a third of a century to leave Wembley as the FA Cup winners, did not look like an over-optimistic side; they were actually 'living the dream'. Kendall was shining and Lawton was running, left arm characteristically crooked, seemingly everywhere. But inevitably it was Moore who was to initiate a retort for the Irons. The flaxen-haired prince pushed his side forward and in the twelfth minute, just 120 seconds after Preston opened the scoring, West Ham replied.

According to Budgie Byrne:

> Bobby moved into Preston's half, changing position with me, and got the ball to Sissons who immediately sprinted down the wing. He passed it inside to me, and as John ran on I sent it back to him sharpish, he picked it up at about knee height. Johnny went past two of the four defenders in the Preston box, and after he cut inside and beat full-back George Ross he screwed the ball hard and low into the bottom right-hand corner of the net, past Kelly's outstretched hand, between the 'keeper and the post. It was a hard shot, one of those where both feet are off the ground as the ball is struck, from a tightish angle.

This made Sissons the youngest player ever to score in an FA Cup final and it meant that both of the goals had been netted by outside rights.

Immediately West Ham were back on the retreat, waiting for the next opportunity to counterattack and avoiding making tackles in no man's land. Kendall was back into things from the restart. Wilson, who had followed up a well-placed Kendall pass, lofted the ball in from the right wing. Watched by the horrified Standen, it rolled almost the length of the Hammers crossbar before it fell harmlessly behind the goal. Just after the quarter of an hour, Brabrook found Byrne on the edge of the penalty area. The Hammers were playing towards the West Ham fans and many of us thought Budgie had scored following his shot, but in fact the ball had gone wide. At the other end a dangerous Spavin drive was blocked by Moore. The cries for handball were ignored by referee Holland. A couple of minutes later, Ashworth, whose presence was now becoming a barometer of the extent that Preston were dictating the game, barged Standen on his own line.

Whilst West Ham, and Byrne in particular, were sending too many passes astray, Kendall was now having an outstanding game and delighted the crowd with his play, nearly scoring a spectacular goal after twice selling a dummy to Ronnie Boyce before unleashing a shot.

Around the mid-point of the first half, Lawton hit a rocket from less than three yards outside the penalty box and Standen did well to clear the ball. The corner that followed was cleared by Brown to the accompaniment of yet more demands for handball. On the half-hour mark, North End could, and maybe should, have had a penalty. Holden had teed up the ball for Spavin and his shot crashed against Brown's arm. The referee decided it was 'ball to hand' and waved play on with the North End supporters roaring for a spot-kick.

Being cut off from midfield supply lines, Byrne had to draw on his individual skill; this was epitomised when he dribbled round three defenders and gave the hard-grafting Geoff Hurst the opportunity to produce a great shot, which was brilliantly saved by Kelly as the half entered its final third; the Preston goalie launched himself the full length of the goal to put the ball around the post; up to that point it was the best save of the match.

With around ten minutes of the first half remaining, the West Ham fans started a mighty chorus of *Bubbles*, swaying *en masse*. It was said at that time that when the Hammers supporters swayed to their theme that West Ham would score and it was almost the case as Byrne's snapshot was only just limited to a corner kick by Kelly, who picked up an injury in the process that was bad enough to require treatment from the Preston trainer Walter Crook (formerly a player with Blackburn Rovers and Bolton Wanderers).

The edge had been taken from the Irons' attack by Singleton's domination of Hurst. At the same time, Burkett continued to struggle to hold Wilson, although Bovington was beginning to get the better of Ashworth, having become a perpetual shadow to the Whites' inside right. But overall it was clear that West Ham's close-passing play, founded on Byrne and Moore, was being read by Preston, forcing the likes of Bond and Moore to rely much more on long balls out of defence, whilst Lawton was making frequent sorties upfield, dragging Moore with him to leave gaping holes in the Irons' defence. Greenwood had seen this, but in the heat of battle was limited in what he could do about it. With Preston throwing themselves forward, the Hammers were not given time to collectively build a counter strategy and were doing all they could, thrown back on a primal fight-back response, which was mirrored in a pass made by Byrne to Hurst whilst Budgie was flat out on his back. For Byrne:

> Our attacks were breaking down before we got within sight of the Preston goal. Lawton kept his strikers pressing forward and Preston weren't looking like the underdogs. Five minutes before half-time they were in front again. Dave Wilson, their left winger, took a corner. Ken Brown stumbled trying to close in and Jim Standen slipped as Dawson, using his strength to hurtle through our defence, headed it in with Standen and Bondy rooted on the goal line.

It was a simple goal, one that the Hammers should not have conceded. This happened just when it looked like Brown was getting the better of big Alex. It was

Dawson's sixth goal of the cup campaign and his thirty-sixth of an excellent season. Dawson recalled with some amusement how Ken Brown claimed foul when the ball hit the net for Preston's second goal, despite the fact that he was sitting with his backside a few feet away. According to Johnny Byrne:

> Preston's half-back line, Lawton, Kendall and Singleton, were making it hard for us to get through. I was doing okay when Bobby was sending up long balls, but Mooro couldn't risk too many runs upfield as Ken Brown had enough to do holding on to Dawson. Preston deserved to go in with the lead. Their distribution had been good. We were not getting on top of Dawson and their wingers, Wilson and Holden, were making good use of the space we had given them.

Lawton spent much of what was left of the half urging his players to calm down, but Nobby was now looking confident and almost arrogant, like a man in control of his own destiny.

Other action in the last eight minutes before the break (there were three minutes of injury time) included a Spavin pass that found Dawson, whose missile-like shot Standen was thankful to punch away. Kelly was unable to hold a Byrne effort, causing Kendall to clear the Preston lines and Eddie Bovington had a couple of long-range attempts. The youthful Howard came close to turning a Sissons cross into his own net, and a shot from the young Hammers winger forced a good save from Kelly that was followed up by a Byrne shoulder barge on the 'keeper. Bobby Moore's great weakness, lack of pace, was demonstrated when Dawson, collecting from Ashworth, sped past the England skipper. Standen did well to save the situation.

At half-time the West Ham players knew they had been bettered in the first forty-five minutes, but they probably looked a little fresher than their Preston counterparts. North End had been doing the majority of the running. It was telling that Standen was perhaps the outstanding Hammer of the first half, but Sissons had also done well, whilst Bovington was coming more and more into the game. For Preston, Spavin, Ashworth and Lawton had excelled. Kelly, Wilson and Singleton had all looked solid, in fact it was hard to fault any of the Preston side, but Kendall had been their star. He had been active in defence and attack whilst showing fantastic positional awareness.

As the crowd were treated to more brass-band delights and a marching display by the massed bands of the Brigade of Guards, there was a West Ham seminar going on. Greenwood had, prior to the final, constantly warned his players against complacency. He had told them that they were in for one of the toughest games of their lives, impressing on them that Preston could only be beaten if the Hammers played to the best of their ability and backed this up with raw effort. Greenwood had predicted that the Lancashire side, with its Scottish flavour, would concentrate on shutting out the roving Johnny Byrne. Ron believed that every team should have a plan, and in the few minutes of half-time he laid out the tactics that would help his young Irons to overcome the intimidating strength and energy of the Preston side. According to Johnny Byrne:

> At half-time Ron Greenwood said that Preston had played well, having taken the lead twice and that they deserved to be in front. He told us that we just had to play better than we had been. He told us to go back out and win the cup even if it killed us. Yeah, fine. But how do you 'play better'? A lot of other managers would have left it at that, maybe after a bollocking. But Ron had a brilliant football brain and told us that we were not finding each other coming out of defence and that we had allowed Spavin and Lawton much too much time and space in midfield and this meant that play was bypassing Mooro, who hadn't done much at all in the first half. Wembley was so big that the usual marking systems were messed up
>
> Preston were running the midfield and we had to do something to counter the threat posed by Kendall and Lawton so Ron told Eddie Bovington to push into midfield to make an earlier impact and speed up the pace of the game, but also to keep an eye on Spavin whilst Lawton would be marked by Ronnie Boyce. Bobby would shift up alongside Kenny Brown to help him with Dawson and Ashworth who had got used to playing on the big pitch better than our attack and were giving Ken problems in the air. At the same time we were to switch to a flat back four, in the 4-2-4 formation. We basically reversed our tactics. Peter Brabrook had got a bit lost in the first half and this brought him back into things a bit.
>
> So we went out looking to make Preston play our way.

But Preston were out to keep the pressure on. A Ross free-kick was punched out by Standen after a clash with Lawton. But West Ham began to find some momentum and pushed forward. A Byrne cross was blocked by Singleton, but he was caught square in the 'bread-basket' and Crooks was recalled to the field to help the ailing centre half recover his 'poise'.

For Byrne:

> Shutting down Lawton seemed to kill their attack and Greenwood's plan began to open the way to goal; we had a number of chances. Having said that about Ron's strategy, our equaliser was just a little bit lucky.

West Ham drew level in the fifty-third minute. Peter Brabrook took a corner on the right that Brown, under extreme pressure from Dawson and Ashworth, headed to

Hurst, who had lost Singleton who seemed to still be feeling the effects of his 'ball-stop'. The powerful West Ham forward caught the ball perfectly with a header of his own. Kelly fingertipped the ball on to the underside of the bar but it cannoned down. Hurst was on his knees as Kelly made a grab for the ball but as he turned it struck his back and trickled agonisingly slowly over the line. Budgie Byrne recalled the moment:

> At that point we all thought they were beaten. They had really dominated up to then but we had gained control of midfield and the attack was getting some service, all we had to do to score more goals was to hang on to this; keep things that way.

Bubbles rang out louder than ever as the match started to move at breakneck pace, going backwards and forwards. Only minutes later, a cutting drive from Bovington flew over the Preston bar and then Kelly saved a Sissons pile-driver. A long, long ball from Bond found the head of Hurst, but the Preston 'keeper had positioned himself superbly and caught the ball with ease just a few feet in front of Hurst. It was clear that the Hammers were making headway as Holden was forced back and into tackling action.

Another huge pass from Bond found Byrne well inside the Preston penalty area, but Budgie caught his studs in the long grass and the split second of delay allowed the ball to be cleared. At the other end of the field, Standen had dived bravely at the feet of Alex Dawson and in the following confusion caused by a high ball from Ross, a Wilson pass allowed Holden a powerful drive that went just over the bar.

Byrne set up a Sissons cross that Hurst somehow missed completely just a few yards from the Preston goal. Budgie recalled:

> Geoff got it at about waist height. The ball went across the goal but Hurst, with Singleton all over him, completely missed it, five yards out! Then Sissons nearly scored his second with a shot that beat Kelly but crawled past the far post.

Preston made it back to the last part of the West Ham half and a slip by Moore made room for an Ashworth effort, but Standen was yet again a safe pair of hands. Another Ashworth chance was, in much the same way as Byrne had experienced, disarmed by the lush Wembley turf.

Although Boyce and Bovington were controlling the midfield in the final quarter of the game, thoughts were turning to extra time (which had not occurred since 1947) and the possibility of a replay (which would have been staged at Goodison Park on the following Thursday at 7.30 p.m.) as Preston were forced to call on their most primitive reserves, producing penetrating runs and battering hard into West Ham's midfield and defence, chasing the Irons attack that was now working with the rest of the side. This all-out effort, drawn up from the very core of the Preston men's battling instincts, gave the stoic Lilywhites opportunities, but it was costing them; they were haemorrhaging energy and West Ham began to take advantage as Hurst beat the man of steel, Singleton. Geoff's header from just a few feet off the Preston line demanded a fine save from Kelly.

Ashworth and Dawson continued to test Standen but their efforts were weakening. Like a raging bull that had for too long been fighting matadors and picadors in an Iberian ring of blood-letting, Preston were faltering. Lawton kept coming forward, he never stopped trying, but a West Ham corner that was almost converted by a thunderbolt of a shot from Boyce, seemed to be the turning point.

With ten minutes of the match left, Brabrook, taking advantage of the space created for him by the change in tactics, centred with Hurst waiting. However, Kelly was determined to reach the ball before the West Ham man and 'keeper and striker collided as Geoff connected and the header went wide. Play was held up as the Preston goalie was treated for a back injury. Crook was back on the field and, with Kelly looking like he was going to collapse, seemed to administer smelling salts.

As the game went on into the second minute of injury time, West Ham were still applying the pressure. But Preston were not dead. Holden got past Bond and hit the ball into the side net. Johnny Byrne remembered those last tense moments:

> I remember Peter Brabrook having his socks around his ankles at that point. You used see a lot of that at Wembley. It was a big pitch, but at least we were a bit prepared for that. I had told Ron about the central area at West Ham dog track. He had no idea what the inside of Custom House Stadium was like, but it was almost as big as the Wembley playing area and we had trained on it. But the Wembley turf was thick and tended to bring on cramp.

Indeed, as Eddie Bovington went down crippled with cramp in the centre-circle on the stroke of ninety minutes, obliging Rob Jenkins to take to the field for the first time, other players were sitting down and Kelly, who had been hobbling since his injury, was getting further attention from Walter Crooks.

Budgie went on:

> Anyway, the referee was examining his watch when Hurst picked up the ball from a goal kick and hurtled forward on a swerving run on the right, breaking through a barrage of challenges. At just the right second Geoff swept the ball to Brabrook and as Peter sent a high ball to Ronnie, Ticker had begun a run towards their goal. That was typical of Boycie. He had marvellous positional vision. He was still running when Peter's cross connected with his head and he kept on running as the ball went wide of Kelly and into the bottom corner

> of the net. It was very like his second goal against United; a similar header from close in. He was completely unmarked. I was just behind him, just in case anything had gone wrong. The crowd seemed to take ages to react. I did a head-over-heels and as I jumped up they started cheering. Ronnie ran round the goal, I think that was the first time I'd seen a pro player do that. The last few minutes felt like about an hour.

Boyce (whose grandfather had been a turnstile operator at Wembley for West Ham's first FA Cup final appearance in 1923), 'Ticker' to his teammates as he was the engine of the side, the man with wonderful timing, the player who so often made the team 'tick', made it work like clockwork, had executed a beautiful movement. When asked about his nickname he said:

> I have no idea why I got that. It might have been the newspapers. Ron probably said something about me being the heartbeat of the team. I don't know. I suppose it stuck because it fitted the way I played. I played one- and two-touch football and I was able to read a game, anticipate things. I got that from playing the holding role that Ron asked me to take.

West Ham's third goal, which meant they kept up their record of scoring three goals in every round of the cup, had been part of a precise and coordinated forward motion of Boyce's body, his head and trunk had moved in unison. He recalled:

> I didn't feel I had a good game but I was in the right place at the right time with just minutes left. Both teams were tired but Geoff got the move started and pushed it out wide to Peter. His cross from the right was terrific. After I headed the ball, I saw it going in, but it seemed like ages before the crowd reacted.
>
> I knew the 'keeper was beaten. Looking back it was like time stood still, then the crowd roared. After you were hit by the noise, everything went so fast. I ran round the back of the goal. I've heard it said that was the first time a goal has been celebrated like that. I don't know, but I never planned it.

Ron smiled as he went on,

> It was just the moment I think. I suppose it looks a bit funny now. I sort of skipped round the goal. I think it was scored at the West Ham end, but I'm not sure. No one wore team shirts and stuff then. Fans were 'supporters' and a lot of them wore shirts and ties.

According to Peter Brabrook,

> We'd been struggling up until then and I had my socks around my ankles because my legs had been tightening with cramp. But then Hursty played a little one-two before playing the ball out. I took a touch before crossing for Boycie to head in.
>
> It was a decent worked goal, actually, and I remember seeing Boycie running around behind the goal and Budgie doing somersaults.

Eddie Bovington is perhaps the great unsung hero behind Boyce's goal. In the second half he had restricted Lawton, and this had done much to cut off Preston's blood supply and was instrumental in the successful application of a Greenwood tactic.

The goal had been scored with Kelly continuing to suffer from an injured left leg and back problems, but like his North End comrades he had dug deep to struggle on. The Lancashire men were not going to give in; they were not that kind of side; they would fight to and beyond the end. This Preston team were truly admirable, every one of them a man of pride, proud to play for 'Proud Preston'. Their collective will to keep on running, to metaphorically stand and fight, not to let each other or their fans down, caused even the most ardent West Ham fan to respect these men as, like a great and terminally holed battle cruiser, they went down… all guns blazing.

With two or three seconds to go, the Hammers had a nervous moment when North End were given a free-kick on the edge of the West Ham penalty area. Ronnie Boyce recalled the moment,

> It was just outside our box, about minute after I'd scored the our third. I was saying to myself, 'Please don't let this go to extra time!'

For Alec Ashworth,

> It was the last of our last chances. Before that I had a chance when John Bond messed up trying to walk the ball out of defence. I was brought down by Ken Brown; he caught my ankle as I was running in. The kick was a yard outside their box. Tug Wilson got the ball to Nobby and then there were about four players all on top of one another, I think all on top of Ken Brown. Anyway, they managed to get the ball away and then it was all over. I think we were unlucky. I think we had the best of it that day. None of us played less than well.

But, in the end, Bobby Moore picked up the first of the three trophies he would lift at Wembley in successive years. West Ham and Preston had been divided not by skill but by preparation and tactics. According to West Ham's vice-captain, Budgie Byrne, his idea of playing practice matches on the centre-field of the huge West Ham Greyhound Track (something of a second home to greyhound-race-loving Johnny) an area at least as big as the Wembley pitch, had proved more than worthwhile.

Bobby Moore and his men succeeded where, forty-one years before, George Kay and his 1923 Hammers failed in that historic first-ever Wembley final. Perhaps the whole event was encapsulated in one moving moment. As the referee blew to signal the end of the match, the two youngest players on the pitch, John Sissons of West Ham and Howard Kendall of Preston, embraced each other in a mutual spontaneous gesture between teammates of the England Youth side that had won the international tournament a few weeks earlier. At such a moment, the purpose and meaning of 'the beautiful game' becomes clear, if unsayable, but it is such expressions that tell us why 'our game' is beautiful.

When All's Said and Done

All the bubbles West Ham fans had blown, for once, didn't fade and die.
Ken Wolstenholme – BBC commentator for the 1964 FA Cup final

As Budgie received his FA Cup medal from the Earl of Harewood, he momentarily turned to the Hammers' fans:

> The thing that hit you was that they were so happy. I'm not sure I'd ever seen, or ever would see, so much joy in one place. I was well pleased we won, but I don't think I'd ever expected that a game I'd play, anything I would do, would cause so much pleasure. It was infectious. And when we got back to the pitch for the lap of honour we were all falling about laughing and passing round a great big Hammer that Bobby had got from someone in the crowd. It was about eight foot high; you'd never get it into an English ground these days! The noise our fans made was amazing.
>
> But as I was going onto the pitch I spotted Nobby Lawton and couldn't help feeling sorry for him. He played out of his skin and had brought his side within a hair's breadth of winning the cup. But that said, we were so relieved we'd done what we went to Wembley to do and maybe the pressure being suddenly off explains the hysteria that followed the match, or perhaps it was just because we didn't totally deserve to win and had. But then, how many matches did West Ham play and deserve to win and didn't? I've heard it said that after the United game that Wembley was an anti-climax, but it wasn't for me. Like everyone says, it is over too soon, but it was a great day. I never experienced anything like it again.

Forty-one years later West Ham beat Preston in the play-off final for promotion to the Premiership. It would be the last play-off final to be played in Cardiff. The

Hammers were once more the 'first and last Englishmen' – the first to play at Wembley and the last to appear at the Millenium Stadium. However, the celebrations in '64 were, unlike in 2005 , motivated more by joy than relief. Preston players looked resigned in Cardiff; at Wembley they were devastated.

Wembley looked a sea of claret and blue after the game, perhaps indicating that some Cockney deals had been done.

It was certainly an experience Ronnie Boyce would never forget, but it did not change his life. According to Ron, little changed for him. A modest book about the players was put together and the team produced an advertisement for milk that showed some of them drinking out of the cup, so there was a small financial benefit. However, when Boyce's contract came up for renewal in the summer he recalled some dispute:

> You'd go to the ground and there was a long line of players waiting to go in and find out what they were being offered, or if they were being let go... I was told that I would be kept on but I didn't sign the contract straight away. The secretary, Eddie Chapman, said in the paper that because I scored the winner in the FA Cup final I thought I was better than anyone else... that was embarrassing so I signed the contract. The clubs had all the power then.
>
> We were making more than the average wage but we weren't making big money. Around the £25 a week mark, but you could pay all your bills for about £5 a week. Ernie Gregory used to say, 'the money you lot are making!'

West Ham's lap of honour was a moment when at last the young men could be boys again just for a few minutes. Eddie Bovington had been passed a huge, seven-foot hammer that Bobby Moore had been given by a West Ham supporter. Ken Brown had picked up a claret-and-blue bowler hat and he told Eddie to hit the top of it. Eddie did, a lot harder than Ken had expected!

John Bond recalled that Ron Greenwood, who was usually reserved and tight-lipped with praise, actually patted him on the back after the game. This unprecedented show of appreciation seems to demonstrate some concurrence with the view of Tony Scott, a young Hammer of the time, who felt that John was man of the match.

The 1964 FA Cup final had produced thirty-nine goal attempts, twenty-one of them on target, with Kelly making ten saves and Standen eleven. Preston's contribution to the match had been so great that the game was hailed by sections of the press as the greatest cup encounter since the Stanley Matthews Final of 1953. Others claimed that it was the cleanest final tie ever, but thought it lacked an outstanding star and that made it one of the least memorable of the great Wembley confrontations. But it was a unique cup final, and the changing fortunes implicit in the match, culminating in its dramatic finale, made it an exciting and entertaining event.

For all this, the 1964 final has long carried the stigma of Bobby Moore's post-match comment on the game:

> We didn't play well and the final was an anti-climax.

This said, for most of the Hammers side, winning the cup was a means to an end rather than an end in itself. Byrne said:

> After the game we didn't say 'We've done it,' we said 'We're there.' We had made it into Europe because that's where it was at for us. It might have been Ron's influence, but we wanted to play at the highest level, where the innovation was happening and that was what European football would offer us.

Greenwood confirmed Budgie's point of view:

> Winning at Wembley was the greatest moment in the life of this club, but it is only a stage in development.

The West Ham team, being 'The Academy', the think tank that produced a whole new generation of managers, men who thought about the game and looked to create the means to make sides play better, were always going to examine what they had done together. Players like Moore, Brown and Bond, who had been influenced by the analytical mind of West Ham's guerrilla leader of the late 1950s, Malcolm Allison, along with Byrne, who had worked alongside Arthur Rowe, Walter Winterbottom, Alf Ramsey and Greenwood, were disappointed in their Wembley performance. The game had been an exciting spectacle and it is true that the final third of the match had enlivened the game as an event, but for Budgie:

> We didn't play well. We didn't do what we had done against United and, having played so well in that game, felt a bit let down by our performance at Wembley. We were probably lucky to win against Preston. I think it says something that on the way home from Hillsborough Ron had cried. I think that was because he had seen his vision fulfilled, and that will always be a bitter-sweet thing. The game against Preston wouldn't have given him the same sort of feeling.
>
> Ron always said that coaching was nothing magical. It was about getting players to think for themselves and take responsibility. Mistakes are never intentional, even the best of players make them; the trick is to learn from your mistakes. The truth is, despite the old saying, many of us don't learn; we make the same mistakes over and over again. The way to begin not making the same error twice is to admit to the gaffes you have made; then you can begin to do

something about preventing them from happening again, and that is part of responsibility taking. It was looking at the 8-2 defeat by Blackburn on Boxing Day 1963 and the FA Cup final of 1964 in that way that I think led to the club winning the Cup-Winners' Cup in 1965.

Other Hammers reflected the feelings expressed by Moore and Byrne. Although Eddie Bovington had played well, especially in the second half of the 1964 cup final, reflecting on the game he commented:

It wasn't as good as the semi-final and it was an anti-climax really... the final seemed to be over too quickly... you never had the chance to savour being in front. Ronnie Boyce scored, the whistle went and that was it... you've won it, get the cup, lap of honour and back in the dressing room. I sat in the dressing room afterwards laughing and joking clutching my medal but deep down inside thinking 'what was all that about?' We had a reception at the Hilton and went to a club.

I never thought I'd play in a cup final and it was magnificent walking up the tunnel and out for the kick-off, but there's nothing there really and a lot of people say the build-up is better than the actual event. It's like a holiday; you look forward to it for six months, then it's not what you expect it to be.

Things seemed to take time to sink in for Jack Burkett too:

It's only when you look back you get a sort of cold feeling going through you that you've actually done it and been a part of it... Those games fly by but what I remember about the cup final, apart from the fact we weren't at our best and Preston played very well, were the spectators after the game. The noise and roars were amazing.

According to Peter Brabrook:

We certainly didn't have things our own way, it was nip and tuck throughout, but we ended up winning 3-2 when Boycie came up trumps again with a header right near the end. It was a great time for the players, Ron and the club, and that was the start of some very successful times.

For Ken Brown:

Everybody said it was a good, exciting game but I don't think we played that well. Deep down, we weren't satisfied because we'd become used to playing good football.

> We'd gone to New York before our FA Cup run and built good rapport and team spirit.

However, these comments need to been seen in context. They have to be understood as being made in the aftermath of a final that caused both sides to fight and neither to totally dominate. This was in sharp contrast to the West Ham semi-final game with Manchester United, maybe the Hammers' greatest ever game. Almost anything following Hillsborough would have been anti-climactic. The match between West Ham and Preston called for totally different qualities from the camp of the Irons than the physical craft needed to defeat the Manchester Reds, which had been almost wholly a battle of technique and dependency on who could hold and use the ball best in terrible conditions. Wembley 1964 was the sight of a war between eras, regions, attitudes and a trail, in the end, of courage and will. North End had a point to prove (unlike Manchester United who seemed to think they had proved their point just by turning up). At points the Lancastrians had played the calmer football, a stance more characteristic of their opponents. West Ham had come out on top, but only just, and in the best tradition of cup football it could have gone either way.

Pathe Pictorial made an 8mm film of the 1964 FA Cup final. A black-and-white silent edition cost £2 15s. It lasted ten minutes so it didn't show the fact that Preston had twenty-three goal attempts, seven more than the Hammers, and that the Irons had spent long periods of the game chasing the match, but it has to be said that West Ham, having played relatively badly, had recovered. They had dealt with anxiety and fear by a belief in themselves. Such qualities would stand them in good stead over the next year. But more immediately, Johnny Byrne, along with Moore, had to report directly for England duty, while Ronnie Boyce married his long-term partner Dawn – Ticker had had a good year.

The West Ham team that had come from behind to take the cup from Preston's grasp was the last all-English side to win the FA Cup. The winning West Ham side of 1975 came close to the feat, but the big Bermudan Clyde Best played in the fourth round and replay against Swindon. The Manchester City side built by ex-Hammer Malcolm Allison almost replicated his old team's accomplishment but they played a Scot, Arthur Mann, in the third-round match at Maine Road against Luton. All-English sides had won before, but the West Ham side of 1964 would be the last all-English XI to win the FA Cup.

Football, like life, goes on though. A special service of non-stop trains was run at frequent intervals after the match between the stadium station and Marylebone. The first train departed at 4.42 p.m., and the last at 6.06 p.m. Soon the great Empire Stadium was empty and dark. Not an echo remained. The 1964 cup final had been ushered into history. The next game at Wembley was England *v*. Uruguay, the dearest ticket was 50s the cheapest was 7s 6d (standing). Both Byrne and Moore were there.

However, the West Ham players did have a chance to celebrate their victory. The players attended a banquet at the Park Lane Hotel. The party was attended by Des O'Connor, the Vernon Girls and the Bachelors. According to Peter Brabrook,

> It was marvellous and we had a very good night.

Ronnie Boyce agreed:

> The celebrations afterwards were great. We had a brilliant reception at the Hilton, then we went to some nightclub that Budgie had recommended.

Ken Brown recalled:

> After the final we stayed at the Hilton Hotel in Mayfair and Peter Brabrook came up to wake me and Budgie. We'd had a good night!

The official banquet at the Hilton after the match included the sixty-nine-year-old West Ham veteran Billy Moore (no relation to Bobby). Billy had played in the last cup final the Hammers had been involved in – the very first Wembley final. However, for Budgie Byrne, the celebrations didn't quite live up to expectations:

> West Ham had kept the guest list on the low side. There were a few hundred people kind of lost in a great big room. It was a bit gloomy and we enjoyed ourselves much more after it was finished.

At the banquet, the recently elected chairman of the Football Association, Mr Joe Mears, gave a pledge to raise the matter of an increased allocation to the competing clubs at the final. Alas, little came of this promise.

The following day, the newspapers portrayed Preston as the brave losers. Peter Wilson, the legendary sports journalist, who wrote under the aphorism, 'The Man They Can't Gag', was one of the few commentators overtly disappointed with the final. He apparently felt that the Hammers' performance had been something less than mediocre and asked rhetorically:

> How do you think this team will fare next season in the European Cup Winners Cup?

The most immediate answer to this question came when Bobby Moore was voted the Football Writers' Footballer of the Year in 1964, aged just twenty-three. He was the youngest ever recipient of the award. Wilson would get another answer a year later, and another the year after that. One thing the Hammers of the sixties were good at was answering questions.

7

Homeward Bound

We lost the final in injury time, which was heartbreaking, especially as Leeds and Sunderland had pipped us to promotion to the First Division, but I just felt a great sense of pride... It was if North End were saying 'We are at Wembley, and we're proud.'

Howard Kendall – Preston North End

All My Dreams Come Back to Me

The East End of London virtually came to a standstill as the Hammers brought the cup home for the first time in West Ham's history. Although the day of the cup final had been one of the greatest in the life of Ron Boyce, he insisted that nothing could have beaten West Ham's homecoming the following day, taking the cup back to the Town Hall on the open-topped bus. He remembered going through Aldgate and there being no more than a sprinkling of people there. Ron thought the whole thing was not such a good idea and that it was going to be 'a washout'. But as soon as the Boleyn boys got to Stratford E15, it all started. As the coach went past the Black Lion at Plaistow, the team was handed a crate of lager. Ticker remembered people kissing him on the forehead and the tremendous atmosphere when he and his teammates got to the Town Hall. Even looking back over the years, Ron thought the whole thing was '... unbelievable, such a wonderful experience'.

For Ken Brown, the sight of the crowds from Petticoat Lane to Barking that welcomed the team back is one his most abiding memories of being involved in football. He recalled the homecoming from Wembley:

> We got on the open-top bus and thought we were going to look stupid if no one was about, but we didn't dream of the number of people who'd be there. From Aldgate to East Ham Town Hall, I've never seen so many people in all my life. Incredible!
>
> We kept on seeing one bloke in different venues – he had a sports car, but how he got through the crowds was a mystery.

Jack Burkett recalled:

> On Sunday we went on the cavalcade to East Ham with 250,000 lining the streets and you wondered where they'd all come from. That's what hits you – the support.

Eddie Bovington 'couldn't believe the amount of people on the streets. Unbelievable.'

Johnny Byrne had told Ron Greenwood that he didn't think anyone would be out on the streets to welcome the cup into the Docklands, but Budgie's memories were quite the opposite:

> First thing, Peter Brabrook woke up Ken Brown and me in our room at the Hilton. We'd had a good night. From Aldgate to East Ham, through Whitechapel and the Mile End Road, the crowds lined the route our coach took. It was eight to ten deep most of the way! Banners out on balconies and the sides of buildings; there must have been a million people out on the streets. It took us four hours to reach East Ham Town Hall, which was normally a twenty-five minute drive. We all loved it. The cup, that had spent the night in Ron's bed, was being passed round and held up for the half-a-dozen miles from Petticoat Lane to East Ham. This was the kind of thing you always dreamed of. It's not the money that motivates you in the end but the chance of glory, the kind of appreciation the supporters gave us that day. It was a nice feeling; kinda that you'd given the fans something.

For many of the tens of thousands applauding as the team coach slowly edged its way down the Barking Road the Wembley triumph was the realisation and culmination of deeply held hopes and long-standing dreams. It made West Ham something, a real place with much to offer.

In Emptiness and Harmony

Howard Kendall recalled:

> When we got back to Preston, the fans had painted the town blue and white and that bus journey from the railway station to the Market Square was very emotional. Everybody had a banner, rosette or flag of some kind and they were singing 'Glory, Glory, Howard Kendall' and 'We want North End'. I got a special cheer from the crowd outside the Guttridge Memorial Church,

> where I'd played the organ at Sunday school. It was a truly special time in my life.

An estimated 80,000 people lined the streets and roads of Preston as the players made a journey of something less than a mile from the station to the Market Square in an open-top coach, headed by the Brindle Brass Band. At points, police were obliged to create a path through the crowds, but the coach never achieved much more than walking pace through a town. As the coach passed Preston Royal Infirmary on its way to Deepdale, the patients who were fit enough to be brought or make their own way into the grounds welcomed their gallant side back. Many supporters who could not get to Wembley attended local cinemas where the film of the match was being shown again in 'living colour'.

The coach got to the Town Hall and every player was greeted by Councillor Cyril Molyneux, Preston's Mayor, as they came out onto the balcony to address the crowd. 'They didn't win the cup,' he confirmed, 'but they won the admiration of the country.' Turning to the Preston side he said: 'You provided one of the greatest shows ever seen at Wembley. Thank you for all the glory you have brought to the town of Preston.'

The great Lancashire throng was made up of a cross-section of the whole town of Preston – men and women, babes in arms, pensioners in wheelchairs. The atmosphere was, in its way, equal to that of Wembley. Rattles cracked a fanfare along with blowing bugles. Tony Singleton told the gathered thousands that North End would try again the following year; Alex Dawson confirmed what everyone already knew, that the Lilywhites had done their best; but perhaps George Ross made the most moving remarks:

> Being a Scotsman [there were huge cheers at this point] I am a foreigner among you [this raised laughter and more cheers] but I feel I'm part of you now [protracted and loud approval was expressed].

Following a civic reception, the procession was recommenced and made its way to Deepdale. As night fell, the breezes of darkness shifted the discarded blue-and-white bunting around the streets of Preston; the dream had finally ended.

Better to Have Loved and Lost…

Nobby Lawton walked to the edge of players' tunnel and, for the briefest of moments, he was alone with his thoughts. Post-match he was to sportingly comment that, 'The better team won', but it was a heartbreaking finish for North End, whose cultured play made a mockery of their underdog label. Indeed, Preston had experienced a fine season under Lawton's leadership.

League Appearances (forty-two games):
Ashworth A. 31, Barber D.E. 5, Barton J.B. 2, Davidson I. 3[T], Dawson A.D. 41, Donnelly J. 9, Godfrey B.C. 11, Holden A.D. 39, Kelly J.A. 40, Kendall H. 9, Lawton N. 38, Lee F. 1, Napier C.R.A. 1, Ross G. 42, Singleton A.J. 42, Smith J.A.G. 33, Spavin A. 40, Wilson D.C. 41.

FA Cup Appearances (eight games):
Kelly 8, Ross 8, Smith 2, Lawton 8, Singleton 8, Davidson 7, Wilson 8, Ashworth 4, Dawson 8, Spavin 8, Holden 8, Kendall 5, Donnelly 2, Godfrey 4.

League Cup Appearances (one game):
Barton, Ross, Smith, Lawton, Singleton, Davidson, Wilson, Barber, Dawson, Spavin, Holden.

Goalscorers	League	FA Cup	Total
Dawson	30	6	36
Ashworth	14	0	14
Wilson	11	0	11
Lawton	6	1	7
Holden	6	1	7
Godfrey	5	1	6
Spavin	4	1	5
Kendall	1	1	2
Davidson	1	0	1
Singleton	0	1	0
Own goals	1 (Kiernan of Northampton)		

Ever-presents: George Ross and Tony Singleton.
Hat-tricks: Alex Dawson, Alex Ashworth and Dave Wilson, one each.
Players used: eighteen.
Chairman: J.H. Ingham Esq. (died February 1964) then A. Harrison Esq. BEM.
Leading scorer: thirty-six goals – Alex Dawson (thirty League, six FA Cup).
Best home run without defeat: fourteen games.
Best away run without defeat: five games.
Longest run unbeaten: eleven games.
Longest run without a win: three games.
Best home attendance: 38,290 *v.* Bolton, FA Cup 27 January 1964.
Worst home attendance: 12,933 *v.* Northampton, 24 April 1964.
Worst away attendance: 6,492 *v.* Scunthorpe, 7 March 1964.
Aggregate and average home attendance: 395,244, 18,821.
Aggregate and average away attendance: 351,080, 16,718.

Debutants: Alec Ashworth, Kit Napier, Brian Godfrey and Frank Lee.
Last games: Barber and Napier.

For all this, missing out on promotion and losing in the final of the FA Cup made 1963/64 a bittersweet season for everyone involved with Preston, its football team and the town. North End had missed both objectives by only the narrowest of margins. On 14 August 1963 Peter Thompson moved from Deepdale to Liverpool for a fee of £33,500. This was regarded as a huge sum at the time and matched exactly the sum North End made from their 1964 cup run. How different the whole history of the club might have been if it had been possible to retain Thompson as part of a First Division, cup-winning side. North End, with their innovative training methods and youth policy, producing the likes of Gordon Milne and Thompson, had a good foundation on which to build a fine team. But Liverpool, led by Bill Shankly, were establishing their remarkable domination of English football, winning the League Championship in 1964 and the FA Cup a year later. It seemed that the old ascendancy of North End's style of football had, in a sense, passed to Merseyside, where it would prosper for most of the second half of the twentieth century.

For all this, Nobby Lawton could still recall that one day in May and the season with fondness:

> Football can be a cruel game, a rollercoaster of emotions sometimes, but that day was my proudest moment in football. When something goes wrong in your life, as it does from time to time, or no matter how many highs and lows you experience, everybody has special memories to savour. 1964 was an incredible time in my life, and nobody can ever take that away.

Tiredness had taken its toll on the Preston players at the same time West Ham had found their rhythm. If the game had gone into extra time the Hammers would have looked the best bet. Afterwards both Alex Dawson and Doug Holden, who had played in five cup finals between them, agreed that the game in 1964 had been the best. Certainly there was no disgrace in defeat. Managers Jim Milne and Ron Greenwood were both pleased with the way their teams had performed and the high standard of football. Bobby Moore praised North End for playing good football and admitted they had worried West Ham on many occasions. Among the neutrals, the game was said to compare with the great 1948 final between Manchester United and Blackpool.

This said, it was a cruel end for the team that had belied their Second Division status for much of the game and, despite being a lower-division side, lived up to their reputation as purveyors of stylish football. Both sides played in a positive, attacking style. However, in the last ten minutes West Ham looked the more skilful overall. In their efforts to find a way back into the game Preston became disorientated and lost shape. For the first time they started to look like a Second Division side. When it was over, some Lilywhites fans shed a few tears, for what might have been as much as for what was.

Nobby Lawton remembered a letter he received from the Deepdale director three days after the FA Cup final:

> I'll never forget the words. It said: 'I want to thank you and the players for a wonderful weekend, because I must confess I thought we'd get murdered!'
>
> That's what a lot of people thought. We were massive underdogs but we played with pride, passion and tremendous skill... Do you know we hardly gave the ball away in that final, and as captain that made me so incredibly proud.
>
> That's what we did and Preston shocked West Ham. Bobby Moore told me afterwards he couldn't believe how well we held the ball and dominated the game until half-time.
>
> Of course the disappointment was immense to lose 3-2 after going ahead twice in the final, but we put on a great show and had a real go. I told the lads in the dressing room, they couldn't have done anything more and they'd done Preston proud.

Jimmy Milne received more than a hundred letters of congratulation from Scotland alone, and a special letter was also received from a beloved Lancastrian character:

> Coronation Street, Wetherfield.
>
> To the lads of Preston North End,
>
> I know nowt about football but I watched you all on Saturday and, believe me, I was very proud of you. It was real bad luck to miss the cup. You certainly deserved it. Ah well, you did your best and that's all that matters.
>
> God bless you, Ena Sharples.

That Preston's reputation had reached the Rovers Return was a sign of the fame the club had attained. The vast majority of North End's supporters had seen the match on television. The media, which would transform football in the future, had only really been a mass phenomenon for about a decade before 1964.

The players who had contested the cup final for Preston received two-year contracts and most remained at Deepdale into the late sixties. A few months after the cup final, the Government announced that the new wonder plane, the TSR2, was to be built at Preston. The town and its football club seemed to be on the move. But the high hopes raised in 1964 were not realised. Promotion was theoretically attainable well into the 1964/65 and 1966/67 seasons, but relegation was a real threat in 1965/66 and 1967/68, and became a reality in 1969/70. Injuries played their part, notably in 1964/5, but North End's form was too often simply inconsistent. In 1965/66, the side enjoyed a good cup run. Having defeated Charlton Athletic 3-2 away, the fourth round revived memories of 1964. A replay against Bolton Wanderers at Deepdale was won 3-2, with two penalties scored by Brian Godfrey. The fifth round saw an epic encounter with Tottenham Hotspur at Preston. Spurs were defeated 2-1, after leading through a Jimmy Greaves goal. The quarter-finals brought Manchester United to Deepdale. In front of a crowd of 37,876, North End took the lead through Dawson, only to see Herd bring the game level with what many saw as an infringement of the offside rule. At Old Trafford, Singleton equalised after Denis Law had given United the lead, but by the final whistle North End had been well beaten 3-1. Perhaps the tie could have been won at Deepdale, but almost 100,000 people saw these two games, and the players had acquitted themselves very well.

The defeat of Cardiff 9-0 in the last League game of the season helped the Lilywhites narrowly avoid relegation. The following term Preston won their first ten home games, but scored just half a dozen goals in the first ten matches away from Deepdale. This could be seen as the start of the long-term decline of the club.

The club's failure to move forward in the 1960s might be seen as a consequence of the Preston board's lack of confidence, which was probably a reaction to barely break-even gates of 15,000, and soaring player costs. Wages and related costs rose from £15,000 to £60,000 in 1963/64, reflecting the team's success, but did not fall back thereafter, and had reached £70,000 by 1967 and £90,000 two years later. In simple terms, by 1967 these costs exceeded gate takings. The bank would not sanction an extension of the overdraft, which had to be covered by the club's property. Past failure to acquire Deepdale outright now became a seriously limiting factor in relations with the bank.

Since neither the directors nor the supporters appeared to be willing to fund expansion, through personal guarantees or high admission prices respectively, the obvious way out of the board's problems was to subsidise the club by selling player assets. By the mid-1960s, requests for transfers had reached an unprecedented level. Dave Wilson got into a long-running dispute with the club, and the League tribunal intervened on his behalf in October 1966. Howard Kendall, who after the 1964 cup final had become an overnight and national hero, also asked for a transfer, which was similarly turned down, but when he turned twenty-one the club was obliged to offer him a new contract and he was free to refuse it and leave the club. On 8 November Kendall made a second request, and Liverpool upped a previous offer to £75,000. It was decided that ultimately Preston had no choice but to transfer him. Knowing that local reaction would be very bad, it was agreed that it would be announced that the player had asked for a transfer that had been rejected. Members were accused of defeatism, and warned that the club was bound for the Third Division.

By the end of January, North End's cup run had ended, and promotion was an increasingly distant prospect. In February, the League tribunal fixed Wilson's transfer fee at just £20,000, a vast reduction on the sort of sum discussed before the transfer of Peter Thompson. He was quickly snapped up by Liverpool. By doing all they could to keep a player, the board had lost tens of thousands of pounds; this was a mistake they would learn from. At this point Kendall put in his written request for a new contract, and Preston offered him one. But by this time the club was feeling pragmatic about selling its player assets; if Preston sold Kendall that would make money available for new signings. This attitude, although perhaps predictable, was to have a lasting impact on the club's history. It was generally agreed that the acquisition of higher-priced players would present too many problems for a club like Preston and for virtually the next thirty years, upcoming prospects would be sold and replaced by older players who, whatever their individual merits, had usually seen their best days and would have little or no sell-on value. A cycle of decline was thus confirmed.

Howard Kendall's transfer was announced on 11 March. As the minutes relate:

> The chairman had met him and asked him what he wanted, but the player had been adamant that he wanted a move to First Division football. His subsequent transfer to Everton at a fee of £85,000 was confirmed. The fee payable immediately.

Fears that the club would be perceived as a 'Liverpool nursery' had apparently weighed against the Anfield offer. Alex Dawson also left, to join Bury FC, so that £115,000 had been raised from sales in just three weeks. Harry Catterick, the Everton manager at the time, was highly delighted with his purchase – he commented: 'Kendall is another splendid investment for our pool of young players' (Howard had joined Alan Ball, recently acquired by Everton from Blackpool).

Although the board had resisted the loss of Wilson and Kendall, relegation three seasons later was the inevitable consequence of such a short-term policy. In the same season, Everton won the championship. Preston, in the space of a few years had moved from being on the verge of a new golden age, to relative ignominy. The wonderful season of 1964 that had ended so sadly, which could have made Preston a club of the future, turned out to be the seed of North End's decades-long demise.

The Men of '64

I attended the 1964 cup final reunion at the Pines Hotel in Chorley early in May 2004. Eight of Preston's final squad, George Ross, Tony Singleton, Howard Kendall, Dave Wilson, Alex Dawson, Doug Holden, Brian Godfrey and Nobby Lawton were there. Their life stories are varied and, of course, most are still incomplete. For many of the Preston team that played in the 1964 cup final, that Wembley appearance marked the height or the swansong of their careers, for others it was just a start. One such was **Howard Kendall**. He was chosen for an FA team in 1964/65 under Alf Ramsey that made a two-match tour of Gibraltar. The team won both games with Kendall scoring in each of them.

Kendall left Deepdale for Goodison Park in March 1967 and picked up his second loser's medal in the 1968 cup final with the Toffees, but in 1969/70 he was a member of the Liverpool Blues' side that won the League Championship. After seven seasons with Everton, having made 233 League appearances, Kendall moved on, first to Birmingham and then to Stoke City, before becoming player-manager of Blackburn Rovers. Kendall took Rovers from the Third Division to the brink of the First within two seasons. He moved into full-time management with Everton and led them to the League Championship in 1985 and 1987.

He arrived at Goodison on the final day of May in 1981. One newspaper commented: 'They're not asking much from Howard Kendall at Everton – only a three-minute mile, a century before lunch and a successful assault on Everest.' Always a modest and articulate man, he had been taken on to restore pride to Everton and help the club move out of the shadow cast by Liverpool FC. Howard recalled:

> One of the first telephone calls I got that day was from a journalist, who just said 'Welcome to Everton – you'll get the sack you know'... I never did, but it was a monumental task. Liverpool were the yardstick then, like Manchester United are today. They were the best club side in the world, and they were just across Stanley Park. I was sat at my desk at Goodison in those first few hours and my only thought was 'how could we overtake them?' and we did it.
>
> I'd come from Blackburn, where a couple of months earlier I was in a board meeting when a director had suggested sending out second-class stamps instead of first to save money, or to order a pint less of milk to try and balance the books. That was the reality; how the game has changed in that time it's incredible.

Over three years Kendall had transformed Everton, but this was not before having to deal with falling attendances and repeated calls for him to be sacked. He returned home from training one day to find 'Kendall Out' daubed on his garage doors. He commented:

> People say don't buy papers when you're struggling. But I did and the stories about how I was going to get sacked just motivated me all the more.
>
> Our gates had fallen, we were getting 10,000 for some games, and the media were on my back. But dealing with the pressure is part of the job. You want to

do it for yourself, but it's really for the fans, for all those people who love the club. Time was the biggest factor in my success at Everton. Billy Bingham and Gordon Lee each had three years as manager and I was into my third season when things turned around.

Today, the demands of the modern job have made it an impossible task compared to my years at Everton. Gerard Houllier was under pressure at Liverpool after two games, but look how many trophies he won. When we won the Championship for the first time in 1985 we lost the first two games but still went on to win it. Today's situation is ludicrous. Now you have until the end of August.

There remains a warm affection for Kendall amongst many Evertonians who were around under his reign at Goodison, and he was the most successful manager in Everton's history. In six years on Merseyside, Kendall delivered the FA Cup, two Championships in 1985 and 1987, and the 1985 Cup-Winners' Cup, Everton's first European silverware. Indeed, only Norman Whiteside's curling effort for Manchester United denied Everton the domestic double and European trophy treble years before Old Trafford could dream of their first victory parade hangover. He had dragged Everton from also-rans to being the best in the world – a fact acknowledged by *World Soccer* magazine, who in 1985 named Everton their 'World Team of the Year' and Kendall the club manager of the year. He reminisced:

It is lovely still to be recognised by people and thought of that way, very special indeed… It was as if we were unbeatable then. I got on the plane to the Cup-Winners' Cup final in Rotterdam and I just knew we'd win that final. I sensed it, but I couldn't transmit it to the players. I had incredible confidence in characters like Peter Reid and Andy Gray who would make it happen for you.

The press called us the team with no stars, but the players had a rare belief that they'd never be beaten. They also showed the same confidence in me and I just felt I could go on and on. It can be a formidable task to control strong men on and off the field, but I believed Everton were the best in Europe and they proved it.

The Cup-Winners' Cup semi-final against Bayern Munich in Germany will live with me until my last day. Bayern were a side of tremendous quality; world-class footballers like Lothar Matthaus, Klaus Augenthaler, and up front they had a fearsome and aggressive striker called Dieter Hoeness. The Olympic Stadium was boiling with emotion; the whole of Bavaria expected them to win. But I'd studied Bayern for several weeks, watching their games and analysing their system. I devised a defensive and tactical plan that turned out to be one of the proudest moments of my career because we kept the

Germans to 0-0. There were 50,000 at Goodison for the second leg and we won 3-1. I don't think I've been overcome by so much noise as that night.

The final in Rotterdam was an incredible day of emotion, yet, strangely, when I think back to that season I remember nearly going out in the first round to a part-time team of students from the University College of Dublin. We could only manage a 0-0 draw in Dublin and a young lad called Hanrahan missed a golden chance in the final seconds at Goodison that would have put UCD through on away goals. It could have been a very different story.

Kendall is a regular at Everton home games and writes a weekly column for the *Liverpool Echo*, but that is as far as his involvement goes these days. He confesses,

I'm happy as I am and I certainly wouldn't want to return as a number one, that's for sure. A lot of people need to be seen on television at games to show they wish to get back into the game. Not me, I am not that interested. I don't miss match days, but what I do miss is putting on that tracksuit and having two hours a day with the players on the training pitch. I have to say, though, that by the end of my final spell at Everton (June 1997–July 1998) I'd stopped enjoying it. The way it was handled by the club at the end really hurt. It soured me. You get spoilt with success and if you're selecting a team you know deep down are not good enough, it's not enjoyable. It was very, very difficult to get motivated. We always had a bit of music on the team bus, and we were down at West Ham that season. We were a couple of miles from Upton Park and I said to the boys get the tape on loud. The track that blurted out was Tina Turner's *Simply The Best*; none of them joined in and I didn't either because I knew we weren't. There wasn't a peep from the players and they just looked straight ahead.

But football has given me so much to savour, from the cut and thrust of management in England to living and working in another country. To this day I'm still convinced I signed the greatest goalkeeper in the world in the 1980s, Neville Southall. I bought Trevor Steven from Burnley for £325,000 and what amazed me was that they had not had a single bid for the boy. Trevor had tremendous vision and was one of my finest signings, I suppose. A couple of weeks later I was sat in the directors' room at Goodison and Bob Paisley came in and said 'You were right about Steven, Howard. Every time I went to see him he never finished a game. He just seemed too weak. But I should have taken a risk on him.' Sometimes you just sense a player is the right one at the right time and Trevor was certainly that.

After his first stint with the Toffees, Kendall took on the job of leading Athletico Bilbao in Spain. He commented:

> When I left Everton for Athletico Bilbao I knew I had to test myself again, because English clubs were banned from Europe and I needed that challenge. After six years something inside me just said go out and start again.

Kendall came back to England to do what he could to cure the ills of a struggling Manchester City side. He returned to Everton, but was not able to meet the expectations of the club's fans and management and started what was to be a string of appointments with Notts County and Sheffield United.

Alex Dawson's twenty-seven goals would make him North End's top marksman in the 1964/65 season and by 1966 he had scored 114 goals in 197 outings for Preston (including his vital goal against Swansea that helped the Whites reach Wembley) a strike-rate comparable only to that of Deepdale legend Charlie Wayman. One of a number of hat-tricks he scored in his North End career included three headed goals in a 3-2 win over Charlton Athletic at The Valley.

In 1967, Dawson signed for Bury and later played for Brighton, Brentford (on loan) and finally Corby Town before he retired. According to his former teammate, England and Manchester United legend Nobby Stiles, 'his fire was allowed to burn out too quickly', having been brought on too soon because of Munich:

> Dawson was strong beyond his years, but soon enough he showed evidence of burnout. He arrived at Old Trafford as a fearless, dark and hugely powerful young man. He was an England Schoolboy international who was a big factor in two of United's Youth Cup triumphs. He scored in his first games for the first team in the League, in the FA Cup and the League Cup and at the age of eighteen years and thirty-three days, just a few months after Munich, he scored a hat-trick in the FA Cup semi-final.

For Stiles, Dawson had 'raw power', but this was not nurtured by United's assistant manager Jimmy Murphy, who according to Nobby was driven by his efforts to keep United alive as a force in football and win something after the Old Trafford side had been so cruelly cut to pieces. In this sense, Dawson was one of the last victims of Munich.

In typical style he scored six goals in ten matches during his short time in West London, but the Bees could not afford his transfer fee. Dawson was on target 212 times in 394 League matches over his thirteen years in the professional game. He was a centre forward after the English tradition and the main threat in North End's striking armoury of 1964. His skipper at Preston, Nobby Lawton, said:

> I'd known Alex since we were both on the ground staff at Old Trafford. He was a bull of a centre forward and was a Deepdale hero. He's a lovely man and I was best man at his wedding. He hasn't changed at all, and we are still great

friends today. Alex and the rest of the team would have graced any Premiership side today.

Doug Holden stayed three seasons at Deepdale before emigrating to Australia and gaining international recognition representing the Socceroos. He was one of the unluckiest players when shooting; often the ball hit the post, the crossbar or a fortunately placed defender. His greatest asset was his skill in limited space. In claustrophobic situations, between line and defender, Holden found a way through.

Tony Singleton never scored in his eight-season, 287-League-game career with Preston. But of course it was his first goal for the club that sent the Lilywhites to Wembley in 1964.

Alan Spavin turned out in 424 League games for Preston; only four players in the club's history had appeared in more League matches. He netted twenty-six times, including two goals against Rotherham United in 1971, helping North End to the Division Three Championship. He was the consummate team player. Alan became player-manager at Morecambe after the resignation of former manager Dave Roberts in 1975. Spavin made thirty appearances for the club before he resigned in 1976 to become player/assistant manager at American club Washington Diplomats. Alan later returned to play briefly for Lancaster City for the 1976/77 term and turned out seven more times for Preston in the League campaign of 1977/78. Spavin had a season at Telford United as player-coach and on retiring from the game as a player he became Youth Officer at Preston North End before returning to the USA to continue his career in coaching and managing in American football.

Nobby Lawton would turn out for Preston on 164 occasions in his half a decade with the club and net twenty-three times during that period. But after 1964, Lawton never hit the same heights again; his career was becalmed by injuries. He missed the last part of the 1966/67 season following a second cartilage operation and, though he returned for the start of the next campaign, he was cruelly barracked by fans who had obviously forgotten his great service over the previous five years. Lawton admits his midfield strengths were on the wane:

> I broke my leg at Manchester United, and although I was in and out of the team at Old Trafford, it knocked the confidence out of me. When I joined Preston everything seemed to click, but those last couple of years were very hard at Deepdale.

Nobby moved to Brighton and Hove Albion for two years before finishing his career at Lincoln City. He reflected:

I came back after the two knee operations at Preston, but I was a shadow of the player I was in 1964. I was thirty-two, and the surgeon sat me down and said, 'if you suffer another injury then you'll be a cripple for life'. I felt a sense of total relief that I wouldn't have to play again. I'd had enough of football then. It was a genuine relief to get out of the game. I was butchered really. Both my knees are shattered and I still can't run today. I've had one knee replacement and I'm waiting for the other to be done.

Nobby looks back on his career with mixed emotions:

Money didn't come into it then. We got £30 a week and everything else went into the cup final players' pool. Life wasn't as complicated. Everything seemed a little simpler somehow forty years ago. It's great to see the modern generation getting paid good money and being looked after, because football was a different world then. You'd be kicked on your ankle in a match and the physio would rush on and put a cold sponge down the back of your neck. I'd be shouting 'it's my ankle' and he'd just rush off.

When I retired I could never believe the way the likes of Bobby Moore, an England great who captained the team to the World Cup in 1966, was kicked into touch by the game he had served so well.

Take the great John Charles, who died recently, for instance. They are talking about building a statue in John's memory now, but years ago nobody wanted to know him.

That's a fact of life, and because football is fashionable again, people want to be a part of it. That's great for the game, but it all seems a bit false somehow.

Many years ago I sat on the PFA Committee with Derek Dougan and Terry Venables and the letters I used to get from ex-players who couldn't pay the bills used to break my heart. Some players endured a bitter struggle to survive financially and many were ill. That was the reality, but now football's revolution has changed everything.

After retiring from the game in the early 1970s, like so many in his profession, Nobby found it tough to readjust to the environment outside football. But he carved out a successful career as a sales director with a Manchester-based imports and exports business, where he still works today.

I remember going for a job soon after I retired, and the guy just said 'you were a good footballer, but you're no use to me pal'. That's the stark reality you have to accept and you either sink or swim. When you come out of football you're a bit thick, I suppose, because everything has been done for you in your previous career. You have to start using your brain again, and to start a new life. I know many players I played with at Manchester United and Preston just couldn't handle that. Some took to drink and went on benders to ease the pain. In some ways I could see why they took that path, because when you finish there is a huge void in your life to fill.

If there's 60,000 paying to watch you every week, then you know you are good at something. You feel brilliant, you've made it. But when you finish, absolutely nothing compensates for that, not even a fortune of money. When you are at the peak of your powers it is a truly wonderful feeling, but later on when young players go past you or you're playing in the Third Division with somebody booting the ball over your head, then it's not so much fun. Players who've had a phenomenal natural gift to entertain can't use that skill anymore.

They get to thirty-five and it's 'cheerio pal', and that's why so many have gone off the rails. Some scrape by, others struggle on, and some just give up.

Of course, like anyone else in life, you have good days and bad days, but I've been a very lucky man… I wouldn't have changed anything. I'd do it all again. It was a special chapter in the history of Preston North End, and it did make me so sad to see Preston struggle so badly in the mid-1980s.

Looking back, the problem, I believe, was the unbelievable tradition that weighed Preston down for so many years. When Sir Tom Finney, the greatest player of all time retired, that was their history. After that, nothing was good enough. It took them a generation to recover from Tom retiring.

Now the club is on a sound footing again, Preston needs to be in the Premiership. Then they can forget about the old days, but for many 1964 will always be a magical moment and it is fantastic to be able to remember it with such pride as North End's captain at Wembley.

Wembley had not proved to be a happy hunting ground for **Alan Kelly**. The cup final had been his second appearance at the national stadium. During his first visit as the Republic of Ireland 'keeper England had put five goals past him. After Packie Bonner, Alan Kelly senior is the most capped Republic of Ireland goalkeeper in history. In a game against Bristol City at Deepdale in September 1975, he sustained a shoulder injury that caused him to lose the power in his right hand and had to learn to write with his left. This bad luck certainly robbed Kelly of many more caps. Alan had made forty-seven full international appearances for the Republic of Ireland up to his injury, which made him second only to Tom Finney (seventy-six caps for England) amongst Preston's most-capped players. He kept five clean sheets in international football and, until recently, was the only 'keeper to have captained Eire (against the USSR in October 1972). His international record shows something of his skill as a goalkeeper and integrity as a sportsman:

1962	*v.* Austria (lost 2–3)
1963	*v.* Iceland (won 4–2), *v.* Iceland (drew 1–1), *v.* Scotland (won 1–0)
1964	*v.* Austria (drew 0–0), *v.* Austria (won 3–2), *v.* Spain (lost 1–5), *v.* Spain (lost 0–2), *v.* Poland (lost 1–3)
1965	*v.* Belgium (lost 0–2)
1966	*v.* Austria (lost 0–1), *v.* Belgium (won 3–2)
1967	*v.* Spain (drew 0–0), *v.* Spain (lost 0–2), *v.* Turkey (won 2–1), *v.* Czechoslovakia (lost 0–2)
1968	*v.* Poland (drew 2–2), *v.* Czechoslovakia (won 2–1)
1969	*v.* Poland (lost 0–1), *v.* Austria (drew 2–2), *v.* Denmark (drew 1–1), *v.* Czechoslovakia (lost 1–2), *v.* Denmark (lost 0–2), *v.* Hungary (lost 1–2)
1970	*v.* Scotland (drew 1–1), *v.* Denmark (drew 1–1), *v.* Hungary (lost 0–4), *v.* Poland (lost 1–2), *v.* West Germany (lost 1–2)
1971	*v.* Poland (lost 0–2), *v.* Sweden (drew 1–1), *v.* Sweden (lost 0–1), *v.* Italy (lost 0–3), *v.* Italy (lost 1–2), *v.* Austria (lost 1–4)
1972	*v.* Iran (won 2–1), *v.* Ecuador (won 3–2), *v.* Chile (lost 1–2), *v.* Portugal (lost 1–2)
1973	*v.* USSR (lost 1–2), *v.* Poland (lost 0–2), *v.* France (drew 1–1), *v.* Norway (drew 1–1), two caps won with Drumcondra
1975	*v.* West Germany (won 3–0), *v.* England (lost 1–5)

Kelly also managed the Republic for one game (when Eire faced Switzerland in April 1980).

Playing 447 League games for North End, Kelly gained the record for the number of Football League appearances in a Preston shirt (he also made sixty-five cup appearances). As he hung his boots up, the players with the highest number of League appearances including substitute were as follows:

1. Alan Kelly	1961–1975	447
2. Peter McBride	1898–1912	443
3. Willie Cunningham	1949–1963	440
4. Tom Finney	1946–1960	433

This record made him the most experienced League player of all Preston's internationals. From 1966 he missed only five of 214 League games Preston played in those five seasons; he was never dropped.

Kelly was once described by Bobby Charlton as 'a truly great goalkeeper' for whom 'no cause was a lost one'. Charlton was manager of Preston at the time that Alan was forced out of the game and the former Manchester United and England international went on to say that Kelly's name would be as synonymous with Preston North End as is that of the club's legendary Tom Finney.

Kelly saw Preston slide from a peak of second place in Division One in 1957/58 to Division Three for the first time in the club's history at the end of the 1969/70 season. But during his years with the club they also won the Third Division Championship title in 1971. In thirteen seasons as a player at Deepdale, Alan Kelly experienced all the traumas, exaltations and drama normally associated with a top-flight club.

After his playing days were over, Kelly became involved in North End's administration. He was appointed coach and assistant to Nobby Stiles before becoming manager in 1983. He resigned the post in February 1985, but later took up a role as part of Everton's coaching staff.

Both Alan's sons followed in their father's footsteps. Gary played in the Football League with Bury. Alan (junior) succeeded his father as a Republic of Ireland international 'keeper and made his first-team debut for Preston on 8 March 1986 in a 2-1 defeat by Crewe at Deepdale. He stayed in the side for the remainder of that season, but spent the rest of his Deepdale career fighting various injuries and having to share the 'keeper's jersey with David Brown and Simon Farnworth. Whilst with North End he won international honours with the Republic of Ireland at Youth, Under-21, Under-23 and 'B' level, as well as making 142 League appearances for the Lilywhites until he left the club to join Sheffield United.

In recent years Alan (senior) has been involved in goalkeeping clinics in Washington DC, but he returned to Deepdale in 2001 as guest of honour when the 'Alan Kelly Town End' was opened.

Dave Wilson won seven England Under-23 caps. After scoring thirty-one goals in 170 League matches, including a hat-trick at Cardiff, he signed for Liverpool. The move to Anfield did not work out as he had hoped. Bill Shankly signed him for cover in case of injuries and he languished in the reserves (according to Shanks the second-best team in England) waiting for a chance that never came.

Dave returned to Deepdale at a bargain price in June 1968 and went on to play in a further 111 League games before going to Bradford City and later Southport.

Alec Ashworth, in the two seasons after the 1964 cup final played in only twelve games after suffering a run of injuries; in particular he was haunted by knee ligament trouble. After playing at Derby County (never getting into the first team) in April 1966, he was obliged to retire from the game.

One of the seminal battles in May 1964 had been the duel between **George Ross** and John Sissons. Ross had played well, but Sissons, at that stage in his career, needed to be free for just a few seconds to wreak terrible damage on opponents. George won a Third Division Championship medal with Preston under Alan Ball's management. He played in all but three matches during that campaign.

During November 1972, George went on loan to Southport, but when he returned to Deepdale he added three more appearances to his fine total of 384 games for the club, the eighth-highest total in the entire proud history of Preston North End – a fantastic achievement for a tough-tackling full-back. A loyal servant of North End, Ross was given a testimonial match in November 1973 after signing permanently for Southport. He played thirty-one League games for the latter. George spent a season in the United States with Washington Diplomats before playing non-League football on a part-time basis with Morecambe and Telford United.

Brian Godfrey had his best term for Preston in 1964/65, scoring twenty-five times in thirty-seven League outings, which included a hat-trick in North End's 5-1 defeat of Ipswich Town at Portman Road. His form was good enough to get him into the Welsh international side but the first of his three international outings was not a glorious affair: Wales lost 2-5 at home to Northern Ireland. His second cap was awarded for his part in the 4-2 win over Denmark in 1965, but his career with Wales finished on a sorry note when Italy came to the valleys and defeated the Dragons 1-4.

During the 1964/65 season Brian and Alex Dawson put away fifty-three of North End's eighty League and cup goals. During 1965/66 Godfrey was the club's leading scorer with twenty nettings, this included the harvest of a golden five minutes in the last match of Preston's League campaign wherein Godfrey scored the fastest ever hat-trick by a North End player in a 9-0 win over Cardiff City on 7 May 1966. The goals came in the seventy-second, seventy-fourth and seventy-sixth minutes. His scoring record in the cause of Preston's League campaigns can be appreciated when looked at alongside other North End internationals:

1. Tom Finney (England)	187
2. Tommy Roberts (England)	157
3. Tommy Thompson England)	117
4. Bobby Beattie (Scotland)	57
5. Alex James (Scotland)	53
6. Brian Godfrey (Wales)	52

Although Godfrey scored the goal that took Preston North End to the 1964 FA Cup final, he was twelfth man at Wembley. That was two years before substitutes were introduced and, to his disappointment, he didn't receive a medal. Just a couple of months into North End's 1967/68 campaign (October 1967) Godfrey moved to Villa Park along with Brian Greenhalgh. Godfrey was to net fifty-two times in 122 League games in his four-season career with the Villains. It was whilst he was with Villa that he achieved his greatest moment in football, when he returned to Wembley to skipper the Villains in the Football League Cup final. His leadership in midfield inspired the Third Division club to victory over Manchester United in the semi-final, but at the Twin Towers Tottenham Hotspur proved too much for the brave Villa.

In 1971 Godfrey moved to Bristol Rovers, one of the teams Aston Villa had beaten on their way to the League Cup final. Godfrey was part of a £58,000 deal that took Ray Graydon to Villa Park. He earned a Watney Cup winners' medal with Rovers.

In 1973, Newport County manager Billy Lucas paid a club record fee of £10,000 for Godfrey's experience and leadership, seeing him as the man to inspire the Ironsides to promotion. Brian linked up with his fellow former Evertonian Brian Harris, Newport's captain and assistant manager. He made an indifferent beginning but over his two years with the club he gave good account of himself. Brian's management career took him to Bath, Exeter City, Weymouth and Gloucester City.

Jimmy Milne became general manager of Preston when Bobby Seith took over the manager's role at Deepdale late in 1967. Jimmy retired from management in 1968 and became Preston's chief scout. With North End he had gone to Wembley as a player, spectator, trainer and in 1964 as manager. Jimmy died on 13 December 1997, still an adherent to Deepdale and its cause.

James Alexander Grant Smith scored two of his thirteen Preston goals in his three matches as centre forward. He played in all three half-back positions and towards the end of his 314 games in the League for North End he was a success at left-back. He moved to Stockport County in 1969, and played seventy-eight League games for the Edgeley Park side.

John Donnelly up to 1966 played fifty-seven times for Preston, scoring a single goal.

After forty-six matches in Middlesbrough, **Ian Davidson** finished his playing career with twenty-seven games for Darlington in the last part of 1967.

The victorious West Ham United team that played at Wembley in May 1964 went on to even greater glory during the sixties and on into the last part of the twentieth century. I have told part of their exploits elsewhere (Belton 1997, 1998 and 1999) but there is still a deal to be said of their glory in 1964 and 1965. This will be another story, one that will follow in due course.

Bibliography

Belton, B. (1997) *Bubbles, Hammers and Dreams*, Derby: Breedon Books.

Belton, B. (1998) *The First and Last Englishmen*, Derby: Breedon Books.

Belton, B. (1999) *Days of Iron*, Derby: Breedon Books.

Belton, B. (2003) *Founded on Iron*, Stroud: Tempus.

Belton, B. (2004) *Burn Johnny Byrne – Football Inferno*, Derby: Breedon Books.

Blows, K. and Hogg, T. (2000) *West Ham. The Essential History*, Swindon: Headline.

Butler, B. (1987) *The Football League 1888–1988. The Official Illustrated History*, London: Queen Ann Press.

Cook, C. and Stevenson, J. (1988) *Modern British History*, London: Longman.

Dykes, G. (1994) *The United Alphabet: A Complete Who's Who of Manchester United FC*, Leicester: ACL & Polar.

Fabian, A.H. and Green, G. (eds) (1961) *Associated Football*, London: Caxton.

Fenton, T. (1960) *At Home with the Hammers*, London: Nicholas Kaye.

Finn, R.L. (1972) *The Official History of Tottenham Hotspur FC 1882–1972*, London: Robert Hale.

Fishman, W.J. (2001) *East End 1888*, London: Hanbury.

Gambaccini, P., Rice, J. and Rice, T. (1996) *Top 40 Charts*, Middlesex: Guinness Publishing.

Gibson, A. and Pickford, W. (1905) *Association Football and the Men Who Have Made It*, London: Football Association.

Goble, R. and Ward, W. (1993) *Manchester City: A Complete Record*, Derby: Breedon Books.

Green, G. (1953) *The History of the Football Association*, London: The Naldrett Press.

Greenwood, R. (1984) *Yours Sincerely Ron Greenwood*, London: Willow Books.

Groves, R. (1948) *West Ham United*, London: Cassel & Co.

Harding, J. (1991) *For the Good of the Game: The Official History of the Professional Footballers' Association*, London: Robson.

Harrison, P. (1989) *Southern League Football: The First Fifty Years*, Gravesend: Harrison.

Hayes, D. (1993) *Blackburn Rovers, An A–Z*, Preston: Palatine.

Hayes, D. (2001) *One Hundred Greatest Preston North End Post-War Matches*, Lancashire: PNE Publication.

Hayes, D. (2001) *Swindon Town Football Club, an A–Z*, Cardiff: Aureus.

Hayes, D. (2003) *For Club and Country – The Story of North End's International Players*, Lancashire: PNE Publication.

Hayes, D. *The Deepdale Story: An A to Z of Preston North End*, Chorley: Sport in Word.

Hogg, T. and McDonald, T. (1995) *1895–1995 Hammers 100 Years of Football*, London: Independent UK Sports Publications.

Hogg, T. and McDonald, T. (1995) *West Ham United Who's Who*, London: Independent UK Sports Publications.

Hugman, B. (1998) *The PFA Premier & Football League Players Records 1946–1998*, Hertfordshire: Queen Anne Press.

Hunt, D. (2000) *Preston North End Football Club*, Lancashire: PNE Publication.

Hutchenson, J. (1982) *The Football Industry*, Glasgow: R. Drew.

Inglis, S. (1987) *The Football Grounds of Great Britain*, London: Willow.

Inglis, S. (1988) *League Football and the Men Who Made It*, London: Harper Collins Willow.

Irving, D. (1968) *The West Ham United Football Book*, London: Stanley Paul.

Irving, D. (1969) *The West Ham United Football Book No.2*, London: Stanley Paul.

Jackman, M. (1994) *Blackburn Rovers: The Official Encyclopaedia*, Derby: Breedon Books.

Joannou, P. (1986) *Newcastle United, A Complete Record 1882–1986*, Derby: Breedon Books.

Joannou, P. (1996) *The Black and White Alphabet. A Complete Who's Who of Newcastle United*, Leicester: Polar.

Johnston, F. (ed.) (1934) *The Football Encyclopedia*, London: Associated Sporting Press.

Joyce, N. (2004) *Football League Players' Records 1888 to 1939*, Nottingham: Soccer Data.

Kerrigan, C. (2004) *A History of the English Schools' Football Association 1904–2004*, London: ESFA.

Kaufman, N. and Ravenhill, A. (1990) *Leyton Orient: A Complete Record 1881–1990*, Derby: Breedon Books.

Korr, C. (1986) *West Ham United*, London: Duckworth.

Leatherdale, C. (1998) *West Ham United from Greenwood to Redknapp*, Essex: Desert Island Books.

Lindsay, R. (1991) *Millwall, A Complete Record 1885–1991*, Derby: Breedon Books.

Lovesey, P. (1970) *The Official Centenary History of the Amateur Athletic Association*, London: Guinness Superlatives.

Lyall, J. (1989) *Just Like My Dreams*, Harmondsworth: Penguin.

Mallory, J. (1997) *Football League Tables*, Glasgow and London: Collins.

Marland, S. (2002) *Bolton Wanderers FC – The Official History 1877–2002. Heroes, Heartbreakers and Headliners*, Harefield: Yore.

Mason, T. (1980) *Association Football and English Society 1863–1915*, Brighton: Harvester Press.

Mattick, D. (1989) *The Robins. The Story of Swindon Town Football Club*, Whittlebury: Sporting and Leisure.

Moynihan, J. (1984) *The West Ham Story*, London: Arthur Baker Ltd.

Northcutt, J. and Shoesmith, R. (1993) *West Ham United. A Complete Record*, Derby: Breedon Books.

Northcutt, J. and Shoesmith, R. (1994) *West Ham United. An Illustrated History*, Derby: Breedon Books.

Oliver, G. (1995) *World Soccer* (2nd Edn), Bath: Guinness.

Palmer, K. (2004) *Tottenham Hotspur – Champions of England 1950–51 & 1960–61*, Essex: Desert Island Books.

Plowman, P. (1981) *Swindon Town First in Wiltshire. A Football History in Facts and Figures. Part 1: Up to 1920*, Swindon: Plowman.

Prestage, M. (2000) *Preston North End – The Glory Years Remembered*, Derby: Breedon Books.

Rigby, I. and Payne, M. (1999) *Proud Preston*, Lancaster: Carnegie.

Shaoul, M. and Williamson, T. (2000) *Forever England – A History of the National Side*, Stroud: Tempus.

Stiles, N. (2003) *Nobby Stiles – After the Ball*, London: Hodder and Stoughton.

Thompson, P. and Hale, S. (2004) *Shankly – From Glenbuck to Wembley*, Stroud: Tempus.

Turner, D. and White, A. (1987) *Fulham A Complete Record 1879–1987*, Derby: Breedon Books.

Turner, D. and White, A. (1998) *Fulham Facts and Figures 1879–1998*, Hampshire: Northdown.

Wall, F. (1935) *Fifty Years of Football*, London: Cassel & Co.

Walvin, J. (1975) *The People's Game. A Social History of British Football*, Newton Abbot: A. Lane.

Ward, A. (1999) *West Ham United 1895–1999*, London: Octopus.

Whitburn, J. (1992) *Top 40 Hits*, New York: Billboard.

White, A. and Lilliman, B. (2005) *Football Grounds of London*, Stroud: Tempus.

Whittell, I. (1994) *Manchester City Greats*, Edinburgh: Sportsprint.

Wigglesworth, N. (1996) *The Evolution of English Sport*, London: Frank Cass.

Willmore, G. (1996) *The Hawthorns Encyclopedia*, Edinburgh and London: Mainstream.

Journals/Newspapers

Daily Mail.

East End News.

East Ham and Barking Free Press.

East Ham Echo.

East and West Ham Gazette.

East London Advertiser.

Evening Post.

Ex-Magazine.

Football Players' Magazine.

Hammers News.

Saturday Night and Football Sun.

Soccer History.

South Essex Mail (this would become the *West Ham Herald*).

Sporting Chronicle.

The Footballer.

The Sportsman.

Sports Times.

Stratford Express.

The Times.

West Ham Guardian.

West London Press.

Other titles published by Tempus

Founded on Iron: Thames Ironworks and the Origins of West Ham United

BRIAN BELTON

The genesis of West Ham United is probably the most fascinating of any professional football club. The team began as Thames Ironworks, the players tough hammer-men who burnt and beat the rivets into the great ships built at the Docklands. This is a tale of philanthropy, religious beliefs, Corinthian ethics, entrepreneurial enterprise and the enthusiasm of working people for the beautiful game.

0 7524 2928 0

Summer of '64: A Season in English Cricket

ANDREW HIGNELL

The halcyon summer of 1964 saw Graveney, Boycott and Wilson all make over 2,000 runs while Shackleton, Harman, Cartwright, Titmus and Illingworth were the most lethal exponents of the art of bowling. After one of the hardest-fought contests in living memory Australia took the Ashes, while Worcestershire finally saw off intense competition to take the County Championship. An affectionate and nostalgic look at one of the finest seasons on record.

0 7524 3404 7

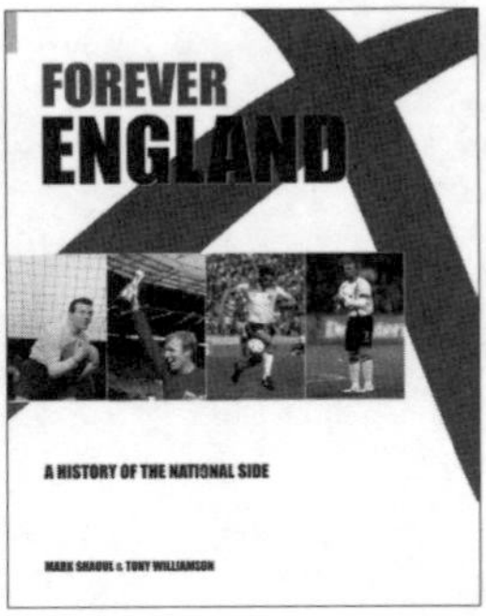

Forever England: A History of the National Side

MARK SHAOUL & TONY WILLIAMSON

This insightful and fascinating account, which covers the careers of England's all-time great players and the team's successes, failures and near misses, is an essential read for anyone interested in the history of the three lions. From the amateur gentlemen of the 1870s to the stars of the early twenty-first century, with many wonderfully evocative illustrations, it is the definitive history of England's national football team.

0 7524 2939 6

If you are interested in purchasing other books published by Tempus, or in case you have difficulty finding any Tempus books in your local bookshop, you can also place orders directly through our website **www.tempus-publishing.com**